# Cinderella Man

## The James J. Braddock Story

*Michael C. DeLisa*

Milo Books Ltd

DeLisa, Michael C.
Cinderella Man: The James J. Braddock Story/Michael C. DeLisa.

Includes bibliographical references and index.

ISBN 1 903854 37 7

First published in 2005 by Milo Books, The Old Weighbridge,
Station Road, Wrea Green, PR4 2PH, United Kingdom

Printed in the United States of America

# Cinderella Man

*James Braddock, newly crowned heavyweight champion, and his family. It was for them that he climbed into the ring to lift the world title. At their home in Guttenberg, New Jersey, are, left to right, Rose Marie, aged two, Howard, three, "Jay" (Jim Jr.) aged four, and the champ and his wife, Mae.*

*For my father and uncle,*
*two fighters, each with his own style*

It may be that race is not always to the swift, nor the battle to the strong – but that is the way to bet.

—Damon Runyon

*A young James Walter Braddock in training in Chicago. His manager changed his name to "James J." in a deliberate echo of some of the great champions of the past.*

# Table of Contents

# Prologue

At four in the morning on July 9, 1932, police captain Louis Bachman, his driver and two patrolmen responded to a call from a house owned by one Anna Quinlan on Bergen Turnpike in Jersey City, New Jersey. Discreetly referred to as a "rooming house" or "tourist hotel," the Quinlan home was actually a house of prostitution, drawing its clientele from young men drinking bootleg beer at the speakeasies operating illegally in the area. Quinlan had called the police when two drunken men broke seven or eight of her windows after she denied them admission. The men then charged her front door, breaking it, before running off.

After hearing Quinlan's story, Captain Bachman – for a reason known only to him went to a local café and arrested two men, Jefferson Bostwick and Al Braddock, brother of a local heavyweight boxer, Jim Braddock. Jim, who had once fought for a world title but was now semi-retired from boxing, owned a speakeasy called Hintz's Place on Hudson Boulevard and Fisher Avenue, and the two had been drinking there earlier.

Someone alerted Jim Braddock that his brother had been taken into custody. The boxer took a friend, Hank Werner, with him to the precinct house to see if he could clear up things. Braddock asked that his brother be released into his custody, but Bachman directed that the two men be booked. Suddenly, Jim Braddock threw a punch in a short arc. It landed squarely on Bachman's nose, the bone snapped, and blood erupted from his face

What had started as a routine investigation into a case of

drunken vandalism now turned into a full-scale riot between four prisoners and the cops at the North Bergen police headquarters.

A dozen cops charged the four men. Hank and Jefferson went down, but the Braddock brothers fought stubbornly. Then the blackjacks came out. Blood splattered on the walls, floors, and uniforms of the cops as they battered and beat Jim Braddock back. But no matter how hard the blow, he would not go down. He was in a rage now, and he continued to fight. Two of the smarter cops dropped out of the melee, hanging back behind the booking desk.

Though he still would not drop, Braddock was forced to retreat, step by step. Finally, with one last rush, the cops forced him into an open cell and slammed the door.

The boxer stood in the center of the cell, as he had stood in the center of many a boxing ring, breathing hard, bleeding from his hands, head and face, but unbowed. In the dank, gray room, his blood dripped onto the dirty cement floor.


In October 1956, Playhouse 90 premiered Rod Serling's *Requiem for a Heavyweight* live on American television. The teleplay – starring Jack Palance, himself an ex-fighter, as a worn-out challenger – recorded in grainy detail the typical end to a boxer's career. In the opening moments, an announcer's voice is heard intoning the time of Mountain McClintlock's loss by knockout. A crowd is seen surging along a concrete walkway, headed by two tough-looking mugs who were obviously also ex-fighters. In fact not only were they ex-fighters, they were former world champions: Max Baer and Max Rosenbloom. The two Maxies had reigned at heavyweight and light-heavyweight during the depths of the Great Depression. By 1956, Serling saw them as embodying the ex-fighter. Besides being world champs, they had one other thing in common. Both had fought Jim Braddock, better known as the "Cinderella Man of Boxing."

By the 1950s, Jim Braddock was all but forgotten. When the big hitter of the day, Rocky Marciano, fought Roland La Starza, several former champs were introduced from the ring. As Braddock stepped up to take his bow, the announcer put his hand over the microphone and asked for his name.

So, why Jim Braddock? What was he like? British journalist Trevor Wignall held a special place for Braddock: "There was never a man I liked more. He was so natural, so totally bereft of the conceit and the hideous vanities that prize-fighting creates. Jim Braddock was one of the very, very few who was not spoiled by the success that dropped on him in his somewhat late days. The only part of him that swelled was the generosity of his nature that grew bigger."

That might make a description of a good drinking buddy. But Braddock was an authentic American hero, at least for a specific time and place. What had he done or said that would resonate? Wignall again: "As a conversationalist [Braddock] was a total loss. There was a natural shyness in Jim, and I feel now that much more remarkable than his winning of the heavyweight championship was his transformation into a hearty, handshaking, talkative public character."

So, again, why Jim Braddock? He fought many stirring professional prizefights and in several, his bravery exceeded his skills. But, as Papa Hemingway wrote, "Guts never made any money for anybody except violin string manufacturers."

The answer perhaps comes when you examine America during the depth of the Great Depression, and the ways that Americans extricated themselves from it. In Braddock's day, his was often referred to as a type of "Horatio Alger" story. Alger's "Strive and Succeed" philosophical underpinnings were akin to Herbert Hoover's notions of government. President Hoover used the phrase "American Individualism" in the title of a book in 1922. Simply stated, he meant to encompass the view that "hard work and self-reliance" were the tools for a man to elevate himself from poverty – and that the federal government should play a minor role. Would Robert Sherwood call Jim Braddock the "last rugged apostle of American Individualism"? Probably not.

In contrast, Franklin Delano Roosevelt and the "brains trust" behind the New Deal of the 1930s advocated a strong government that would take an active role in shaping society. The hand of government would be a helping hand for the poor. That difference would shape the nation. "This comparison is more than just a debate between two men," Hoover said just before Election Day in 1932. "It is more than a contest between two parties. It is a contest between two competing systems of government."

Braddock's core story played out in a few concentrated months at the nadir of the Great Depression. For some mystical reason, his life mirrored the nation's. He rose to the top of the bubble during the Roaring Twenties. When that bubble burst, his life deflated too, along with the lives of most Americans. As he made his comeback, it was clear that he was not an "individual" working alone. He was a member of a family – his own, his profession's, and the American family. And so it was that a nation turned its eyes to a prizefighter's life.

# PART ONE

# The Fists of Polydeuces

Club-footed Hephaestus toiled before the flames of his golden forge, shaping the weapons of the gods. Polydeuces, twin of Castor and brother of Helen, burst into that infernal workshop and placed his hands upon the distressed anvil. Hephaestus understood, and with one swift blow lopped off both hands at the wrist as his golden handmaidens averted their eyes. Polydeuces left with two new weapons – white-hot metal beaten into the shape of fists by a god. With these hands, Polydeuces would be able to hammer out victory against the greatest of odds. Polydeuces had sacrificed a mortal part of himself to become an unbeatable warrior, the greatest boxer on Earth.

*Joe Gould, the dapper, quick-tongued Jewish boxing manager who stood by Jim Braddock in his darkest moments and shared the good times.*

CHAPTER 1

# The Forging of a Fighter

"All of life is six-to-five against."

—Damon Runyon

Hell's Kitchen. Rarely was a slum more aptly named. A notorious grid of factories, grog shops and tenements, it sprawled out from the West Forties of Manhattan to reach from 34th to 59th streets, and from 8th Avenue to the Hudson River. Its evocative name first appeared in print in 1881, when a *New York Times* reporter used the phrase to describe an especially vile housing block he visited, with police escort, to write up a multiple murder. Here drunken sailors were waylaid and robbed, prostitutes and barefoot children thronged the alleyways, and the Gophers gang held sway from their hideouts in basements and cellars, emerging to terrorise the streets or do battle with rival mobs. In his famous work *The Gangs of New York*, social historian Herbert Asbury would call it "the most dangerous area on the American continent."

Hell's Kitchen teemed with large families, living in cramped conditions, and on June 7, 1905,[1] Joseph and Lizzie Braddock added one more child to the neighborhood – a son they named James Walter. He was their sixth child: they already had Nellie, Julia, Ralph, Joe and

---

[1] Not a single contemporary report ever got Braddock's birthday correct. He "was born on June 7, 1905. The December 6, 1906 was incorrect." Undated letter from Mrs. James J. Braddock to author.

Jack. A later biographer reported that James weighed seventeen pounds at birth, a dubious claim, as it would make him one of the heaviest babies ever born.

Like many of their neighbors, Joseph and his wife, originally Mary Elizabeth O'Toole, were immigrants. They had arrived in the United States separately but both, by coincidence, from the same place: Manchester, England, the world's first industrial city. Manchester was not so much hell's kitchen as hell's forge, an equally overcrowded, squalid metropolis where merchants made fortunes from Britain's domination of the international cotton trade while children slaved in unspeakable conditions in their noisy, smoke-belching mills.

The Braddock family was of Irish descent but, like many from the Emerald Isle, had migrated to England to seek work. Joe was actually born in Mottram, a village south of Manchester in the county of Cheshire, and worked as a porter for London and North Western Railways before, in August 1886, joining Manchester Police. He was described on his joining papers as twenty-two years old, of sallow complexion, standing five feet, eleven inches tall, with brown eyes and black hair – and a Catholic.

Joe worked the east side of the city, a tough area plagued at that time by bizarre youth gangs known as "scuttlers," who wore clogs and bell-bottomed trousers and fought with heavy belt buckles. He didn't stay in the service long, however: in January 1888, he was "dismissed" for reasons unknown and within weeks was on a ship bound for America. In later years, Joe Braddock would claim he sailed on the same vessel as two renowned bareknuckle fighters, Jake Kilrain and Charley Mitchell, as if that somehow contributed to his son's proficiency with boxing gloves. Kilrain was on his way to challenge the great John L. Sullivan for the world heavyweight title.

Elizabeth O'Toole was also of Irish descent: her father, Thomas, being a native of Sligo and her mother, Mary Oates, coming from Galway. She left Manchester for the New World a couple of years before her husband-to-be. The couple married in Manhattan on April 28, 1895, and set up home in a tiny set of rooms in a tenement on

West 48<sup>th</sup> Street. Most residents couldn't wait to escape Hell's Kitchen, and when baby Jim was about a year old, Joe moved his family across the river to the Monitor Park section of New Jersey, where he operated a trucking business. A fifth son, Alfred, was born after the move.

One later friend and biographer described James Walter Braddock's childhood in the kind of terms used when there is little original to say: "Like other boys, Jimmy Braddock played marbles. Like other boys, he played 'three-ole-cat.' Like other boys, he played baseball – and was an outfielder ... Like other boys, he loved to go down to the river and plunge in for a swim. Like other boys, he wanted to be a fireman or a locomotive engineer. Like other boys, he saved those small, brightly colored pictures of prize fighters, ball players, warships and birds – then to be had with every purchase of cigarettes by their elders. Yes, and like other boys he positively hated books."[2]

He attended St. Joseph's Parochial School, where he apparently "hated arithmetic like it was poison" but showed a certain aptitude for spelling. The older Braddock boys learned to box, and Jim too must have learned to defend himself at an early age "There were about thirty-five boys in my class," he later recalled, "and they could all fight a bit" – but through most of his teens he took no interest in boxing. He had a bit of the wanderlust in him, which, after he became famous, would lead to various stories of his "hobo" days. For the most part, though, his travels took him no further than western New York. One "frolicsome" night in 1921, the teenage Braddock and several of his buddies wound up on New York's Bowery. Braddock capped off the evening by having his forearm tattooed in a baroque amalgam of a naval anchor and other military detail, perhaps in honor of his brothers, both of whom had served and boxed in the Navy.

[2] *Relief to Royalty*, by Ludwig "Lud" Shabazian, 1936. Stories of the youthful Braddock's high jinks with his friend Marty McGann, which would later appear in accounts of his life, may owe as much to the imagination of press agents as to fact.

Jimmy left school without a diploma and worked in 1919 as a messenger boy for Western Union, where one of his most vivid memories was of standing outside the offices of the *Hudson Dispatch* newspaper, holding his batch of telegrams to be delivered, and listening to a vivid round-by-round description of the Jess Willard-Jack Dempsey world title fight being announced through a megaphone.

Most biographies of Braddock claim that his interest in organized boxing was sparked after a street fight with his brother Joe over a borrowed sweater. The sportswriters of the day were prone to gild the lily, and in all likelihood Braddock simply started hanging around the gym as Joe surged through the amateur ranks, winning the State Welterweight Championship in 1923. Joe turned professional shortly thereafter, and at one of his matches, an aspiring politician, Harry Buesser, convinced his younger brother to fight a short-notice "smoker" bout with local tough guy Tom Hummel. Hummel must have enjoyed the sensation of hitting someone because he went on to become a Jersey cop. The taste of leather must have appealed to James Braddock also, because he began his own amateur boxing career shortly afterwards, joining a gym in Jersey City, New Jersey.

Jersey City of the late twenties and early thirties could be described in the pulp parlance of the day as hard-boiled. Most New Yorkers were uncomfortable there, though perhaps certain Brooklynites less so. Doyen humorist Ring Lardner needed just a few trips from Manhattan to the foreign precincts of Jersey to form his view: "Present defenders of the dorp joint point with pride to the fact that though the State of New Jersey is famous for murders, hardly any occur in Jersey City itself. My theory is that the returns are in – because the police don't consider such pranks worth reporting, and that a thorough investigation of the slayings which take place elsewhere would reveal that nearly all the assassins had just been to Jersey City and talked to a cop."

The mayor and political boss of Jersey City, Frank Hague, came from an Irish-immigrant slum area to govern his city for thirty years, from the end of World War One until after World War II. A firm exponent of the peculiarly American blend of political favoritism and social welfare known as "bossism," he assured the city's reputation as one of the most corrupt in the country. Two of his most frequently quoted statements were, "I am the law," and, "I decide, I do, me!"

Tough as the streets of New Jersey were at that time, the world beneath those streets was even tougher, as many a basement doubled as makeshift boxing gym for thousands of young men. So it was that one day a lanky youngster named James Walter Braddock began his boxing career in fellow amateur Freddie Huber's basement, which doubled as headquarters for the Irish-American Athletic Club. The head trainer in this subterranean gymnasium was an ambitious, truculent small-timer named Barney Doyle.

Braddock stood well over six feet tall but weighed only one hundred and sixty pounds, not exactly a muscle-bound bruiser. He also began boxing fairly late, at age eighteen, when most serious boxers start training before fifteen, but had already imbibed the rudiments of the sport from his brothers. He showed instant promise and, despite his skinny frame, had a naturally hard punch. After an appropriate period learning the basics, he began boxing in amateur competitions throughout New Jersey, even venturing from time to time into New York. Thanks to his punching power, he swiftly compiled an impressive knockout record.

In March 1925, skinny Jim impressed even the most cynical of critics by winning amateur titles in two weight divisions. First, he won the New Jersey amateur light-heavyweight (175-pound) championship by stopping Johnny Emmerson, who broke his ankle after a crushing Braddock right sent him spinning to the canvas.

Two nights later, Braddock kayoed two men to win the heavyweight title as well. It was an extraordinary display of both bravery and talent: both of his opponents outweighed the 161-pound Braddock by about forty pounds. The boxing officials presented Braddock with an expensive watch as token of his victories, and Barney Doyle carried it with him for months thereafter, showing it proudly to virtually every reporter in northern New Jersey.

New York City's heavyweight champion, Kaiser DeWitt, eventually stopped Braddock's winning streak. Going into their bout, Braddock had a string of nineteen consecutive victories, but DeWitt stayed away from his power right and danced to a decision. In February 1926, Braddock returned to Newark to defend his New Jersey titles. Thousands of eager fans packed National Turner Hall, curious to see if the young star could repeat his audacious feat of winning titles in two weight divisions. Eleven months on, Braddock had gained weight – a full eight ounces – to scale 162 pounds, just two pounds over the middleweight limit, yet again he seemed undeterred at tackling much bigger, stronger men.

The 175-pound competitors quickly fell before Braddock's power punches. But the heavyweights were expected to present a different type of challenge. In the championship bout in the heavyweight division, Braddock would face a 215-pound stove maker named Frank Zavita. Stove making was no job for sissies, and seconds into the first round, Zavita whipped a left hook to the body that jack-knifed Braddock and sent him backwards, gasping for air. Zavita continued his onslaught throughout the three minutes of the round, only an occasional jab by Braddock staving off a knockout.

Between rounds, Barney Doyle and Braddock's brother Joe advised their fighter to use the jab to keep Zavita at bay. Braddock followed their counsel, jabbing Zavita repeatedly. His persistent pecking angered and frustrated Zavita, who dropped his guard for a moment. *Thud.* Braddock knocked him down with a blistering overhand right. Zavita jumped up and ran smack into another right that dropped him again. In all he was dropped eleven times before the referee belatedly waved it over in round three and awarded the fight to Braddock.

Such exciting wins made the young Braddock something of a local hero, and Barney Doyle capitalized on his growing popularity by matching him in a series of fundraising bouts for the Palisades Knights of Columbus building fund. At the same time, Doyle began preparations to have him enter professional boxing, under his management. Joe Braddock, however, was adamant that his brother would have a manager other than the self-dealing Doyle. He felt that his brother needed a manager who would stick by him if times got tough; in professional boxing, tough times were a given.

Braddock's friend and biographer, Ludwig Shabazian, ascribed Joe's reticence to appoint Doyle to the manager's behavior at one of Joe's own bouts. Doyle had managed and trained Joe to the New Jersey amateur welterweight title in 1923, then continued to handle him when he turned pro. Andy Lake, another local pro, was a natural opponent for Joe, since Lake had won the 1922 welterweight championship. Doyle agreed to a match between them in January 1925, and it drew over 1500 fans to tiny Amsterdam Hall.

Joe Braddock suffered a demoralizing loss. In the fourth round, Lake landed a right-left combination that dropped Braddock for the full count. Doyle, rather than assist his fallen fighter, stalked away from the ringside, leaving an embarrassed Joe to fend for himself. Joe's contract with Doyle still had some time to run, but he vowed that night that Doyle would not manage his brother's professional career.

In March 1926, Doyle rematched Jim Braddock with Kaiser DeWitt, the New York Metropolitan Amateur Athletic Union champion, who had handed Braddock one of his few amateur losses. It seems that the Jersey City fighter agreed to this last amateur bout in order to gain revenge. Any such notion that Braddock had ended when DeWitt failed to show at the Knights of Columbus Hall for the scheduled bout. Braddock instead went on against last-minute substitute, Frankie Anderson, so as not to disappoint the record-breaking crowd that had shown up for the card. He came out slugging and ended the bout with a resounding knockout after just thirty seconds.

Doyle's plans to use Braddock's popularity to enrich himself were crushed in early April when Braddock decided to turn professional under the management of Alfred J. Barnett, a sportsman based in neighboring Union City. Barnett's role in the Cinderella Man story has been buried for over seventy-five years, and outside of a few references to him in the Jersey papers of the day, he has been completely overlooked. He made one major contribution to Braddock's career, however, by arranging to have him train at a Union City boxing gymnasium managed by the great African-American pugilist of the Jack Johnson era, Joe Jeanette.

The transition from amateur to professional was anything but smooth. Braddock signed to make his professional debut against Tom Brennan at Amsterdam Hall in Union City, the same venue as his brother's humiliating loss to Andy Lake. The Braddock-Brennan bout would be promoted by George Broad, owner of the Hall and known as the "man with many headaches." Broad usually ran his shows on a weekly basis during the cooler months. There was a hitch, however: Braddock had already agreed to appear on the next Barney Doyle amateur show. Since that was scheduled for two days after the Brennan fight, ticket-buying fans were hard-pressed to decide which card to attend. Broad was given another headache to justify his nickname when his main event failed to materialize and he was forced to cancel Braddock's pro debut. Doyle continued to advertise that Braddock would fight on his promotion, and a large crowd turned out, only to be disappointed when the fighter did not appear.

According to the *Jersey Journal*, James Braddock ended his amateur career with a string of twenty-one kayos in twenty-two bouts. Though still to make his debut, he was now a professional boxer.

The rules governing boxing in Braddock's hometown were much different than today. A New Jersey State law made illegal the rendering of official decisions in boxing matches, apparently on the notion that gambling would be discouraged if no official verdict was given. Except for those ending by foul or knockout, bouts would be officially listed as "no decision." By contrast, in New York official decisions were permitted under that state's Walker Law, named after Mayor Jimmy Walker, who helped guide its formation and enactment. Five months prior to Braddock's debut, New York's scoring method was changed from points to a system in which two judges would award a fight to the boxer winning the most rounds. If they disagreed, the referee's scoring would be used to break the tie.

Newspaper reporters often gave their own decision to readers the following day. For the most part, these "newspaper verdicts" for no-decision bouts were unreliable. Many sportswriters supplemented their incomes by accepting "contributions" from local boxing promoters, which led to many a house favorite being lauded in the press, no matter how badly he performed. Even honest sportswriters could differ in opinion, and it was not uncommon to find several different newspapers reporting different results. Wire service reports were especially unreliable, since often the stringers feeding the stories to the wire were associated in some way with either the promoter or the boxers. One favorite ruse of fight managers was to hurry to a Western Union office immediately after a fight and send out a story stating that the manager's fighter had just beaten his opponent – regardless of the merits. The race between managers to the telegraph office was often more competitive than the fights they sought to report. Sometimes a manager would report his fighter's win before the end of the bout.

At about the same time as young Jim Braddock was beginning to make a name for himself in boxing, the *Jersey Journal* sought to address the credibility of newspaper decisions in the state. The *Journal* collected a list of potential "fan judges," and at each fight would have five such judges score the bouts. These fans would submit their opinions in a sealed envelope to the *Journal* reporter at ringside, and he would select two at random, combine them with his own and reach a result. Braddock's early professional fights in New Jersey would be judged by this fan-panel procedure until decisions were legalized in 1928.

Headaches notwithstanding, George Broad announced the lineup for his April 13 card. Jim Braddock would fight a special four-round bout against Al Settle, "colored heavyweight of Harlem." As so often in his amateur bouts, Braddock, who was little more than a heavy middleweight, would be fighting a bigger man. The experts at the *Hudson Dispatch* did not expect him to have an easy time against Settle, but believed that the bout would give "a true line on Braddock and indicate whether he is going to cut any ice on in the professional ranks."

In the event, Braddock barely avoided a loss. Settle's pushing and mauling had him fatigued and blowing hard at the end of only four rounds. The *Jersey Journal*, which had been very supportive during his amateur career, expressed a tinge of disappointment: "To say that Braddock's debut was a success would be stretching a point too far. Jim started well but was going very badly as the bout progressed and when the bell sounded seemed about ready to drop the verdict to Settle." Officially a no-decision in the record books, the *Jersey Journal* ruled it a draw.

Braddock happily picked up one significant difference between the amateur and the professional ranks: "I was supposed to get a medal, but instead I got ten berries [dollars]," he recalled. Ten bucks went a long way in 1926, and he had future visions of entire bushels of berries.

Braddock didn't have much time to dwell on his slow start as he had already booked to fight the following week. His second pro contest took place at the Knights of Columbus Hall in Ridgefield Park, New Jersey. His opponent, George Deschner, the "German Oak" of North Hudson, was managed by former fighter Babe Orlando and was considered a good prospect in the middleweight division. For one of the few times in his early career, Braddock would be fighting an opponent roughly his own weight.

Braddock wrecked Deschner, knocking him down twice in the first round. Just moments into the second round, he flattened Deschner once more, and the referee halted the bout, awarding him a technical knockout. Braddock received $35 as his share of the purse. The berries had begun to multiply.

During this time, Joe Jeanette took an interest in Braddock that went beyond giving him a place to train. Believing that Braddock had within him the makings of a solid fighter, he began teaching him the finer points of boxing. There was little the forty-six-year-old Jeanette didn't know about the sport. No one knew how many times he had fought, but the record books said more than 150. One of the best of a talented group of pre-War black heavyweights headed by the controversial champion Jack Johnson, Jeanette could box, punch, move or brawl as the situation demanded, and was only ever stopped once, by the fabled Sam Langford. Like the rest of the group, he was avoided by white boxers, and had to fight certain black rivals repeatedly to earn money; his bitter series with the rock-jawed Sam McVey culminated in an astonishing 1909 bout in which Jeanette was knocked down twenty-seven times, only to force his opponent to quit after forty-nine rounds, or nearly two and a half hours of combat.

The sport had changed in the fifteen years since Jeanette's heyday. Fights to a finish were a thing of the past. Most bouts were now held over ten rounds or less, and gloves held more padding, affording more protection to the hands. Fighters threw and took more punches, changed the way they stood and moved, and suddenly the stances and postures of the turn-of-the-century champions on the old-time movie reels looked cumbersome, even comical. The electrifying Jack Dempsey had brought a surge of high voltage to world boxing, and blasted it into the modern era. Brilliant lighter men from the bursting city ghettos, like New York's Benny Leonard, added refinement and technique. Yet the basic principles remained the same, and of those Jeanette was a guru.

Though he had long been retired, Jeanette fought an exhibition on the Deschner card, helping to draw a larger crowd to see his protégé. On April 29, 1926, boxing fans attending the monthly social of a private club called the Zem-Zems were treated to an exhibition between Jeanette and Braddock at the Grotto Auditorium, a Jersey City fight club. Jersey boxing fans were already well aware of

Braddock through his amateur career. His appearances with Jeanette demonstrated that Braddock was laying the groundwork to become a top-flight professional. He was now a full-time prize-fighter, and the time spent with this cagey old mentor would pay dividends throughout Braddock's career. His punch came to him naturally, but his boxing skills had to be acquired through hours of intense training by an old-school professional. It was no coincidence that Braddock evolved a stand-up, relaxed style, evocative of an earlier era when masters such as Jack Johnson – and Jeanette – dominated the game.

Whatever ambitions Jeanette had to play a role in Braddock's career ended when Alfred M. Barnett was squeezed aside by a cigar-smoking whirlwind named Joe Gould. It appears that Braddock's contract with Barnett ran for one year, but even though he would be manager of record into 1927, Gould took over in June 1926.

Joe Jeanette would hone Jim Braddock's ring identity; Gould would dominate his life. On first sight they made the oddest of couples. Gould was everything Braddock was not: small, dapper, talkative and fizzing with nervous energy. To veteran *New York Daily News* sportswriter Jack Miley, he was "a cocky little guy. For years he didn't have a quarter, but you'd never know it, for he's the sort of chap who can strut sitting down and make a noise buttoning his vest."

Joe Gould had been around boxing virtually his whole life. He was born August 14, 1896, in Poughkeepsie, New York, the fifth of nine children to Ida and Benjamin Goldstein; the family's correct name was actually Biegel, but upon arrival in this country, a mix-up caused the Biegels to be renamed Goldstein. They soon moved to New York City, and their children grew up bright and energetic: two became lawyers, one a schoolteacher and another an accountant, while Harvey and Joe would work together in the boxing business.

In their 112th Street apartment building, young Joe became

friends with a skinny kid called Benjamin Leiner, while another pal, Robert Lippman, lived a block away. Leiner became Benny Leonard, the world lightweight champion and a hero to the New York Jewish community; Lippman, under the name Doc Robb, became his trainer. Leonard had perhaps the greatest ring intellect of any boxer who ever lived, compensating for his slight physique by inventing moves and tricks never seen before. Trainers would crowd around the ring just to watch him spar, and his influence on the entire sport – not least on Joe Gould – would be profound.

Gould's family moved again, to Jersey City, where he came to know two brothers, Lou and Sammy Diamond, both of whom made their living in the boxing business. After a short stint on the Erie Railroad, which ran between Jersey City and Haverstraw, New York, Gould joined the Navy with Sammy Diamond, and began staging fights as entertainment for the sailors in and around the naval base at Newport, Rhode Island, where he was stationed. On leaving the service, Gould worked temporarily as meat inspector – despite knowing next to nothing about food hygiene – before handling Lou Diamond's fighters in their out-of-town bouts. He had found his calling. By 1925, Gould had a small portfolio of fighters under his own management, including such fighters such as Frank Carbone, Johnny Reisler and Harry Galfund.

One of his better-known boxers was a sloppy heavyweight named Emilio Buttafochi, who fought under the *nom de glove* of Italian Jack Herman. Gould liked to tell the story of how he matched Herman with Luis Firpo in Havana, Cuba, after an approach from the game's biggest promoter, Tex Rickard. Having agreed to the fight, Gould rushed out to find his fighter, who he had not seen in several months. He tracked Herman to a rooming house in Hoboken, but on arrival found that the boxer had been taken to the hospital. Gould shot to the hospital, woke the slumbering Herman and told him of the pending bout. Herman refused, saying he had stomach pains that the doctors thought might be appendicitis.

"Are you out of your mind?" yelled Gould. "For $5,000 how can you afford to have appendicitis?" Herman made the trip to Havana and was promptly knocked out in the second round. On his return, Gould discovered he had spent an enormous amount on ice to apply to his stomach. "Are you nuts?" he said, on seeing the invoice. "For that kind of dough I can buy a whole iceberg!"

Gould took pride in managing fighters who, regardless of talent, would always give their best. The gym rats of the day were familiar with a story about one of the heavyweights he managed. During a tough bout, the fighter returned to the corner, complaining of a broken hand.

"Look here," Gould told him, "You're not going to quit in my corner. If you want to quit, go out in the middle of the ring and do it, not here. I'm the gamest manager in the business."

Another Gould boxer was a spunky Jewish welterweight, Harry Galfund. He trained at Jeanette's gym, and saw what the old trainer and others saw in James Braddock – an aggressive, tough young fighter with a very hard punch. He spoke highly about Braddock to Gould, who soon began stopping by Jeanette's gym to watch the young man train.

Galfund's high praise brought Gould and Braddock together. Gould's version was somewhat different and Galfund would have to endure years of its retelling. Gould claimed he had arranged to sell Galfund's contract to some "beer barons from Hoboken." These investors visited the gym, wanting to see Galfund work out before concluding any deal, so Gould offered the first fighter he came across – Jim Braddock – $5 to spar with him. Big mistake. Braddock supposedly cuffed around the seasoned veteran for three rounds. The sale was still made, but at a reduced rate. Until his dying day Galfund denied Gould's fiction, but the colorful nature of the tale won out.

Gould did have good connections in the fight game, while Barnett apparently did not. Just days after meeting Braddock, he spoke with promoter Charlie Doesserick about a match for his new fighter. Doesserick was booking fights at Boyle's Thirty Acres, a rambling pine structure built to host Jack Dempsey's historic battle with French war hero Georges Carpentier in 1921. Doesserick took a chance on Braddock, offering him $75 to fight a power-punching black fighter named Leo Dobson, who outweighed him by over twenty-five pounds. Although Gould was leery of such a large weight discrepancy, Braddock put him at ease by recounting his amateur success against bigger men.

Gould's nimble mind made one change before the Dobson fight, a change that would last for Braddock's entire career – he decided to change his middle initial from a "W" to a "J." It was typical of the fast-thinking Gould: Jim Braddock would henceforth be announced as "James J. Braddock," a deliberate echo of James J. Corbett and James J. Jeffries, great champions of yesteryear.

Braddock later recalled the win over Dobson, attributing it to a clever trap he set. "Dobson was a whale of a puncher," he said. "In those days I was taught to believe never to let the other fellow start a punch. Sometimes I'm amused when they say I can't think or move fast. The strange part about this fight of mine was that I walked out and deliberately feinted my opponent into throwing a right cross, and then I knocked Dobson's brains out with a left hook."

Over the next few months, Braddock fought often, mostly at Boyle's Thirty Acres, racking up a string of knockouts, including seven in the first round. His victims included Mike Rock, Phil Weisberger, and Carmine Caggiano – tough journeymen heavyweights of the day.

Gould decided that Braddock was ready to fight in New York City, the next step up in his fistic education, and matched for a $75 purse at the venerable Pioneer Sporting Club on 24th street. Gould did not select a patsy for Braddock's Big Apple debut; Lou Barba was an undefeated, iron-jawed heavyweight from Greenwich Village which, odd as it would later seem, had a reputation for producing good fighters, including reigning heavyweight champion Gene Tunney.

The six-foot-tall Barba outweighed his opponent by nearly

twenty pounds. A well-conditioned, thick-limbed teenager, he pressed Braddock throughout, but the New Jersey novice handled him with finesse and, according to the *New York Times*, "established his right to the decision rather handily." Braddock earned $75, matching his biggest purse to date.

Gould kept Braddock busy, having him fight three times during the first three weeks of December 1926. Confident of the progress made by his fighter, he matched him once more with Al Settle, his first professional opponent, this time at the Walker Athletic Club in New York. Braddock proved that he had improved markedly from his debut, whipping Settle over six swift rounds.

Just four days later, matchmaker Joe McKenna paired Braddock against Joe Hudson, yet another heavyweight prospect based in Greenwich Village. Their Hudson six-rounder was advertised as a "special bout" on a card featuring six other bouts. Braddock won his third six-round decision in a row. After his string of early knock-outs in New Jersey, he was finding that the more talented competitors would not simply fall down.

Braddock finished his first year as a professional by returning to Jersey City to fight on a Christmas Fund Show promoted by Humbert Fugazy, a promoter with big ambitions. Profits went to help the needy during the Holiday season. Braddock waltzed through a four-round bout with middleweight Doc Conrad, one of the few times he met an opponent near his own weight.

The *Jersey Journal's* year-end boxing issue contained a profile on Braddock that included some high praise, and made specific mention of the magic value of the "J" that Gould had added to his name: "James J. – it may only be a hunch but who can tell – is expected to some day fight his way up the ladder and sit on the throne James J. Corbett, James J. Jeffries, and James J. [Gene] Tunney have occupied at one time or another." Yet even while predicting a heavyweight championship for the tyro, the article described him as "awkward and seemingly crude," concluding it was "Braddock's ability to hit that has spelled ruination for many another aspirant."

Braddock's good work during 1926 paid dividends in his first bout in 1927. Gould secured a four-round preliminary bout for Braddock against heavyweight George LaRocco. More important than the choice of opponent was the venue – New York's famous "mecca" of boxing, Madison Square Garden, which had recently relocated to 50th Street and Eighth Avenue. It was a place boxers dreamed of fighting, and Braddock found himself climbing into the ring before more than 20,000 fans, though most had turned up to see the main event between two former light-heavyweight champions Mike McTigue and Paul Berlenbach. They were astonished to see the lanky Braddock roar out of his corner and flatten LaRocco in one round.

In the main bout, the aging McTigue overcame great odds to beat the younger Berlenbach. Damon Runyon viewed McTigue's comeback as somewhat mystical and gave all credit to his *de facto* manager, Jimmy Johnston. "Not until he dropped the title and fell victim to the hypnotic influence of Mr. James J. Johnston, the man with the suspiciously black hair, did McTigue start to do some real fighting. Scientists are still endeavoring to discover the prescription Mr. Johnston employed."

February found Braddock in Wilkes-Barre, Pennsylvania, pounding out a decision win on the undercard of a main event featuring yet another of the top light-heavyweight contenders. Tommy Loughran was just three years older than Braddock but was entering his ninth year as a pro, and was already regarded as a phenomenon. Today, many experts consider him one of the best boxers of all time.

Born in Philadelphia on November 29, 1902, he began boxing professionally in 1919, and by age nineteen, after just a handful of bouts, was holding his own with world champions such as Mike McTique, Harry Greb, Gene Tunney and Brian Downey. Loughran prided himself on his ring acumen and scientific approach. "Nobody is going to 'think me' into a licking," he would say. "I've got a brain that works too." He spent thousands of hours in the basement of his home teaching himself to box, studying himself in mirrors while he shadowboxed, sealing off any openings he saw in his defense. "I knew exactly how I appeared to every fellow that I was boxing, and I would set him up for certain punches that he'd be taking at me," he later told writer Peter Heller. "See, he didn't know how he looked to me. All he saw was me. But I saw what he saw ... from studying it in the mirror." Though he couldn't hit hard enough to break an egg – he would stop only seventeen opponents in 174 recorded contests – he could sucker an opponent into almost anything, and his defense was virtually impregnable.

A devout Catholic, Loughran made fighting his profession but not his life. "I make a living with my fists," he told one reporter. "I consider it an honorable way to make a living, but I do not have to take it into my life outside the ring. I like people and I enjoy talking to them about other things." The only blot on his record would be that in 175 career fights, he never met a black opponent.

In Johnny Risko, a heavyweight contender nicknamed the "Cleveland Rubber Man" for his ability to take punishment, Loughran would be fighting a heavier man. That night in Wilkes-Barre, however, science prevailed over brawn. Loughran danced around Risko for ten rounds and used his unerring left jab to win a clear-cut decision.

If Jim Braddock was to win a title, he would have to get past Loughran first.

*A young James Braddock receives instructions on the taping of his hands from right legend Jack Dempsey. The old Manassa Mauler was the idol of an entire generation of boxers.*

# CHAPTER 2

# Diamonds and Hard Rocks

And blest forever is she who relied
Upon Erin's honour and Erin's pride.

—Thomas Moore

E arly in 1927, Jim Braddock caught the eye of the nation's most influential sportswriter, Damon Runyon. In a column on potential heavyweight title contenders, Runyon wrote:

I really should have mentioned a young man in Jersey, James J. Braddock by name. I have seen James J. Braddock on a number of occasions, and I think well of him. However, I believe he is only a light heavyweight as yet, though certain to get bigger in another year. James J. Braddock has a considerable natural class, and a bit of a punch. His manager is taking him along with great care, for James J. Braddock is still under twenty-one, and has much to learn. I am inclined to think, however, that James J. Braddock will go far.

Not too shabby a write up – two paragraphs, and five mentions of "James J. Braddock." Runyon evidently liked the rhythm of the name as much as he liked the young fighter. Gould's savvy was paying off.

Braddock continued his string of consecutive knockouts. On the heels of a scintillating first-round demolition of Stanley Simmons, Gould matched Braddock in his first ten-round bout. As was becoming the norm, Braddock's opponent, Jack Stone, outweighed him by twenty-five pounds. Stone was a grizzled veteran of many a ring war, with years of experience against every manner of fighter, including such all-time greats as Mike McTigue. Braddock's fans packed the West New York Playgrounds for this stern test. Cheering loudly in the crowd was his best friend, Howard Fox, and Fox's sister, Mae.

After a quiet first round, Mae Fox and the rest of Braddock's supporters watched horrified as Stone sent him sprawling on the canvas in the second. Braddock jumped to his feet at the count of three, a sign of his inexperience. Good fighters would take a full eight or nine seconds to recuperate before getting up. Still, youthful stamina, sheer guts, and a previously undisclosed ability to take a punch enabled Braddock to survive the round. The rest of the fight was nip and tuck, and the newspaper "judges" were divided over the winner.

Mae Fox, who worked as a telephone operator, had met Braddock several years before – he worked with her brother – but they were not especially close. Their first meeting was so uneventful that Mae would later say she scarcely remembered it. "One night in 1924, my brother … brought him home to dinner," she wrote. "[B]eing fond of music, I happened to be playing the piano when I heard them coming into the house." Looking up from the piano as they came in, Mae recalled she "hardly gave a thought to the big, shy fellow Howard had brought home that night."

In June, Braddock was matched with a gritty middleweight from Union City, Jimmy Francis. The night of the bout, Braddock ate dinner at the Foxes' house with Howard and the rest of his family, including Mae. Howard was taking a date to the fight and decided to have his little sister join them. "Jimmy'll lay this guy in the sawdust," he said. "Come with us Mae. After the fight we'll all go out somewhere."

Mae had enjoyed the excitement at the Stone fight, so she agreed to go along to watch lanky, shy Jimmy Braddock fight the main event at the West New York Stadium. She picked a good fight to attend; more than sixty years later, the performance by the two boxers was still being recounted in Jersey newspapers and among hardcore boxing fans. Mae would also pinpoint it as the moment her love affair with Jim Braddock began.

Nearly 7,000 fans thronged the stands, a decent crowd for that arena. Gould plotted Braddock's strategy, telling him, "This guy is a right-hand puncher, and he will rush you continually … you've got to keep circling away from his right and you've got to poke him steadily with your left hand as you do so."

Francis surprised Braddock in the first round by attempting to counter-punch, and in the second landed a stiff right hand. Rather than circle and box as had been the plan, Braddock abandoned all ring science and tore angrily into his foe. For the next four rounds the pair fought like hyenas, to the roars of the crowd. Even Mae was caught up in the delirium, as Francis slowly faded in face of his youthful opponent's onslaught. Braddock won the newspaper decision, to a crescendo of applause.

Afterwards, Howard, Mae, and their friends picked up Braddock in his dressing room. He was flush with the joy of victory, and a career-high purse of $1,000, a relative fortune. Tired but happy, the boxer insisted on hiring a private car to take the group out for dinner and an evening of dancing. The Braddock party had a great time. After an exotic meal of "Chinese food," Jim even tried dancing with Mae, who described his attempt as "pathetic." The evening emboldened Braddock to begin revealing his feelings for the pretty Irish sister of his best friend.

"I'm going to buy you a dinner ring tomorrow," he told Mae. "What does a rich guy like me need with all that money I won tonight?" Until that moment, Mae had been unaware of any interest in her at all on Braddock's part.

"Quit kidding me Jimmy," she said. "Just because you beat Jimmy Francis … "

"Honest," Braddock cut her off. "I mean it. Wait and see."

The next day he showed up at Mac's house as she was getting ready to leave for another date. Braddock gave her a small ring box, but his swagger of the previous night had evaporated, and he was too embarrassed to say he had gone out and bought it for her. "Here Mae," he said, "here's something I found on the ferry. You can have it."

Mae looked down and saw a ring glittering with diamonds. Throughout her date that evening, all she could think of was the young fighter who had given her a ring she had dreamed about. Braddock's story of finding the ring on the ferry was so transparent as to be endearing.

Over the next few months, Braddock courted Mae in his typical, shy, low-key way. She stopped attending his fights as her own feelings deepened, unable to watch someone she cared about be hit or hurt. "I was a telephone operator," she told Marguerite Marshall of the *New York Evening Journal*, "and he used to call at the office and take me to dinner. Then we'd go to a movie down in Newark. Once in a while we'd go to a ball game. If he was going to fight, I'd go with him to the gates of the park or the entrance of wherever the bout was held. But he could not persuade me to go farther – not ever." On many nights, Braddock would visit and they would sit in her parlor listening to the radio, or Mae would play the piano for him."

In virtually every interview that she was to give, Mae could not help but express the fear that absorbed her during each of Braddock's subsequent bouts. "What I couldn't bear would be to see him hit and hurt," she said. "To watch anyone hit him, to hear the blows and see the blood, to know that he was suffering and I unable to help – oh, I couldn't bear it."

Braddock repeated his win over Francis in a rematch just three weeks after the first. Gould then landed what would be Braddock's most important bout to date – a slot on the undercard of Jack Dempsey's bout against Jack Sharkey at Yankee Stadium. The attraction of the veteran Manassa Mauler attempting to beat the rising Sharkey and earn a crack at his old title drew one of the biggest crowds ever seen at a boxing event: 80,000 fans, paying up to $27.50 at ringside. No one could pull them in like Dempsey, and the excitement spread down to the undercard.

In the view of the normally staid *New York Times*, Braddock's third match with LaRocco, played out against the massive crowd, was "a thriller from the opening bell." Braddock was outweighed by fifteen pounds, but "showed a nice left hand and electrified the crowd by unleashing a right with dynamite in it. This punch sent LaRocco to the canvas for a count of nine in the second round."

Driven by the roars of 80,000 people, LaRocco got up and made Braddock work hard through the rest of that round and the third. In the fourth, Braddock's right landed once more on LaRocco's chin for another knockdown. LaRocco tried to force his way back into the fight, but Braddock boxed superbly to take an easy six-round decision.

Just fifteen months after his first, desultory professional bout before a slim crowd at a New Jersey dance hall, Braddock had developed into a cool, well-conditioned pro boxing before a record-breaking attendance. With such impressive progression, Braddock could now dare to aspire to his own main event championship bout, outdoors in a New York City ballpark.

Later that evening, the ageing but still fearless Jack Dempsey lumbered through six rounds while a motivated and focused Jack Sharkey battered the former champion around the ring. In the seventh, one of Dempsey's increasingly erratic body blows seemed to land squarely in Sharkey's groin. When he turned to the referee to complain, Dempsey, the merciless opportunist, shot across a left hook that caught Sharkey blind. That single blow was enough: the old Mauler still hit harder than anyone, and Sharkey dropped like a stone. Bill Duffy, Dempsey's second, yelled, "Count him out, count him out," and the hesitant referee did, before lifting Dempsey's hand in victory. Sharkey's corner men had to drag him, insensible, back to his stool. He had become a victim of the most fundamental rule of boxing: Protect yourself at all times.

★

In October, Gould was able to land Braddock a semi-final bout to a world championship fight at Madison Square Garden. Mike McTigue, who through the lobbying efforts of his manager, Jimmy Johnston, had been named light-heavyweight champion by the New York State Athletic Commission a few weeks prior, would be defending against Tommy Loughran of Philadelphia. The winner would become Braddock and Gould's number one target.

First, however, they had to negotiate Joe Monte, a tall, experienced fighter from Boston who carried the ominous nickname "Iron Head." Monte had been a top amateur throughout the early 1920s. He missed the 1924 Olympics, but did beat Harry Mitchell of England, the gold medallist at his weight, in a special bout after the games.

The Monte bout would drastically affect the rest of Braddock's career. It ended in a ten-round draw, but that mattered little. More importantly, Braddock had fractured his right hand on Monty's iron head. A fighter's fists are his tools, but the twenty-seven bones in each hand – the carpals, metacarpals and phalanges – are not built for punching, and even tight wrapping with yards of bandage is no guarantee against sprains, dislocations, breaks, premature arthritis and other hazards of the trade. Many a promising boxer has seen ambition thwarted by bad hands.

Braddock was forced to take nearly three months off while his hand healed. The purses he had recently earned were more than enough to tide him over, but at the end of that rest period it was discovered that his hand had been set improperly. He could not box with it; it would have to be re-broken and reset.

Gould would later say that the doctor's fee to break and reset the hand was $1,000. Instead of paying out such a large sum, Gould got Braddock a bout on the undercard of new champion Tommy Loughran's first defense. Gould's idea was that Braddock should break his hand intentionally in the ring, thus saving much of the $1,000 fee.

Braddock would use the head of Paul Swidereski as his medical assistant. Swidereski, known variously as "Sad-Eyed Paul" and "The Syracuse Pollack," was a slim, six-foot, three-inch light-heavyweight who packed a punch. In the first round Braddock tossed several looping rights at Sad Paul's head. One landed solidly, and a stab of pain shot through Braddock's arm – he had re-broken his hand. The spectators jeered as Braddock fought a one-handed, conservative battle during the rest of the bout, but Gould was content. Not only had his boxer eked out an eight round decision, but he had avoided some of the medical costs. Braddock, who hated to let people down, was less happy. "It was hard taking such a razzing from the mob," he would recall, "but fight fans aren't interested in excuses, so I made none." The hand was reset, although Braddock would be forced to sit out for another four months.

While Braddock was being hustled off to have his hand repaired, Tommy Loughran was facing Leo Lomski in what would be one of his toughest fights. Lomski started boxing as an amateur soon after joining the United States Navy, and had his first recorded pro bout in 1922, two years after his discharge. By late 1924, he was living in Aberdeen, Washington, and was labeled the "Aberdeen Assassin." Lomski dominated the Northwest boxing scene, fighting an average of once a month and racking up win after win. In January 1927 he beat a former middleweight champion, Tiger Flowers, and came to the attention of Bill Duffy, who quickly became his "East Coast" representative. In New York, he beat top contenders Maxie Rosenbloom, Harold Mays and Yale Okun, wins that clinched his shot at Loughran's title.

Lomski shocked the packed Garden – and Loughran – by knocking down the unhittable champion twice in the first round. Loughran survived each knockdown by taking a nine count on one knee, giving himself every available second to recover. Then he comprehensively outboxed Lomski for the remaining fourteen rounds to retain his title. Loughran told reporters afterwards that he could not recall the second knockdown, nor anything from the first four rounds.

After two more fights, including a successful rubber match against Jimmy Francis, Gould agreed to put Braddock in for a return bout against the iron-headed Joe Monte at Madison Square Garden on June 7, 1928, Braddock's twenty-third birthday. Any planned celebrations were ruined by a ten-round decision loss, the first official defeat of Braddock's thirty-seven-fight career. More painful still, one of Monte's right hands landed squarely on Braddock's ear, which ballooned as blood flowed into the damaged area. The blood would solidify and for the rest of his life Braddock would carry with him Monte's birthday present – a cauliflower ear.

Gould realized that Braddock's fistic education depended in great part on the quality of his opponents. For that reason, he matched him against talented fighters during the first two years of his pro career. Now, in order to expose his charge to an even higher level of boxing, Gould now agreed to have him serve as a sparring partner for heavyweight Tom Heeney, who was preparing to challenge Gene Tunney for the world's title.

Heeney, who hailed from Gisborne, New Zealand, was something of a brute, known as the "Hard Rock Down Under." Born in 1898, the ninth of ten children, he excelled in his national sport of rugby before focusing on boxing. He had an interesting explanation for his great durability. "Much of my present hardiness and toughness I owe to the thrashings I had as a kid," he told an interviewer. "My mother gave me at least twelve million wallopings, all of which I deserved; but my father gave me only one. His idea was to give a child one good licking at an early age that he would always remember, then when he was spoken to there would be obedience and attention and he was right as far as I was concerned. The one thrashing he gave me was the toughest of my life."

Turning professional, Heeney quickly ran out of opponents on home turf, and for the next two years he shuttled between New Zealand and Australia, picking up whatever fights he could. In 1923, he seriously considered giving up the game when one of his opponents, Cyril Whittaker, died after their bout. Instead, Heeney left the Southern Hemisphere to try his luck in England and South Africa. He met with only middling success, even losing a twenty-round decision to "Phainting" Phil Scott, an English heavyweight much lampooned for his delicacy. Heeney left England for the United States, but after trying unsuccessfully for months to get a match, decided that he would take the proceeds from his first fight in the States and return to New Zealand.

And then he met a man with an ostentatious moustache. Charlie "Handlebars" Harvey, one of those larger-than-life managers that boxing seems to produce by rote, saw in Heeney the rugged sort of heavyweight that could give Gene Tunney, the world champion, lots of trouble. He obtained a match at Madison Square Garden for Heeney against a black heavyweight from Chicago, Charley Anderson, and when Heeney won in five hard-fought rounds, suddenly he was a contender. Over the next thirteen months, Heeney established himself as the top contender, beating Jim Maloney and Johnny Risko and drawing with Paulino Uzcudun and Jack Sharkey.

Tex Rickard, the promoter in charge of Madison Square Garden, was not exactly enthralled with the notion of awarding a title bout to the squat, rugged Heeney, not least because they did not want the title – and the income it brought – to go abroad. No overseas heavyweight had held the title for thirty years, and Rickard gave Harvey the runaround. Handlebars Harvey went to work, traveling to Florida where Gene Tunney was vacationing and personally persuading him to defend against Heeney. The Garden had no choice, and made the match for July 28, 1928 at Yankee Stadium.

Charlie Harvey set up Heeney's training camp at the Fairhaven, New Jersey, estate of wealthy sportsman Raymond Hoagland. Hoagland's barn became the gymnasium, while the field beside it was fitted with an outdoor ring. Eddie Harvey, Charlie's brother, served as head trainer. Heeney had a difficult time adjusting to the sweltering July heat and ubiquitous mosquitoes, which only served to increase his natural surliness.

The camp was run in an extremely professional manner. The fighters would arise at five in the morning for roadwork. After breakfast and a nap, the fighters would exercise, jump rope, shadow box, and hit the light bags. Following these warm-ups, Heeney would usually spar at least four hard rounds. Braddock worked out with the Kiwi through most of the camp.

In mid-July, Heeney began the last phase of intensive sparring in preparation for Tunney. His sessions with Braddock took on added intensity. Braddock, perhaps wanting to impress the throng of newspapermen or perhaps forced by Heeney's relentless pressure, fought as hard as he could. A week before the fight, the Hard Rock was nearing top form. In one two-round sparring session, he seemed to disdain the effects of others' punches. One right cross by Braddock was so hard it drew whistles from the ringside, but Heeney "paid no more attention to this than if he had been hit by a toy balloon."

Braddock was learning as well as assisting. In one session, rather than rely on his booming right crosses, Braddock surprised Heeney by jabbing repeatedly before opening up with both hands, knocking Heeney's protective headgear askew, before slamming a punch directly on Heeney's jaw. The truculent New Zealander picked up his work pace in the next round and nearly ran Braddock out of the ring.

Word circulated about the skinny light-heavyweight who was unafraid to rumble with the bull-like challenger, and for their next sparring session an extraordinary crowd of nearly 10,000 people showed up at the camp. Heeney was now approaching his peak, and although Braddock was able to land the occasional hard blow, he simply used his weight and size to walk through the punches and belabor the lighter man to the stomach, ribs and kidneys. Braddock tried to box at long range but obtained only a moment's respite before Heeney was on him again. After the session, Braddock seemed slightly dazed as he told reporters that he found it almost impossible to slow Heeney.

Four days before the title match, in one of their last encounters, Braddock could hardly land a glove on the bobbing, weaving, slugging New Zealander. He left camp having helped Tom Heeney get into the best shape of his life. The time with Heeney had given Braddock a good look at a well-run training camp. The brothers Charlie and Eddie Harvey, along with the rest of the staff, all worked together with the best interest of the fighters foremost in their minds. Charlie Harvey had little time to celebrate. On the last day in camp, somebody picked his pocket for $400, and later that day, he slammed his hand in a car door and broke three fingers.

Despite Gould's best efforts, he had not been able to get a fight on the Tunney-Heeney card. Instead, Braddock boxed against a tough Connecticut Italian, Nando Tassi, at Ebbett's Field, Brooklyn, under the promotional banner of the Garden's foremost competitor, Herbert Fugazy, the night before the big show. Tassi danced a tarantella for the bulk of the fight, which ended in a draw after ten rounds.

The next day, July 26, 1928, Heeney finally got his shot at the title with Charlie Harvey looking on, his hand bandaged with more gauze than his fighter's. In Heeney's hometown of Gisborne, loudspeakers were mounted on every available spot so that his countrymen could listen to the radio broadcast. Heeney pressured the elegant Tunney in the first round raising several lumps and a bruise on the champion's face. He won the first round by a wide margin. But from the third round on, Tunney marshalled every bit of his experience and talent to torment Heeney in front of 60,000 fans. By round eight, Heeney's left eye was swollen shut and his face streaked with blood from several cuts, but he still pressed forward, "a bloody Cyclops," snorting crimson from a battered nose.

Finally, in the eleventh, the bull was felled; the bloody Heeney dropped to the canvas. Tunney had retained his title. He retired a few days later, one of few boxing champions ever to bow out with laurels intact. The Hard Rock never really recovered from what AP sportswriter Charles W. Dunkley called "one of the worst beatings a challenger ever received," and although he fought for six years afterwards, he lost more often than he won.

Joe Gould, meanwhile, had been encouraged by Braddock's work with Heeney. His restless gaze now fixed on the light heavyweight title, held by the formidable Tommy Loughran.

*Notorious Hell's Kitchen mobster Owney Madden (left) leaves the gates of Sing Sing Prison in July 1933 after spending a year behind bars for violation of parole on a manslaughter sentence. There to greet him – either hiding his face or tipping his hat to photographers – is his friend Joe Gould. Madden was the secret power behind the New York fight scene in the 1920s and 1930s.*

CHAPTER 3

# Title Contender

"Never try to be ordinary – there is always room at the top."

—Joe Gould

By 1928, the twenty-three-year-old Jim Braddock was regularly tussling with world-ranked boxers. Joe Sekyra, a curly-haired light-heavyweight from Dayton, Ohio, garnered a little publicity for himself by boldly claiming Gene Tunney's vacated heavyweight title a few days before his bout with Jimmy Braddock. He looked to solidify that claim by knocking off the popular Jersey fighter.

Sekyra, born in 1906 to Bohemian parents, had excelled at football in high school but declined offers to play college ball because he had his mind set on a world boxing title. He learned the rudiments of the game from a local pro fighter, and showed early promise in reeling off forty-two consecutive wins in the amateurs, while working at a drug store as a soda jerk. He turned professional in 1925 and met similar success until a bizarre health problem sidetracked him: after one bout, he had a fifty-two-foot tapeworm removed from his system. By 1928, when he was matched with Braddock, he was regarded as a talented, tough-to-beat light-heavy with designs on a world title. Few beyond Sekyra's immediate circle, however, gave any credence to his claiming Tunney's crown, least of all the 5,000 fans present at Everett's Field for his ten-round contest with Braddock.

Sekyra came in several pounds over the contracted weight, leading Joe Gould to seek payment of a forfeit. Braddock, an extremely light 168 pounds, for once seemed crude, awkward, and hesitant. For some reason, he fought almost exclusively as a counter-fighter, waiting for Sekyra to lead off. Braddock did deliver the best punch of the fight, an overhand right in the first round that rocked Sekyra to his heels, but after that he rarely landed a solid punch, while one of Sekyra's blows split open his eye, cutting him for the first time in his career. The bout was a stinker, and Braddock lost the decision.

His career seemed to be going backwards. In his past four fights, he had lost to Monte, fought an unimpressive ten rounds with Tunney sparring partner Billy Vidabeck, drawn with Nando Tassi, and now lost to Sekyra. The power seemed to have gone from his right hand, a legacy of those bad breaks that must have preyed on his subconscious.

At some point after the Sekyra bout, Gould apparently sold part of his interest in Braddock to "Pete the Goat" Stone, an associate of, and front for, Bill Duffy and Owney "Killer" Madden. Stone was a scary character, his backers even more so. Madden had once led the Gophers gang of Hell's Kitchen, and was reputed to have killed several men, becoming one of the nation's most notorious, and successful, gangsters. He now ran Harlem's popular Cotton Club, home to Cab Calloway, Duke Ellington and many more of the great black musicians of the day. His sidekick, the beetle-browed Duffy was known as one of the few fight managers who could knock out any fighter he handled. H. McGinty helped burnish his reputation: "Few New Yorkers know what a wonderful fighter Bill Duffy was in his younger days. He never took a back answer from any of the good fighters. He took them in a room and always fought fairly and there are few fellows Bill Duffy could not stop." Duffy and the slender, sinister Madden – who preferred to remain in the shadows – became hugely influential in boxing, and would later take over the boxing career of the giant Italian heavyweight

Primo Carnera, resulting in a caravan of fixed fights and dubious results.

Duffy and Madden did not get involved directly in controlling Braddock's career, and Gould seems to have kept any knowledge of their help or interference from Braddock – who never asked too many questions anyway. "If they got anything," Braddock would say, "they got it out of Gould's share."

Gould and Pete the Goat were a strange team. "Peter never gave up his first nickel and Joe could never keep a dollar," wrote Jack Miley. Importantly, however, the Goat and Bill Duffy served as East Coast managers for light-heavyweight contender Leo Lomski, who Braddock would almost certainly have to meet to move up the rankings.

Gould's new association paid off immediately. He was able to match Braddock against Pete Latzo, the first ex-champion he would fight. Latzo had jumped two divisions from his title-holding days – from welterweight (147lbs) past middleweight (160) to light-heavy (175) and was looking for a tune-up for his pending match with contender Tuffy Griffith.

Latzo had been a fighter for nearly a decade and more than seventy-five battles. He had beaten the great Mickey Walker for the welterweight title, and as a light-heavy had defeated such top fighters as Maxie Rosenbloom, Leo Lomski, and Charlie Belanger, but had lost twice to the champion, Loughran. His plan was to re-establish his credentials by beating both Braddock and Griffith.

The Latzo-Braddock tilt was held at the Newark Armory. The first three rounds were up-tempo but indecisive. In the fourth, Latzo came alive, bullying Braddock around the ring, and going into the ninth held a slight edge. Braddock finally up, hurting Latzo and sending him reeling to his corner at the end of the round. In the tenth, the match became a mugging as Braddock bounced punch after punch off of Latzo's head. Moments before the final bell, a sickening crack signaled Latzo's jaw snapping, and he dropped in a heap.

The newspapers awarded the no-decision bout to Braddock, while doctors needed eleven feet of silver wire to re-assemble Latzo's jaw. "Braddock hits harder than any fighter I have ever met," Latzo said once he could talk.

The night after, a sportswriter for the influential *Ring* magazine encountered Gould at Broadway and 47th Street, searching for a taxi. The pair shared a ride uptown and for the entire journey Gould extolled Braddock's virtues to his captive listener. He was still talking even as the cab dropped off the reporter. "The kid's found his punch and watch his smoke now!" he yelled out the window.

A week later, Gould was hounding Tom McArdle, the match-maker for Madison Square Garden, for a bout in the big arena. Perhaps to discourage the visions of sugarplums dancing before Gould's eyes, McArdle offered to substitute Braddock for the inca-pacitated Latzo against Gerald "Tuffy" Griffith, expecting Gould to reject the bout out of hand.

"Trot out the contracts," said Gould. "Braddock is ready for Griffith."

It was a bold statement. Griffith's purported record inspired awe – and incredulity – in those who heard of it: fifty-five wins and over forty knockouts. Fortunately Braddock was as fearless as his manager, and voiced no qualms – though what he saw when Griffith finally arrived in New York, two days before the bout, must have given even him pause for thought. The Iowan went straight to Stillman's Gym in midtown to work out for the press, boxed five hard rounds with several sparring partners, and flattened each of them. His power shocked even the hard-bitten trainers in atten-dance. In the back of the gym, Jim Braddock looked on, evaluating the visitor for weaknesses.

Griffith entered the fight a dead-cert five-to-one betting favorite. "Looks like they are picking a casket for you," Braddock's mother told him after reviewing the newspaper predictions. "Don't let that stuff worry you. Go in there and try to knock him out with the first punch."

Promoter Tex Rickard took the opportunity to showcase another unbeaten boxer, the fabulous Cuban featherweight Kid Chocolate, and over 19,000 fans paid into the Garden to see the two hotshots. Surprisingly, Chocolate's winning streak was halted when unheralded Joe Scalfaro held him to a draw.

In the main event, Griffith soon had the crowd standing on the scats as he chased his opponent around the ring in the first round, looking for a quick finish. But adversity brought the best out in Braddock. He boxed superbly, and neither fighter did any real damage. Returning to his corner at the end of the round, Braddock had seen something. "I'll take him in a round or two," he calmly told Gould.

In round two, the boxers sparred at ring center for about a half a minute. The aggressive Griffith soon moved in – and as he did, he dropped his left hand. Braddock saw the opening, and flashed over a straight right that catapulted Griffith to the canvas. Clearly dazed, he staggered up at the count of three. Braddock measured his man and knocked him down again. Once more Griffith rose at the count of three and once more he was driven to the canvas by a booming right hand. Four times in all Griffith crashed to the canvas. Finally, the referee Kid McPartland intervened and stopped the contest.

Boxing writer Hype Igoe dispensed with all technical analysis to describe the upset in a few colorful words: "Tuffy came charging out at the start of the second round. Bam! That right landed on his whiskers, and then he was on the floor as stiff as a frozen mackerel." Gross receipts totaled over $53,000, resulting in a purse to Braddock of nearly $9,000, a huge jump from the $300 he received for whipping Latzo. And Tex Rickard rewarded Braddock with a make-or-break match against Bill Duffy's fighter, the Aberdeen Assassin, Leo Lomski. The winner would likely fight Tommy Loughran for the light-heavyweight championship of the world.

At the end of 1928, Tex Rickard, head of Madison Square Garden and the most powerful person in boxing, ranked the light-heavyweight division. He named four fighters that stood out above the rest: champion Tommy Loughran, Leo Lomski, Jimmy Slattery and Mike McTigue. Braddock was grouped in with about twelve other fighters in a second tier behind them – but at least he was ranked.

Joe Gould's fighter had hit the big time.

The Lomski-Braddock decider sold out the Garden, much to Rickard's delight. The crowd paid over $60,000 into the box office to watch the two men battle for a title shot.

Braddock boxed calmly against his aggressive opponent to carry the first round easily. The second round was fought on even terms: Lomski peppered Braddock with left jabs before launching thudding hooks on the inside but Braddock came back to score with a fierce flurry.

In the third, Braddock kept his rival back with his low, rising jab, and several times countered Lomski's swings with hard rights. One of these split Lomski's left eye and blood began to ooze out. Out of necessity, Lomski stepped up his attacks and carried the fight to Braddock. His most effective targets were the heart and ribs, but he also mixed in a jab, a new element to his arsenal.

In the seventh round both fighters tried for a knockout. Braddock ended the round with a right cross that stopped Lomski in his tracks at the bell. In the eighth and ninth Braddock once more held Lomski at bay with his longer reach, but Lomski could not be discouraged and pressed forward throwing hard, short punches. In the tenth round Lomski seemed to be the fresher of the two and drove in relentlessly, walking through the occasional bomb from Braddock.

The result lay with the judges. Charles F. Mathison tabbed it a draw. Tom Flynn and referee Arthur Donovan voted for Lomski, giving him a majority decision. They said Lomski had won five rounds, Braddock four and the second round was even.

The loss should have ruled Braddock out of immediate title contention. In March 1929, however, Lomski lost to both Tuffy Griffith and Maxie Rosenbloom. This left a contest that same month between Braddock and the highly rated Jimmy Slattery as the elimination fight for a challenge to Tommy Loughran's title. It was a chance he could not afford to miss.

Jimmy Slattery loved life. "I tried to hold him down but it was like trying to sit on an active volcano," rued his exasperated manager, Red Carr. Even Slattery recognized the debilitating effects of his candle-burning lifestyle, admitting, "when you dance you have to pay the fiddler. That fiddler always has his hand out. And I did a lot of dancing."

He could certainly fight, though. He had briefly held the National Boxing Association's version of the world light-heavyweight title, and his friend and roommate, Newsboy Brindis, penned a poem about him entitled *The Most Natural Boxer of Modern Times*, the last stanza of which summed up his view of Slattery's career:

> You can shout about Joe Louis, the Bomber of the day,
> Of Armstrong, the tiger, of Braddock and his sway;
> Of Greb, of Baer and Carnera, the "Big Battery"
> But all of them together would make one "Jimmy Slattery."

A capacity crowd, paying over $60,000, packed Madison Square Garden for the Slattery bout. The loudest cheers were for the now-retired Jack Dempsey, who was introduced before the start. Dempsey was in negotiations to take over as promoter of boxing at the Garden, following the sudden death of the pioneering Tex Rickard in January 1929.

Slattery was the seven-to-five betting favorite, even though he had weighed in 168½ pounds to Braddock's 173¼. In the early rounds, he capered fluidly around the ring, using lateral movement and quick punches to befuddle Braddock. Though comparatively flat-footed, Braddock did manage to cut off the ring several times, forcing Slattery to the ropes and attacking to the body to slow him down.

Time and again Braddock launched hard, looping right hands at Slattery's head, drawing gasps and groans from the ringsiders as Slattery slipped most of them by fractions of an inch. In the third round, Slattery varied his approach by moving inside of Braddock's wide punches and landing several swift combinations on Braddock's jaw. The pattern continued through round six. Referee Lou Magnolia had little work as the fighters rarely clinched.

By the seventh round, Braddock appeared to be losing confidence and vigor in the face of Slattery's continuous flurries, but Slattery's lax approach to training lifestyle and Braddock's body punches were taking their toll. In the eighth, Braddock twice rocked his opponent with sweeping left hooks. When Slattery sought to dance away from the ropes, Braddock went after him, throwing hard punches with both hands, and won the round by a clear margin, the first he had won in the fight.

Entering the home stretch, Slattery still seemed to have a comfortable lead, and at the start of the ninth his second wind seemed to kick in, as he maneuvered around the ring as fast as he had at the start.

And then Braddock landed his right hand.

The blow hit Slattery's jaw with an audible thud and sent him stumbling backwards to the ropes. Braddock advanced for the finish. Taking measure, he battered the helpless Slattery with punch after punch. Slattery's body hung on the ropes, the force of Braddock's punches stopping him from falling. He feebly raised his hands to cover his face, but Braddock slapped the gloves down with his left hand and poured in another half dozen thundering rights. After what seemed like an eternity to the screaming throng, Slattery wilted sideways to the canvas and Lou Magnolia waved it off. Jim Braddock had taken apart a beautiful fighting machine and left it in pieces. More importantly, he was now in pole position to challenge the champion.

Braddock's superb win was all the more impressive because it was against a boxer who, despite his lifestyle, was far from finished. Within a year, Slattery would outfight Lou Scozza to win a version of the world title, and he would end his hall-of-fame career with over 100 wins. Unlike many, including Braddock, he would not lose his money during the Great Depression. He spent it first. "Suppose I had invested my money," he recalled, "I'd only have lost it in the crash, wouldn't I? I have had a hell of a good time. What the hell, Jack, one can't eat that stuff."

Taking careful note was the forensic Tommy Loughran. The savage beating of Slattery impressed the champion, who even wrote an analysis of Braddock's style that was syndicated to several newspapers. Loughran also gave his imprimatur to Braddock as a worthy challenger. His keen eye pinpointed one subtle change in Braddock's style from their evenings fighting on the same card in Wilkes-Barre. "Joe Gould, Jim's manager, has changed his style somewhat," he wrote. "Braddock used to stand as straight as the goddess of Liberty. Gould has him crouching and weaving a little more."

Nat Fleischer, the highly influential editor of *Ring* magazine, also noticed a difference. "Braddock, ordinarily a counter-puncher who waits for the other fellow to do the leading, knew that his only chances for victory lay in forcing the action and adopting a new plan of attack, relentlessly kept after Slattery. Braddock was the aggressor throughout. He pressed forward constantly and took all that Slattery had to offer, but never let up in his attack."

The *Philadelphia Ledger* also noted the change in style, but damned Braddock with faint praise: "As late as last January, when he dropped a close decision to Leo Lomski, Braddock was strictly a one-handed fighter who relied on counter-punching with his right.

Since that time, a great change for the better has been made in Braddock's style. He has been made into an aggressive two-handed battler, a sort of glorified club fighter."

Braddock's title challenge was scheduled for July 18. Having learned valuable lessons in Tom Heeney's training camp, he trained at Saratoga Springs, New York, far from the distractions of the city. He had also learned from his work with Heeney that good sparring partners were crucial to adequate preparation, so Gould hired some of the best. Allentown Joe Gans led the crew. A fast light-heavy of near limitless ability, Gans had difficulty obtaining big fights because he was black. Even worse for him were the rumors were that he had once dropped Jack Dempsey in a sparring session; no-one wanted to fight a light-heavy who could floor the great Dempsey. Joe Hanlon of Bridgeport, Connecticut, Joe Barlow, a spark plug from Boston, and Braddock's brother Al rounded out the team. Al had succeeded his brother by winning the New Jersey Amateur Light-heavyweight Title in 1927, but had flopped as a professional.

Braddock's sparring was intense. One particularly brutal session, a few days before the Loughran match, saw him club Barlow without let up, crumple Allentown Joe to his knees with a left hook to the body, and knock out Hanlon with a left hook. In the final round, "there was no brotherly love shown in the lively combat" with brother Al, according to one witness. Braddock was sharpened to a razor's edge, and would have no trouble making the weight, as he consistently weighed 172 pounds. Support for the "Irishman" was high, and Gould was ebulliently confident.

"I have the next light-heavyweight champion of the world," he told the press. "Jim will punch Loughran's head right into your lap Thursday night."

Loughran, in contrast, struggled each day to reduce to the 175-pound limit. Visitors to his camp saw him swathed in "rubber lingerie" as he sought to sweat off the extra weight. Win or lose, Loughran moaned to all who would listen that this would be his last bout at light-heavyweight. He spent the night before the fight on a yacht anchored on the East River, and the next morning sought to reassure his fans and backers. "Making weight was a tough job," he said, "but I did it and am strong enough to retain my title after a sensational fight." Perhaps nausea occasioned by the insistent rocking of his berth during the night led him to make an uncharacteristic boast: "Braddock may knock me down but I'll get up and give him the worst licking he has ever received." The reference to a knockdown did, however, suggest a healthy respect for his young challenger.

Loughran had been the betting favorite right up to fight night, but late money on Braddock drove the odds down to about even, and a sudden – not to say suspicious – surge of bettors laid one to win three that Braddock would win by knockout. Whether or not this strange activity had anything to do with Joe Gould's mob connections, there was nothing to suggest the contest had not been arranged on the level; indeed its proceeds would benefit the Home of the Daughters of Jacob nursing hospital. Ticket sales at Yankee Stadium reached $140,000, making the night a successful one for the charity, with thousands of Loughran fans from Philadelphia adding to Braddock's hefty New York–New Jersey contingent.

The weigh-in was held in the afternoon of the fight, and Braddock came in at a surprisingly light 170 pounds, leading to whispers that inexperience had led him to over-train. Loughran's rubber lingerie had served its purpose and he scaled a pound below the division limit.

Though an overcast sky threatened rain, some 25,000 fans made their way to Yankee Stadium for the bout. Just after the fighters entered the ring, but before they could be announced, a group of "musicians" calling themselves the Tommy Loughran Marching and Chowder Club and Fife and Drum Corps paraded twice around the infield, singing battle hymns and pounding on makeshift drums. One suspects that a few had not heard about Prohibition. According to one ringsider, the announcer, the venerable Joe Humphries, "expressed his withering critical opinion of the Loughran Legionnaires' artistic efforts by declaring 'now that the armistice has been signed I will announce the next contest.'" Also at ringside, Texas Guinan, the queen of the nightclubs, was telling anyone who would listen that she owned ten percent of Braddock. When Loughran's band spotted her, they broke out in an ironic chorus of "Let Me Call You Sweetheart."

Finally, somehow, the fight got underway. In the first round, Braddock walked to Loughran who inexplicably backed to the ropes. Braddock stuck out a jab and crossed a right that split Loughran below the eye. Thirty seconds into the match, Braddock had already drawn first blood, but Loughran calmly brushed it from his face and continued to box his challenger.

In the second, Loughran showed his mettle, exchanging blows with his power-punching opponent. When they separated, both were bleeding from new cuts on the face, and Braddock's aggression carried the round. By some accounts, it was the last round he would win in the fight. The pattern had been set by round three: Loughran dancing away from Braddock's rushes, circling to his right, away from Braddock's counters, and jabbing at every opportunity. In close, he wrestled and clinched, not letting Braddock do any good work. Loughran had figured out his challenger in just two rounds, and Braddock could do little about it. His frustration and embarrassment mounted as the contest wore on.

In the sixth, Braddock opened a small cut on Tommy's lip with a right hook. Loughran responded by opening up with both fists and pounded Braddock about the head. Braddock couldn't seem to get past the champion's guard, and took a left hook and two hard rights to the face; his eye poured blood after the exchange.

Extant film of the fight does not convey the bloody nature of the contest. "Tommy made the challenger a mess," reported the *Philadelphia Record*. "Coming out of a clinch, the champion's left eye began to spurt blood as a result of a butt from Braddock's head. Tommy's face was a crimson mass. Between rounds, Tommy's face was covered with blood and his seconds worked furiously to stop the flow."

Gould could see that his fighter was in for a long evening. "You have to stop some of those left hands," he implored.

"You don't see any of them going by me, do you?" snapped Braddock in response.

Throughout the middle rounds, one noisy Loughran fan kept up an incessant one-sided conversation with Braddock. In the seventh, he shouted, "Why don't you smile, Jimmy?"

Braddock dropped his hands and turned to the crowd, sarcastically shouting, "Oh, I just love this."

Loughran capitalized on Braddock's lack of focus and quickly clipped him with several hard punches. In the ensuing clinch, he admonished the younger man. "Watch yourself. Pay attention."

In the ninth, Loughran sent Braddock back on his heels with several left hooks, then cleverly made the challenger hit himself with his own glove. In the tenth, he backed Braddock to the ropes and faked him into throwing the left hook. Loughran stepped inside it and shot across a right hand that snapped Braddock's head backwards. As he came forward, his head hit Loughran's, opening yet another deep cut at the champion's hairline. The blood ran down Loughran's forehead.

"I couldn't see anything, my eyes were filled with blood and he threw a right hand at me and I put my head to the side and as I did, my eyes began to roll," Loughran recalled years later. "The blood in there acted like a lubricant and I couldn't raise my eyes. If I put my head this way, they'd roll that way. I couldn't control my eyes. The only thing to do is move in close. I moved in, got ahold, and I wouldn't let go of him. If I got away from the guy I couldn't see where I was going so I stalled through the rest of the round, I got back to the corner, when the round was over I walked into the ropes and my manager came and got me. He said, 'What's wrong?' I said, 'Joe, wash my eyes out, the blood.' ... I got my eyes cleared out, well, from then on he couldn't hit me to save his life."

The last five rounds were a rout. Braddock never stopped charging but Loughran's left hand had locked in on his face. In the fourteenth, Braddock stopped at the ring's center, dropped his hands and invited Loughran to come forward. Loughran ignored him and stuck out another jab. There was no doubting the decision: at the end of fifteen rounds, referee Eddie Forbes held up Loughran's hand in victory.

The report in the *Zanesville Signal* sang Loughran's praises:

> To those who can appreciate the master tactician in action, Loughran was a treat for granulated eyelids. His was the "infinite variety" of which Shakespeare wrote so feelingly. Sometimes he elected to stand in a corner and smother Braddock's leads, sometimes he merely used that intelligent left to jolt the challenger back where he belonged, again he slipped the punch and countered his man with short bruising punches inside, and occasionally he crossed a right to the head, prompting Braddock to blink those small penetrating eyes in amazement.

In his dressing room, Loughran told reporters "he was trying all the time with his right, and he did not land, but look at the bruises on my shoulder; they are from his left jabs. Jim has a real good left, if he could learn to use it."

Braddock was shattered, but there were compensations. He had fought bravely, and his share of the purse, $17,000, was a small fortune when the average annual income was $750, and for farm workers, just $253. In one bloody evening, the twenty-three-year-old boxer had earned more than the average worker would make in twenty years.

After such a hard contest, he could have expected a decent summer break, but within six weeks he was taken to Los Angeles to fight Yale Okun, whose manager, the flamboyant Jimmy "Boy

Bandit" Johnston, managed to steal the headlines by flying from New York to Los Angeles, at a time when air travel cross-country was a risky novelty. Whether it was a publicity stunt or not, it was unusual enough to cause a stir.

Okun, a seasoned veteran with over five years experience and more than sixty fights under his belt, was a difficult opponent to follow Loughran, and outworked a seemingly distracted Braddock over ten rounds to win on points. *Ring* magazine's report, buried in a compilation of the out-of-town results, said, "Braddock's big right hand made no impression on Okun, who took 'em without a quiver. The hairy-chested Jew was just too smart and tough for the harp." Braddock's whopping purse of $7,500 was some consolation.

Despite the back-to-back losses, Jim Braddock had come a long way in a short time. He was even mentioned in a financial survey of the top boxers of the day by press agent extraordinaire, the gnomish Francis Albertanti, for *Ring* magazine, in an article entitled "What Price Cauliflowers?" a pun on the title of the 1926 war movie *What Price Glory?* In his usual lively style, Albertanti recounted the spending habits of some of the game's top names – "Mike McTigue wouldn't spend a nickel to see the Statue of Liberty do a dance," and so on – before concluding: "Some more who are wealthy and for whom they'll never have to hold benefits to get them back on their feet are … James J. Braddock, Joe Jeanette, Leo Lomski, and Tommy Loughran."

Braddock indeed seemed to be in good financial shape. He had paid off the mortgage on his mother's house with the proceeds from the Slattery fight. Cash on hand totaled about $10,000. The bulk of his money, some $20,000, was invested in a taxicab company in Jersey City and a bar-speakeasy named Henke's. He was twenty-three years old, fit and strong, with money in the bank, a sweetheart, a well-connected manager and time on his side. Life was good.

★

On Monday and Tuesday, October 28 and 29, the U.S. stock market crashed, bringing to an end the excesses and optimism of the Jazz Age and the Roaring Twenties. A prolonged, speculative boom in stocks and shares, fuelled by borrowed money, came to a violent halt. By the end of November, investors had lost more than $100 billion in assets, triggering the worldwide economic slump that would come to be known as the Great Depression.

The Crash did not have an immediate crushing effect on Jim Braddock's finances. True, like many others, he lost some on the stock market, but his capital was chiefly invested in the taxi company and his bar.

In time however, only wily Joe Jeanette of the fighters named by Francis Albertanti would escape the most onerous effects of the Depression. Jeanette owned the building housing his gymnasium and an adjacent garage from which he ran a limousine service. All of the others would suffer along with millions of other Americans who exited the Roaring Twenties well off but who quickly lost their economic footing as the nation plunged into economic despair.

Two weeks after "Black Tuesday," Braddock headlined at Madison Square Garden, and matchmaker Tom McArdle served up an eccentric fistic genius named Maxie Rosenbloom as his antagonist. He was judged a poor choice of opponent for someone who needed a confidence-boosting win. "Joe Gould is being censured for accepting a match for his fighter, James J. Braddock, with Maxie Rosenbloom," was the view of boxing writer John Romano. "Braddock has shown to be a deadly hitter but too deliberate to cope with a fast-moving, rapid-fire hitting fighter like Rosenbloom."

Rosenbloom was a great fighter with a great slogan: "I don't drink, I don't smoke, and I don't stay away from girls." He began boxing after George Raft, the future movie star, saw him in a street brawl over a dice game. Raft, then an aspiring "hoofer," managed Maxie during his amateur career and at the start of his professional one, until Raft got his big break dancing in Texas Guinan's floor show. Frank Bachman took over as Rosenbloom's manager, and Rosenbloom's career began to flourish.

Though Rosenbloom was an all-action fighter, he often slapped with an open glove rather than punch hard, earning the nickname "Slapsie Maxie." His flurries were accompanied by a dancing style that kept his chin out of harm's way. Rosenbloom explained his take-no-chances strategy in a bit of doggerel he would trot on occasion:

> Prunes are black, oranges yeller
> Nobody likes to get hit on the smeller.

Proud of this impromptu verse, Rosenbloom would assert that although his poem was not as good as anything by Byron or Shelley, it was as good as the best by Keats. Then he would point out that sportswriter Fred Keats covered horse racing for the *New York Daily Mirror*.

The fight turned out to be a disaster for Braddock. He entered the ring having put on twelve pounds from his title fight, none of it muscle. Though he plodded after Rosenbloom for the entire ten rounds, he barely landed a solid punch. Any lessons in cutting off the ring learned from Loughran had been forgotten.[1]

Mae Fox, Braddock's pretty fiancé, attended the fight, and found it deeply unsettling. Any joy or excitement she had felt during the previous bouts she had watched were now replaced with a sickening horror at her husband-to-be being hit. Mae ran from the arena after the first round. She never again watched Braddock fight.

Braddock, in contrast, didn't appear to care about the decision, and seemed disillusioned with the fight game. "I'm disgusted with it all," he confessed to Mae. "Let's get married and settle down. I'll devote all my time to the taxicab business." He and Mae planned to marry that January.

[1] Loughran was *Ring* magazine's Fighter of the Year for 1929. Despite his three consecutive losses, Braddock came second in the voting, with one first-place vote and fourteen for second position.

Ten days before the wedding, Jack Dempsey called Joe Gould offering Braddock a rematch against Leo Lomski. The fight would be in Chicago – the day before his wedding. Dempsey's purse offer of $6,000 was too large to turn down; Mae postponed the wedding for a week. She didn't want to walk down the aisle with her groom sporting a black eye.

A tiny crowd of 5,232 paid just under $16,000 at the Chicago Coliseum to see Braddock return to form. He decked the thick-necked Lomski for a short count in the second round, and in the fifth, sent him down again. At the conclusion of the bout, one judge voted for Braddock, another for Lomski, and the referee, Davey Miller, called it a draw. Dempsey lost over $10,000 on the promotion, but by the time he had finished counting his receipts, Braddock was on a train back to New Jersey.

James J. Braddock married Mae Theresa Fox at St. Joseph's on the Palisades on January 25, 1930. One of Braddock's brothers was best man; Mae's sister the maid-of-honor. After the ceremony, the couple hosted a wedding breakfast at Radio Frank's Rendezvous on Hudson Heights. Fifteen hundred people attended the reception, including newspaper editors, sports writers, famous sports figures, friends and relatives. The wedding cost several thousand dollars, all paid for by Braddock. In the coming years Mae would wonder where the fifteen hundred friends that had attended her wedding had gone.

The *New York Daily News* listed the gifts given by Braddock to his bride, noting that his finances were in good shape. Braddock "presented Mrs. Braddock with an elegant coupe of expensive make, a diamond ring which his manager Joe Gould swears has six carrots on it, and he also gave her another fine present which Joe says is an elegant broach with fifty-four diamonds on it."

The newlyweds left on Monday to honeymoon in Florida. The next day, Gould received a telegram from the Illinois Boxing Commission. The commissioners, eleven days after the Lomski bout, claimed to have discovered an error in the scorecards. Instead of a draw, Braddock had lost to Lomski. The error was attributed to the scorecard of referee Davey Miller, a man with notorious gangland connections, who had incorrectly tallied his scoring. His corrected ballot gave Lomski four rounds, Braddock two, with four rounds even. Gould's response made sport pages across the country: "I have received from you today a letter notifying me that Lomski has been declared the winner over Braddock 10 days after the fight. May I and Braddock, who has just been married, thank you for the wedding present."

Journalist Dan Parker pulled no punches in the *New York Daily News*: "Referee Davey Miller, a power in Chicago's underworld, always used to get 40 in arithmetic in public school. Adding up a column of figures was one of the things Davey could never do correctly. Throughout life, this failing haunted Davey. And the night of the Lomski-Braddock bout it got him into a jam."

Braddock seemed to lose interest in the fight game after his marriage. In June 1930 Braddock lost a ten-round "newspaper decision" to Harold Mays, a former sparring partner of Gene Tunney. It was his third loss in a row, though it was largely buried in the agate type. The important boxing news came out of Detroit, where Primo Carnera knocked out K.O. Christner, the first time in five years of fighting that Christner had been put on the canvas. Under Bill Duffy's keen guidance, the lumbering Carnera was learning to fight.

Braddock, however, had now lost seven of eight fights. In July, he rebounded slightly in a rubber match with Joe Monte on Monte's home turf, Fenway Park. Braddock won all ten rounds. He jumped on his foe at the outset, stabbing Monte with a long left and then rapping him repeatedly with right hooks. In several rounds, Braddock was able to land as many as a dozen straight lefts without Monte being able to avoid or counter. Old Iron Head would not give ground so he was forced to take a ten-round beating. Monte never fought again. No doctor or commission would permit it; the courageous Italian had fought Braddock even though he was blind in one eye.[1]

---

[1] Monte's nephew, Arthur Mercante, would become one of boxing's most prominent referees, handling the first Ali-Frazier bout, among thousands of other fights.

In August, Braddock returned to Boston to take on heavyweight "Babe" Hunt, a towering Texan, who a short time before, had been the first fighter named as *Ring* magazine's "prospect of the month." Outweighed by fourteen pounds, Braddock once more put in a good effort; indeed the *Boston Globe* described the fight as the most "intense heavyweight battle as a local ring has seen in years." Braddock held his own with a bigger, heavier fighter for the first eight rounds. "Punch and counterpunch, charge and counter-charge, the two young heavyweights thrilled the crowd of 10,000 with their mad orgy of punching," reported the *Boston Post*.

In the eighth round, Braddock staggered Hunt and went all out for the knockout, but his man would not go down. "Holding Braddock when he could, fighting back like a cornered rat when forced to, the big man from Ponca City reeled throughout the three minutes and walked to his corner, the victory as well as won."

Braddock was simply too exhausted to fight well in the last two rounds. "Fourteen pounds were too much, legs were too weary, arms were limp leads, and Hunt stormed through the tenth playing a vicious tune on Braddock's body, ripping and tearing and slashing at close quarters, winning the desperate battle with a last-minute attack." Hunt won the fight, but Braddock won the crowd. "Many of the pew holders booed lustily when the decision ... was announced." Hunt earned the decision if not the glory.

Boston fight fans enjoyed Braddock's slam-bang style, so he was brought back for a bout against heavyweight trial horse Phil Mercurio. Finally fighting a heavyweight of his own size, Braddock pulverized Mercurio in just two rounds. He didn't fight again that year.

Just after Thanksgiving, 1930, an up-and-coming boxer from California was set to make his first appearance in the Big Apple. After negotiating with Joe Gould, his manager agreed to a December date against Braddock at Madison Square Garden. The Garden put in a request for the bout's approval; James A. Farley, chairman of the boxing commission and later Postmaster General under Franklin Roosevelt, had the power to reject any proposed contest. On this occasion, Farley rejected Braddock as a suitable foe, believing that he would be no fit match for the Livermore Larruper, Max Baer.

Max Baer, the broad-shouldered, big-hitting champion from California, whose huge right-hand punch was blamed for the death of two opponents, including the promising young heavy Frankie Campbell [inset].

CHAPTER 4

# The Livermore Larruper

There was a young scrapper named Baer
Who had the most beautiful hair
He could flirt, he could fight
He could dance all night
That fantastic fast puncher Max Baer
—Anonymous 1930s limerick

Heavyweight fighter Max Baer stepped off the 20th Century Limited at Grand Central Station in the Fall of 1930 carrying with him a reputation as a murderous puncher, a wild playboy, and a boxer with a "million-dollar body and a ten-cent head."

Gunslinger-turned-reporter Bat Masterson had once observed, "The average professional boxer has a brain that does not make more than one revolution every twenty-four hours." From the variety and diversity of Baer's antics, it was likely that his brain revolved twenty-four times in one hour.

Baer's grandfather, Aschill Baer, a French Jew from Alsace-Lorraine, migrated to America as a young man. Family lore held that soon after his arrival, Aschill was reviewing a friend's photo album when he saw a photograph of a beautiful young girl. Aschill decided then and there that the girl should be his wife. Shortly after, he paid Fannie Fischel's way from Vienna to the United States. The couple had seven sons, one of whom, Jacob, became Max Baer's father. Neither Aschill nor Fannie insisted on any of their children following the Jewish faith, and Jacob, free of any religious or tribal requirements, married Dora Bales, of Scotch-Irish ancestry.

Jacob was a big, strong man who earned his living as a butcher in a slaughterhouse. Max Baer's brother, known as "Buddy," would recall proudly how their father set a record when he transformed "a 1300-pound bull into steaks and chops in just three minutes and twenty-six seconds." Dora was no less an impressive physical specimen, standing six feet tall and weighing 200 pounds, just slightly smaller than her husband.

In 1909, Jacob and Dora were living in Omaha, Nebraska, where Jacob was working as a cattle buyer for Swift and Company. On February 9, Dora gave birth to their second child and first son. She named him Max Adelbert (to honor her hometown, Adel, Iowa) but called him "Mickey." Shortly after, Swift and Company transferred Jacob to Denver, Colorado, to head up a slaughtering plant there.

The Baer family moved to Durango, Colorado, from Denver soon after the end of World War I. Jacob then held the position of manager of an independent meat packing plant. By age thirteen, Max would be described by his brother Buddy as "something of a loner, more of a introvert than anyone in the family." Max had a hard time adjusting to the macho streets of Durango. He avoided street fights, using the excuse that his father had warned him against "street brawling," and became known as a physical coward. Several stories of Max's youth ended with him running from a schoolyard bully, and his older sister, Frances, often had to intervene to protect him.

Finally, Jacob became aware of his son's pusillanimous behavior. He was shocked.

"A son of mine won't fight back when attacked in his own yard? Are you sick, Max?" he roared.

"I guess I am sick," said Max. "I can't seem to avoid a fight without running and the more I run the more I feel like a coward. That's what makes me sick."

"You ought to feel sick," said his father. "I thought you were old enough to know the difference between avoiding a fight that isn't worth fighting and running from a fight that can't be avoided. Get to your room and I'll talk to you later."

When things cooled down, Jacob took his son aside and explained that sometimes a person was justified in fighting back. After that day, Max Baer would no longer run from a fight.

At about that time, Max got his first job, building wooden crates to transport lard. Later, he was hired as apprentice sausage filler. The Baer family then relocated from Colorado to the farming town of Hayward, California, where Max worked alongside his father swinging a meat axe. "Up to my knees in gore, I had the glorious feeling of physical power, and afterwards the satisfactory fatigue from a job well done," he would recall.

Max excelled in sports at his California high school, playing baseball, football, and basketball for his school teams. He never graduated, however, leaving school to work the ranch with his father. By age seventeen, the sports and the physical labour had built him into a minor Adonis over six feet tall and approaching 200 pounds, but he still had no interest in boxing. That would change one night outside a roadhouse near Galt, California.

Max and several friends congregated in the parking lot outside the bar. One of the group pointed out a nearby car. "That belongs to Eddie Overholt. He nearly always keeps a jug of something in there. I know, because he's given me drinks. Maybe I should take a look."

The rest of the gang agreed, and soon Max and his friends were sharing a gallon of wine – until the owner confronted them about the missing jug.

"Who stole it?" demanded Overholt. "One of you bastards stole my wine."

Max stepped forward and answered, jokingly, in a high falsetto voice: "I did sir. Please be gentle."

Overholt charged, seething with rage.

"Honestly, I was scared to death," Baer later wrote. "My heart pumped furiously, I shivered in fright. [He] grimly advanced and as in a dream I saw him pull back his chunky fist and let one go. It caught me smack on the chin and I had the greatest surprise of my life. I had been hit with a punch that would have put most men out for the night, but I was still standing, and my brain was clear."

Instinctively, Baer swung a wild overhand right at his attacker's jaw. Overholt collapsed in the dirt, and lay "quivering on his back." When he came around, he told Max, "Christ, I say I have never been hit like that by anyone or anything. You ought to go into boxing."

The idea clung to Max for several months. Meanwhile, in March 1928, the Baer family moved to Livermore, a railroad town in an area of vineyards and ranches east of San Francisco, where Jacob leased a hog farm he named "Twin Oaks." Livermore had one important civic amenity that Galt did not – a gymnasium. Max bought a punching bag, gloves, and trunks, and installed them at the gym. Soon, a local instructor, Persey Maden, was tutoring the young giant.

Max began "sparring" with anyone he could entice into the ring, but his sparring consisted of all-out attacks, with no semblance of technique. Maden couldn't get anywhere with his tutoring of the aspiring slugger, so he suggested that Baer train with Ray Lockwood, who fought under the name Ray Pelkey and who ran a gym in Oakland. Soon after, Max left home and moved to East Oakland where he worked in the spare parts department of J. Hamilton Lorimer's Atlas Diesel Engine Company.

Pelkey tried to explain basic boxing theory to Max. "The main idea is to keep from being hit, and to hit the other guy," he said, patiently. "To avoid punches, you must be able to dance, to duck and jab. It's what we call boxing. Have you heard of it?"

Max and his father attended fight cards at the local Oakland fight stadium. As they sat in the gallery, studying the matches, Baer became fascinated by the "color and glamour" of the ring. He pictured himself down there on the canvas, under the gleaming lights – the center of attention.

"Some day you are going to see my name up there, dad, just like that, only it will be 'See Max Baer, here tonight,'" he told his father.

"I'll have to see it to believe it," responded Jacob Baer, unconvinced.

If Max had any amateur fights, it could not have been more than one or two. Certainly his first recorded fight was a professional one against a colorfully named veteran heavyweight, Chief Caribou, in Stockton's Oak Park Arena.

Diesel engine magnate J. Hamilton Lorimer, Baer's boss and *de facto* manager, supposedly set up the fight because he wanted to teach him a much-needed lesson and to encourage him to leave the sport. "Max worked for me," Lorimer said. "He was always talking fight. I listened, and when he began to train in an amorous sort of way, he asked me to hold the watch for him. He was big and powerful, but I thought him too good-looking to go in for fighting. I wanted to cure him of his nonsense so I lashed him with Chief Caribou, an Indian heavyweight in Stockton, the toughest fellow around."

Before the fight, Max got a case of dry mouth that he tried to relieve by drinking several bottles of soda. Minutes later, the bloated Baer found himself in his first professional boxing match. The Chief realized that Baer could be hurt to the stomach but Baer's raw power proved to be too much for him. Buddy Baer described the end: "[Max] summoned all of his fading strength and in a final, desperate effort found Caribou's chin with a right uppercut that laid the Indian low for several times the ten-count." Baer closely avoided an unanticipated gastrointestinal episode to win the fight.

Baer biographer, Don Gardiner, added a poetic coda to the Chief's end: "The Chief said later [he] dreamed of beautiful maidens leaping off high cliffs, all for his sake. He heard birds singing in cool water tingling into shaded pools. He didn't know the water came from buckets his seconds were swashing over him. And all this while Maxie Baer clung to the ropes, draped like the laundry the Mexican women of his father's ranch put out each Monday morning."

Baer earned $35 for the fight. His weekly salary at the diesel plant was $10 less.

The free-swinging, fun-loving young fighter from Livermore quickly became a fan favorite and popular drawing card in Oakland, San Francisco, and Stockton. One of those who saw him in Oakland was Al Jolson, the comedy and singing star of vaudeville and radio. He had gone to one of Baer's bouts with Ancil Hoffman, a wealthy avocado grower from Sacramento who was dabbling as a fight promoter and manager. Hoffman began advising young Baer on his career while trying to buy his contract from Lorimer.

Baer's energetic approach to the game added to his popularity. When he lost his ninth fight by fouling Jack McCarthy, the *Hayward Review*, instead of panning Baer for his foul tactics wrote, "The Max Baer and Jack McCarthy scrap was the real feature of the night. McCarthy, draped on the ropes, didn't want to fight any more. Baer stepped aside and motioned him to come out. McCarthy refused the invitation. Thereupon Max grabbed him around the waist and threw him forcefully to the floor. McCarthy got the decision on a foul, Baer got the raspberry. There is no doubt that Baer lost his head, but McCarthy was somewhat provoking. He tried to lay down earlier in the fight but the bell forestalled him. If promoter Parente would only match up the pair for a four-round main event and line up some strong preliminaries he should pack the hall. Four rounds should be the limit, it wouldn't go any further."

By his tenth fight, he was making $4,000 a match. In his fourteenth fight, with Tillie Taverna, he earned $7,500. Max's popularity had other benefits too. As brother Buddy delicately put it, "Max had many girlfriends. He was literally surrounded by women, who lured him into chasing them to bed, yet another sport in which he excelled. For adventurous women, Max had it all, brawn, personality, a sunny disposition, a flashy car, glory and fame, and money."

Max's adventures had their price. He earned $50,000 for seventeen fights in and around Oakland and San Francisco during 1929, but, as 1930 dawned, Max was $10,000 in debt. Like Jimmy Slattery, Max Baer hadn't waited for the stock market to crash to go broke; he had spent his money first. Half went on wine, women, and song; the rest he wasted. On his twenty-first birthday, Baer's employer presented him with a gift of a new, expensive car – and a promotional contract. Max signed, making J. Hamilton Lorimer his manager.

Fourteen months into his career, in his twenty-sixth fight, Baer faced a rough and tumble "veteran rookie" named Meyer "K.O." Christner. Christner had been a classmate of Babe Ruth's in Baltimore before gaining fame as a member of the Goodrich Giants, a football team composed of deaf-mutes. When it was discovered that Christner could both hear and speak, he traded his football jersey for a pair of boxing gloves, at the relatively advanced age of thirty-three. In contrast to Baer, Christner treated his finances carefully: he saved $800 of every $1000 he made in boxing.

Baer's popularity soared when he became the first person to floor the granite-chinned Christner. He sent Christner crashing to the mat three times in the second round, and the fight was stopped.

Baer was then matched with another young heavyweight from northern California, the only one considered to have a chance against him. Francisco Camilli, brother of local baseball star Dolph Camilli, boxed under the name Frankie Campbell and was riding a fourteen-bout winning streak of his own. In total, the Italian had racked up thirty-four wins, twenty-seven by knockout or stoppage, against just three losses. He had also fought two draws – one against Braddock victim Mike Rock. Baer-Campbell was a natural.

Lorimer and Hoffman reached an agreement with Campbell's managers for a fight at Recreation Park, home of the San Francisco Seals baseball club. Baer's purse was to be $10,000, win, lose or draw. At the weigh-in the day of the fight, Baer was 194 pounds; Campbell, who normally weighed around 185, was just 179 pounds. The bookies had hot action both ways, with Baer a two-to-one favorite. Campbell, the smaller of the two men, realized he needed to get inside of Max's long arms to do any damage. He was particularly concerned with Baer's right-hand punch, which had led him to twenty-three wins in twenty-six bouts.

The aging ballpark groaned with the weight of a capacity crowd of 20,000 fans. In the first round, Campbell bobbed and weaved to the inside, where he leveled several jolting hooks to Baer's head. As Campbell backed out of the exchange, Baer clipped him on the jaw with a right, sending Campbell down for a count of nine.

In the second round, the fighters continued their slugfest. Suddenly, Baer went to his knees at ring center. He sprang back to his feet without a count.

"We reeled to the center of the ring, and it was here that Campbell's supporters yelled their heads off in high voice when they saw me on the floor. They jumped to the conclusion that Frankie has knocked me down.... I had slipped and gone to my knees ... I think Frankie must have thought it was one of his punches, because when I leapt angrily to my feet, he was walking away to a neutral corner.

"He seemed to be looking out over the crowd when I rushed over and hit him on the side of the jaw, and he dropped back against the ropes spinning dizzily. I put all I had into that punch and I knew he must have been hurt, but at that moment the bell rang."

Campbell made his way back to his corner at the end of the round. He seemed dazed.

"Something snapped in my head," he told his corner men as they worked hard over him.

"Feel like going back, Frankie?" one asked. "Sure you can go back?"

"I'll go back all right," growled Campbell. "I'll murder that guy."

In the third and fourth rounds, Baer punished Campbell terribly. Campbell fought back, but the thing that had "snapped in his head" bothered him. Baer must have sensed it. In the fifth, he drove Campbell into a corner, forcing him back with punch after punch. An uppercut snapped back Campbell's head. The crowed gasped as his neck whipped his head back across the ropes. But Campbell charged once more.

"Campbell came at me in a rush and as his hands were held low, I saw my chance," recalled Baer. "I put fire and brimstone into the long looping right hand that I unleashed, and it went just where I wanted it to go – flush on my foe's chin."

Campbell sagged but he couldn't fall as his arm was hung over the middle rope. Baer continued to pour in punches. The referee, Toby Irwin, stood transfixed as many in the crowd yelled for Irwin to stop the fight. Finally, a limp, devastated Campbell sunk to the canvas.

Baer dressed quickly and returned to see a small crowd around Campbell's prostrate form. He was still unconscious. One of his seconds tried an old, sometimes effective, but always brutal boxing trick to bring him out of the coma: he ran the blade of a penknife up and under his thumbnail. Campbell did not stir.

As was typical at fights during the 1930s, no ambulance was at the venue, and it took a half hour for one to arrive. Campbell was taken to St. Joseph's Hospital, where they tried to save his life. But at 11:45 a.m. the next day, Frankie Campbell died.

"Campbell's brain was knocked completely loose from his skull," Dr. T.E. Tilman told reporters. "If it had been a case of one cerebral hemorrhage or two, or even three, we might have saved his life. But his brain was literally one huge mass of bruises. There was nothing to be done."

Campbell was the second boxer to die in San Francisco in a week, and the backlash against those connected with the fatal bout was intense and immediate. Baer was arrested on homicide charges, and held on $10,000 bail while a grand jury was impaneled to investigate the incident. "They branded me as if I were a blood-thirsty criminal," Max later said. "And God knows I was innocent of any wrong-doing ..."

While he sat in his cell, promoter Ancil Hoffman posted Baer's $10,000 bail. Much of it was paid in quarters, half-dollars, $1 and $5 bills – Hoffman had taken the box office receipts directly from the venue to the jail. The clerk counted it all before releasing Baer.

For several weeks after his release, while the grand jury investigated the circumstances surrounding the bout, Baer holed up in his parents' house, depressed, and unwilling to see any family or friends. "Max was emotionally demolished," said Buddy Baer. "He cried uncontrollably for hours. Mother and Dad tried to comfort him, explaining that this tragedy could have befallen any fighter, but it was no use. Still weeping, Max visited Frankie's widow at the hospital, and she, in much worse condition than Max, found it in herself to put her arms around him and say, 'It could just as easily have been you who died.'"

The *Oakland Tribune* quoted a letter from Baer to his managers: "If this is the fight game, I want no more of it. I'd be happier back in the Livermore hills tending pigs. I'm sorry I ever drew on a glove. I'm through … with the racket forever. I could never forget what I've gone through since poor Frankie went down in the fifth round."

Campbell's death would haunt Baer for the rest of his life. "My father was not a violent man. His personality was really gregarious," his son, the actor Max Baer Jr., told the *San Mateo Times* in 2001. "He would cry a lot [over Campbell's death]. My mother told me my dad used to have nightmares, even twenty years later."

In his home state at least, Baer would not have a choice about whether to continue boxing or not. The California Boxing Commission suspended him, his managers, the referee, and Campbell's managers for one year. "Baer was criticized adversely in some quarters for having hit Campbell that punch in the second round, after Max had slipped down and his antagonist had turned to walk to a neutral corner," Nat Fleischer later wrote. "But in so doing, Baer was acting within his rights, as the rules specified that a fighter must take care of himself at all times nor was there proof that the punch in question had any particular effect on the outcome of the battle, as Campbell fought on vigorously after receiving it."

Max had to get away from his hometown, but he needed money to do so. So he sold a piece of himself to Ancil Hoffman. "Early in October, Lorimer told me he could get $5,000 for me, if I consented to turn over sixteen-and-two-thirds of my sixty-six-and-two-thirds percent in my fistic future to Ancil Hoffman. I was broke and in debt. I had never saved any money, although I had loaned, or rather gave away, plenty. So I was glad to make the deal and did so. This was a way of temporary escape from my troubles, I took the $5,000 and headed for Reno, Nevada, where there was a big boom on and the gay life was in full swing. That dough lasted me just one week, and then I came back to California."

In his short stay in Reno, however, Max fell in love. He met the beautiful woman Dorothy Dunbar, a well-to-do divorcee described by Fleischer as "a thoroughly sophisticated woman of the world." Dunbar had been a silent screen actress in the 1920s – she had appeared as Jane in 1927's *Tarzan and the Golden Lion* and in a 1926 boxing film, *An Amateur Gentleman* – before retiring on the occasion of one of her seven marriages.

Baer first encountered her in the lobby of one Reno's several casinos, where she was staying while awaiting a divorce from Don Jaimie Garsony Barrette, a Latin American diplomat. The sophisticated Dunbar did not reciprocate Baer's lusty attention. "She started off with a smashing punch under the belt when she calmly told me she had never heard of me, and for once in a way I was stuck for an answer!" said Baer.

Hoffman looked at the lovesick Baer and realized that his fighter needed to fight. In early November, he arranged for Baer to make his New York debut at Madison Square Garden, where he would face twenty-two-year-old Ernie Schaaf.


Frederick Ernest Schaaf was born in New Jersey to German parents but grew up in the small town of Waltham, Massachusetts. A quiet, honest boy, "Ernie" was devoted to both his mother and the Catholic Church, even considering a career as a priest. He also possessed an outstanding physique, growing to six feet two inches and close to 200 pounds. At age fifteen, he joined the Navy and served alongside a fighting gob nicknamed "the Battling Ski," whose real name was Joseph Paul Zukauskas. Zukauskas changed his name on leaving the Navy to the more marketable Jack Sharkey, an amalgam of the names of his favorite fighters, Jack Dempsey and "Sailor" Tom Sharkey. He would go on to become both the world heavyweight champion and Schaaf's co-manager, buying his contract for $12,500 in 1930.

Schaaf boxed as an amateur around New York while still in the Navy. He turned pro in 1927, managed by former shipmate Phil Schlossberg, and fought seventeen times in his first year, losing just once, when he accidentally fouled his opponent, Yale Okun. Schaaf's progress continued into 1929, when he hit a rocky period, winning six out of nine but losing to difficult opponents Tommy Loughran, K.O. Christner, and Johnny Risko. The German "Sea Tiger" turned it around in 1930. In January he beat Al Friedman, for the fifth time. Friedman, better known for his commentaries on the Talmud than his fighting abilities, nevertheless provided a good tune up for Schaaf.

Schaaf then faced K.O. Christner, who had beaten Schaaf in October 1929, for a second time. Their rematch before a packed Boston Garden revealed the new Ernie Schaaf – cool, meticulous, and tough. He won a convincing ten-round decision.

Tommy Loughran entered his April 1930 match with Schaaf having lost just once in five years and forty bouts. Yet Schaaf shocked Loughran's Philadelphia fans by dominating the ten-round bout and winning a convincing decision. Loughran, as stunned as anyone else, clamored for an immediate rematch – only for Schaaf to repeat his victory and establish himself as one of the top prospects in the game.

Schaaf lost his next bout, however, a ten-round snooze fest to Babe Hunt. His manager, Phil Schlossberg, frustrated at Schaaf's regression, accepted Jack Sharkey's offer to take over as his manager. Sharkey, who in June 1930 had fouled out against Max Schmeling for the heavyweight title, was contemplating retirement from active boxing. Schaaf would be his first venture as manager and trainer.

Sharkey worked with Schaaf for three months, changing his style in subtle ways. Schaaf became more willing to "mix it up". Doc Almy, a veteran Boston boxing scribe, wrote that the new Schaaf was "full of action, a menace to any heavyweight." His first bout under new management would be against killer-clown Max Baer.

In New York, Baer's training consisted of hitting the nightspots with Dorothy Dunbar. "Don't worry about this bum Schaaf," he told Ancil Hoffman, "I'll knock him stiff like I did the others."

"With a baseball bat, maybe," Hoffman replied. "You're stepping into the big league now. You know a little bit more about defense than you did a year ago and every once in a while I think I actually see you using your left hand but if you aren't in 100 percent shape, you're due for a rough, tough evening."

Baer couldn't resist clowning even as he changed for the fight in his dressing room. He told a reporter that he had never been seriously hurt by a punch. "In support of this assertion, he suddenly arose and banged his head enthusiastically against the radiator; 'there!' he chortled triumphantly. 'If that couldn't daze me, what do you suppose I care about a wallop from a padded mitt?'" he later related in *Topical Times*.

Baer's fight with Schaaf would be seen by about 10,000 cynical New Yorkers curious to see whether Baer was for real or just another West Coast false alarm. "Having done no training to speak of I made my bow in the Madison Square Garden," Baer would write, "waving merrily to Dorothy who was sitting in a ringside seat, and taking my first real look at Ernie Schaaf."

The sight of the grim, prepared Schaaf must have unnerved Baer a little. "He had pale blue determined eyes and a shock of blond hair," Baer described. "He was beautifully built and heavily muscled. He was also a grim serious fighter, and in that way we sharply contrasted."

Schaaf made Baer look like the novice he truly was. He battered the Californian for most of the ten rounds, having him on the verge of a knockout on several occasions – though Baer could take a punch as well as any man. Schaaf's rapier-like left jab also closed his right eye as "tight as a snare drum."

Baer was unrepentant about his lack of preparation. "I went the distance," he wrote later, "and though I had to absorb a worse pounding than had been given to me in all my fights, I wasn't hurt, just tired, never so tired before. Humbled? No, not me. I hadn't lost any faith in myself. I told Schaaf that I would pay him back the next time."

Even in defeat, Baer's obvious punching power and colorful style impressed most of the boxing press. Damon Runyon, though, was more reserved: "[w]hile I am impressed with Baer's desire to please, I am not going to get excited about him until I see more of him. He is scarcely the second coming of Dempsey that the ringworms have been hoping for."

William F. Carey, head of boxing at Madison Square Garden, brought Baer back a month later against former title challenger Tom Heeney. This time, Hoffman set up Baer's training camp in the country, supposedly away from the lure of the New York lights.

"For the first couple of sessions, a rock-like Heeney crowded me, hitting short and sharp to the body," said Baer later. "I couldn't get a long shot at him, and he mussed me up and held and clinched."

In the third round, Baer charged at Heeney, who retreated, and then fell through the ropes, landing on top of a couple of scribes. Pulp fiction writer Jack Kofoed was one of them. "His big body plunged through the ropes, and rode off the apron on top of [a friend] and me. Instinctively we held up our hands punching against the sweaty body ... Tom squirmed back on the apron, grinned widely, and said, 'I'm all right.' Then he wriggled through the ropes, dropped on one knee and waited for Jack to count."

Referee Jack Dempsey counted up to eight, and Heeney and Baer were about to resume fighting when Arthur Donovan, the knockdown timekeeper, called "ten" and directed Dempsey to halt the bout. Dempsey had counted to eight, but only once Heeney had climbed back into the ring; he had forgotten to count while the Kiwi was out of the ring. Adding the eight count to the time outside the ring totaled ten. Heeney was out of time.

"Dempsey had nothing else to do but to declare me the winner by a knockout," Baer said. "Those are the rules. He pleaded and I implored. I didn't want to win that way… Dempsey was apologetic but I was credited with a knockout victory in the third round over Heeney."

Baer's attention turned once more to his pursuit of the elusive (when she wanted to be) Dorothy Dunbar. "After the Heeney fight I was even more preoccupied by Dorothy, and the popping of champagne corks was even sweeter music to my ears than the thud of gloves on punching bags and I hit Broadway harder than ever."

Baer would have the opportunity to hear plenty of thudding gloves in his next fight. William H Carey, president of Madison Square Garden, summoned Baer and Hoffman to his office.

"Who would you want for your next bout?" Carey asked.

"I'll take anybody at all," said Baer.

"How about Tommy Loughran?" Loughran now was campaigning exclusively among the heavyweights.

"Swell."

When Baer and Hoffman exited Carey's office, Hoffman told him, "You asked for it, now you've got it."

"What do you mean?" Baer asked.

"This fellow you are so hot to fight is the smartest guy in the ring. Maybe he isn't a puncher but he knows an answer for every wallop. You had a lot of trouble hitting Schaaf. Unless you're in better shape, you won't hit Loughran with a handful of buckshot."

Jim Braddock would be ringside for Loughran's ten-round thrashing of Baer. Loughran would later say that Baer tagged him just one solid punch in ten rounds. "He hit me one punch in the second round, I thought he broke all my ribs," he told writer Peter Heller. "He had a terrific punch. But Max was the most misunderstood fighter of them all. He was the nicest guy, he had the heart of a lion."

For the rest of his life, Baer would sing Loughran's praise: "I clipped him with a couple of lefts and swung my right arm again, trying to corner him against the ropes. But he ducked fast and I couldn't hang another right on him. Suddenly he wasn't there and I began to understand why they called him the 'phantom.' In fact he was right behind me and I hadn't seen him move!

"Tommy made such a monkey out of me that the fans tended to laugh at my feverish and foolish attempts to nail him and it was miraculous the way that fellow could avoid punches. I wasn't hurt but I was flustered. I was out tricked, out boxed, and out speeded."

"He had five hundred and seventy-five left hands in my face all night long and it was a long night," he told reporters. "Ancil warned me if I hit him six times in ten rounds I should get a Congressional Medal of Honor. He understated the case. He made me look and act so much like an amateur that I just had to stop and laugh, not like crazy laugh, but a laugh such as a fellow uses when he has tried his best, failed and is not soured by his failure. It was my sentiment to a better man."

The three New York bouts had made Baer a national figure. Hoffman received telegrams offering fights in a dozen different cities. Baer lost a ten-round decision to the "Cleveland Rubber Man," Johnny Risko, and then traveled to Reno, Nevada for a July the Fourth bout against Spaniard Paulino Uzcudun. Jack Dempsey, the promoter and referee, scheduled the bout for twenty rounds, an old-time distance rarely fought anymore. In the grueling Nevada heat, Baer tired in the last few rounds to lose on points.

Four days later, Max married Dorothy Dunbar in Reno. Their marriage was anything but tranquil. "It would require two certified public accountants and an adding machine to record the number of separations and reconciliations that punctuated the marital history of Mr. and Mrs. Baer," wrote Don Gardiner.

Notwithstanding the hardships being endured by millions across the nation in the Great Depression, Max Baer seemed determined to live up to saloon keeper Texas Guinan's advice that "an indiscretion a day keeps the Depression away."

Shortly after his wedding, he was sued for breach of promise by a waitress in his hometown of Livermore. Olive Beck's $250,000 lawsuit was settled after weeks of damaging publicity. Similar actions were brought by a succession of women. Dee Star, a circus trapeze artist, claimed that Max had reneged on his promise of marriage. An attractive Broadway chorus girl, Shirley LaBell, was next to claim that Baer had made "amatory suggestions" and therefore she was deserving of recompense.

Even the famous fan dancer Sally Rand was included on Max's list of supposed conquests. Baer however, denied them all, at least until he met Edna Dunnam, an attractive New York divorcee. This time, Dunnam was the one who denied the relationship. Indeed, a short time later, she married millionaire Philip Plant, former husband of actress Constance Bennett.

Baer's consecutive losses to Risko and Uzcudun derailed his immediate title aspirations, and he went back to California to rebuild his career. He would return to New York's spotlight, and in a big way.

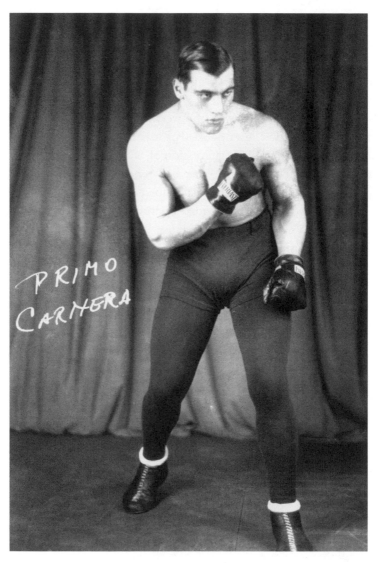

PRIMO CARNERA

*The immense Italian heavyweight Primo Carnera, a former circus strongman who stood over six-and-a-half feet tall. His career was controlled by a New York crime cartel and many of his bouts were rumoured to be fixed.*

# CHAPTER 5

# The Slide

"[T]he only thing we have to fear is fear itself – nameless, unreasoning, unjustified terror which paralyses needed efforts to turn retreat into advance."

—Franklin Delano Roosevelt

After more than a year's absence from boxing's most important venue, Madison Square Garden, Jim Braddock returned in January 1931 to fight Ernie Schaaf. The good payday took on added importance, as Braddock's first child, a son called Jay, had been born a few weeks earlier. Mae and the baby needed to be cared for, and Braddock would earn the money as he always had – with his fists and his blood.

Once more, he would be the underdog in the betting, but by now this was considered to be almost a good thing for Braddock. "There have been – and are – horses that win only when the odds against them are long," wrote one scribe. "Some fighters are like that. James J. Braddock is one. James is set to box Ernie Schaaf, the fighting gob of the stable from which Jack Sharkey has been talking in the garden tomorrow night. Schaaf probably will be made the choice. If the odds are long enough against Braddock, watch out for him."

In Schaaf he faced a true heavyweight, one who outweighed him by eighteen pounds. Yet he fought with customary courage, winning over the crowd with his effort. The two judges split their voting, leaving the deciding vote to referee Patsy Haley. When Haley declared Schaaf the winner, most of the 6,000 in attendance booed lustily for minutes, but the record books would show that Braddock had lost again.

John Kiernan of the *New York Times* deftly explained why Braddock seemed to be on the losing end of so many close decisions:

> After watching James J. Braddock in his bout with Ernie Schaaf, the impression is stronger than ever that James J. would make a great chess player. He has all the necessary speed for that game.
>
> Braddock has a willing disposition and a durable chin, but like the big clock in the Metropolitan Tower, he strikes every quarter of an hour, which isn't often enough for pugilistic purposes.

He didn't explain the mystery of Braddock's reticence. Could it have been that damaged right fist?

In February, Braddock watched from ringside as Tommy Loughran out-boxed Max Baer at Madison Square Garden. Still smarting from the Commission's vetoing him as an opponent for Baer, Braddock told Gould, "If I ever fight that guy, I'll fight him just like Tommy. I'll jab him to death."

Gould took this observation coolly. Braddock's bread and butter was his right cross. His left was hardly the sharp tool that Loughran possessed. No, if Braddock were ever to beat a big lug like Baer, he would need a big right to do so.

The fight mob are a cold-blooded bunch. For that reason, many of them migrate south in the cold weather. Gould's connection with the Cotton Club crowd, Owney Madden and Bill Duffy, helped him secure a match for Braddock in Miami, and boxer and manager headed south in February 1931 for a fight at Madison Square Garden's Florida facility. By no means would Braddock headline the bill. A six-foot, seven-inch Italian leviathan named Primo Carnera had filled that spot. Carnera's backroom team also included a hidden interest for Owney Madden and a more prominent spot for the giant's beetled-browed manager – Bill Duffy.

Every racketeer worth his weight in fedoras attended the March 5 card, which featured a cast of some of the world's top boxers. The entire affair was a lark for a gaggle of mobsters, molls, and wannabe wiseguys. Braddock got into pretty good shape in Miami; for him, at least, socializing took a back seat. He did, however, meet the boss of all bosses, "Scarface" Al Capone, who considered himself a tough guy and therefore loved fighters, who actually were tough.

"Slapsie" Maxie Rosenbloom, who loved the nightlife, appeared before the main event, putting on an extravagant display of feather-dusting and dancing to win an eight-round decision over journeyman Marty Gallagher.

Then came Carnera. The freakish heavyweight was fighting his twenty-seventh bout in thirteen months in America, as the boys sought to capitalize on his novelty before he lost his appeal – or consciousness. Carnera outweighed his opponent, Boston's Jim Maloney, by an incredible 73½ pounds. More incredibly Maloney had outpointed Carnera just five months prior. This time Carnera had no problems with the spunky Irishman.

As the crowd headed out of the stadium after Carnera's victory, Braddock entered the ring for the "walk out" bout, so-called because it came at the end of the evening when many spectators were making their way home, against local boxer Jack Roper. Roper fitted in well with the crowd in Miami; after his previous fight, he had been arrested for stealing a $500 ring. For someone who had fought for a world title, a walk out bout was an embarrassment, and Braddock entered the fight in a foul mood. Two punches into the fight, he was exiting the arena with the rest of the crowd. Roper had lasted sixty-eight seconds.

The featured fighters – Carnera, Rosenbloom and Braddock – would all go on to win world titles. The crew in Miami, at least, got value for the Annie Oakleys.

Returning home, Braddock beat Jack Kelly in New Haven, then

spent the next five months looking for another fight. Finally, in September, with Mae heavily pregnant with their second child, Braddock got a bout in Detroit. Once more, Braddock failed to win, or to impress, though he escaped with a ten-round draw against Andy Mitchell.

Gould kept hustling for his fighter, though, continually hounding the brass at Madison Square Garden for a fight in the big arena. His salesmanship finally paid off, although it was a tiny crowd of about 4,000 that paid their way into the Garden to see Braddock take on the blond Bohemian Joe Sekyra for a second time.

Over the first seven rounds, Sekyra flicked out jab after jab, forcing Braddock into a defensive shell from which he could not emerge. An angered Braddock charged out of his corner in the eighth, pounding Sekyra to the body with both hands. This brief offensive interlude could not overcome Sekyra's early work, and the judges awarded him a unanimous decision.

Even worse was to follow. Braddock's purse for the fight was attached to satisfy a judgment against him relating to his failed taxicab business. Braddock seethed at this maneuver because it was the ex-night manager for his own company that had filed the levy against his purse. With his purse siezed and the judgment not fully satisfied, Braddock was forced to throw in the towel and fold his company. He lost his entire investment of over $30,000. He still owned his speakeasy in Jersey, though the take could only get tighter as the Depression bit. With careful budgeting, and perhaps a few good wins, he hoped to husband his family through the bleak times sure to lie ahead that winter.

A bout on the Sekyra-Braddock undercard illustrated the cruel indifference of Depression-era boxing. The dry entry in the record books reveals that novice heavyweight Steve Hamas won by technical knockout in two rounds over Brooklyn's Tommy DeStefano. But that entry cannot begin to convey the violent battle fought by those two men. Hamas, who would later figure in important ways in Braddock's title ambitions, hammered DeStefano to the canvas five times in the first round. Nearly all bouts today are stopped automatically when a fighter is knocked down three times in a round, but DeStefano was allowed to continue. Moments into the second round, Hamas slammed home another left hook on a defenseless DeStefano, who dropped again. Incredibly, the Brooklyn heavyweight climbed to his feet once more only to be dropped for the seventh time. The referee finally stopped the fight at fifty-four seconds of the second round.

Allowing an inexperienced fighter to take such savage, excessive punishment made sense only to the bloodthirsty crowd. As a demonstration of the sport, it had no value. Yet bouts such as the Hamas-DeStefano debacle were commonplace through the 1930s as hungry, inexperienced fighters climbed into the ring seeking a shortcut out of poverty, or, at the very least, money enough for a decent meal. Too often, these young men served as fodder for more likely prospects.

The type of cruel beating administered by Hamas was repeated thousands of times across America during the five years after the Great Crash. If a fighter's luck held out, he would be driven from the game with only slight damage: a broken nose, scar tissue in his eyebrows, a cauliflower ear. The unlucky would be carried from the ring, dying slowly as blood leaked into their skulls, sometimes squeezing the life from them. No fewer than seventy-five boxers died from injuries received in the ring in these years as a flood of young men laced on gloves out of economic necessity. It was only because many fight clubs were finally forced to close during the depths of the Great Depression that more boxers were not killed.

As the death toll mounted, a cold fear began to overwhelm Mae Braddock. What would become of her and her three children, she thought, if her husband was maimed or killed in the ring?

Braddock's next bout nearly ruined his reputation for giving an honest performance in every match. Braddock traveled to Minneapolis where he agreed to fight his old foe, Slapsie Maxie

Rosenbloom. Rosenbloom, who had won the world light heavy-weight title from Jimmy Slattery in August 1930, was on a barnstorming tour of the Midwest, boxing twice a month in over-the-weight matches in which his title was not at stake. Economics forced Maxie to make up for the lower purses being offered by fighting with astonishing frequency, including twenty-three fights in the twelve months. The Depression had literally decimated boxing purses. Braddock's end was to be $996 and Rosenbloom, as the bigger draw, $1195. In their first bout, the fighters each had earned ten times that amount.

It is probable that, given the small purses, the fighters agreed to "go easy" on each other, especially since Rosenbloom's title was not on the line. What is certain is that the bout was a stinker from the outset, with few legitimate punches thrown. The referee, George Barton, was a former fighter and long-time boxing official. The shenanigans of the pair did not amuse him, and he twice warned them to quit stalling. When their volume of punches failed to increase, Barton slung them both out of the ring in round two, declaring the fight "no contest." Both of their purses were withheld pending a hearing by the Minnesota commission.

At the hearing the following day, Braddock and Rosenbloom protested the stoppage, offering to fight again at a later date without additional compensation to prove they had tried their best. But George Barton's opinion carried more weight with the commission. He testified that the match had been "the worst I have ever seen in twenty years of officiating," and the commission ruled against the fighters. After allowing each $350 for training and "getting out of town," the commission directed the balance of their purses be given to charity, increasing the community chests of Minneapolis and St. Paul.

Rosenbloom headed south, where he fought in warm-weather Florida from December through March. Braddock fought just once more until the spring of 1932, a ten-round loss to New Haven's "Black Panther" Al Gainer.

During this time, his taxicab company having failed completely, he spent more and more time in his bar, trying to recoup some of his losses, or perhaps just forget them.

In the spring of 1932, America was consumed by news of the kidnapping of the baby of flying ace Charles A. Lindbergh from his home in Hopewell, New Jersey. It was still dominating the headlines when, that June, Madison Square Garden opened an open-air boxing arena in Queens. The Long Island City Bowl could seat up to 70,000 for a boxing event, and the Garden would make back its investment with its first show – Jack Sharkey versus Max Schmeling for the heavyweight title.

The undercard was a virtual who's who of former Braddock opponents and sparring partners: Lou Barba, Hans Birkie, Charlie Retzlaff, and Jack McCarthy all fought before the main event. In the main event, Sharkey beat Schmeling by a split decision, and Schmeling's manager, Joe "Yussel the Muscle" Jacobs, went down in the annals with his assessment of the verdict: "We wuz robbed."

Once more, Braddock was relegated to fighting the "walk out" bout after the main event. In five dismal rounds, he managed to outpoint Argentine heavyweight Vicente "Frankenstein" Parille, who earned his nickname from the phlegmatic, stiff-kneed way he stalked his opponents.

Braddock was in a seemingly terminal slump. It was only his first win in seven bouts, he seemed utterly uninterested in boxing, and his cab company had failed. Still, his speakeasy in Jersey City was doing fairly well, and many believed the economy would improve soon.

Then, on July 9, 1932, someone told Braddock that his younger brother, Al, was being held at police headquarters after a disturbance at a house. Braddock went to see if he could straighten things out. An exchange of words with Captain Louis Bachman quickly escalated into an all-out brawl between Braddock, his brother and two friends on one side, and a house full of cops on the other. The police beat the prisoners with lead-filled slapsticks and blackjacks, but Braddock and his brother could not be brought down. Finally they were forced into a cell. Medical treatment was administered to the others, but the Braddocks were deemed "too violent" and were left until morning, untreated, behind bars.

Captain Bachman was treated at hospital for a fractured nose, and one patrolman for a cut eye. One of Braddock's friends needed stitches to four lacerations of the scalp, and had a broken index finger. The other friend also was cut badly on the head from the force of the blackjacks.

Upon hearing of the brawl, a Captain Marcy sent a squad of cops to raid Braddock's speakeasy on Fisher Avenue. They arrested the bartender, confiscated the slot machines, and placed the joint under padlock.

The next evening, Braddock, his brother and their pals appeared at a hearing in night court. Nearly 600 people tried to view the proceedings in a courtroom that held only 250. As a precautionary measure, the police chief, anxious to prevent any outburst among Braddock's friends, placed a score of patrolmen at various points about the courtroom, in the corridors and out in front of the municipal building. The police kept strict order in the court, and any time waves of murmurs started through the crowd they were quickly checked by the rapping of the recorder's gavel.

Ms. Quinlan identified Alfred Braddock and Jefferson Bostwick as two of the men who had stoned her house and broken a number of the windows. Jim Braddock testified that he had not been near the Quinlan house at all; he had been drinking at his speakeasy on Fisher Avenue. The fight, it seems, started when Ms. Quinlan had shown up at the precinct with a man named Sheeler. Braddock blamed Sheeler for nudging his cab company to failure.

Sheeler had been employed as night manager at Braddock's cab firm. Harry Buesser was a local politician and longtime "friend" of the Braddocks, the man who encouraged Jim to fight his first "smoker." However, when Buesser formed a rival cab company, he hired Sheeler as his manager. At Buesser's direction, Sheeler began soliciting Braddock's best drivers. The two of them had been relentless in driving Braddock's company out of business, and it was Sheeler who had attached Braddock's purse after the Sekyra bout several months before.

It was the sight of Sheeler at the station that drove Braddock wild. He must have seen someone who was taking milk from his children.

The recorder sentenced the men to ninety days in county jail for using profane and abusive language at police headquarters. He also ordered them held on $2,500 bail pending the action of the grand jury on a charge of assaulting the police captain. Jim Braddock appealed the ninety days, and his appeal was assigned to Judge Robert F. Kincaid, in the Court of Common Pleas. Luck finally broke Braddock's way. Kincaid had followed his career from the time he was an amateur and was one of his biggest fans.

Judge Kincaid postponed the appeal until the following September. Braddock would not serve any time in jail. However, with his bar padlocked, his main source of income was cut off, Jim Braddock turned to the one place he could to earn money. He laced up the gloves again.

Max Baer fought Ernie Schaaf in August 1932. The blistering heat in Chicago that summer kept the crowd under 5,000, and gate receipts totaled just $15,000. For three rounds, Schaaf advanced on his heavy-hitting opponent, but in the fourth he was forced to retreat to the ropes by blows to the head. The heat and fast pace forced the fighters to slow down in the fifth, but the referee warned them to become "a little more warlike."

In the seventh Baer walked through Schaaf's punches to get in to close range. By the eighth Schaaf was tiring, struggling to keep Baer off with his jab, and in the ninth he wilted further as both men went toe to toe in the heat.

At the start of the tenth round, Baer got home a heavy right hand to the jaw that staggered Schaaf. For the next two minutes, he beat Schaaf, until a terrible blow to the temple dropped him to the canvas, unconscious. The bell sounded a moment later ending the fight. Baer won the decision and it took Schaaf several terrifying minutes to regain his senses.

"Once again I was back in the frame of mind which I had undergone after Campbell's death," recalled Baer. "Although this time I saw things in better perspective and I remembered the words of Campbell's widow: 'It might have been you Max.'" Schaaf survived, and would box again, but no one knew at what cost.

Baer's win, his eleventh win in a row, solidified his position as one of the top two or three contenders. In his next bout, he savaged Braddock's former foe, Tuffy Griffith. Griffith had continued to fight, winning most and losing some of the most exciting fights of the early 1930s. His popularity remained high in the Midwest and his August 1930 exhibition in Chicago against Stanley Harris became the first boxing match to be televised, on Station W9XAP, with the audio broadcast over normal radio channels.

Against Griffith, Baer started slowly and "wasted a lot of effort showing off his perfect physique and assuming classical poses." By the seventh, though, he had Griffith on the verge of a knockout. "With Griffith leaning helplessly across the room, Baer humanely halted his attack and looked pleadingly at the referee to stop the bout ... the crowd loudly applauded his sportsmanship after having booed him for not fighting in earlier rounds." The death of Frankie Campbell may well have been weighing on Baer's mind.

It was his twenty-seventh knockout win in forty-four bouts. The next day, he began pushing for a fight with former world title holder Max Schmeling. With the number one contender's position in sight, Baer wouldn't fight again until he got Schmeling in the ring the following June.

*

That Fall, with Braddock's appeal in the protective hands of Judge Kincaid, Joe Gould decided that a trip far from the vengeful glare of the Jersey City cops would be a tonic, and set up a series of fights in California. Their West Coast tour had its first stop in San Francisco, where Braddock would fight John Henry Lewis, a budding African-American superstar at the Civic Auditorium. Lewis was a hot talent, undefeated in twelve bouts, although his managers beefed up that total by including amateur fights. He had been raised in Arizona, where his father worked as an athletic trainer for the University of Arizona. His father also operated a gym in Phoenix, where Lewis learned to box, often battling his brother Christy in "midget boxing" exhibitions. He became a fast, clever and skilful boxer who could punch with both hands. In his third fight, he battered Sam Terrin with a left hook-right cross combination. Terrin dropped to the canvas just feet from his horror-stricken wife and never recovered, dying before he could reach hospital.

Braddock was Lewis's first "big name" opponent. In the first round, as John Henry sized up his "veteran" foe, Braddock whipped across two of his patented right hands, sending the youngster reeling. For the next five rounds, Lewis boxed on the retreat while Braddock tried to catch him. In the seventh, Braddock got home several more crushing blows but Lewis was again able to weather them without going down, and boxed superbly to the end of the contest. The sole judge, referee Eddie Burns, awarded the fight to Lewis. Sportswriter Harry B. Smith agreed, giving Lewis eight rounds, though some at ringside had scored it a draw.

From San Francisco, Braddock journeyed to San Diego, where he beat Dynamite Jackson, an average fighter with an above-average name, for a $206 purse, most of which he wired home to Mae. Three weeks later, he struggled against heavyweight Tom Patrick, who butted Braddock in the face, opening a gash "that you could lay your finger in" over his left eye. He then compounded the insult by hitting squarely below the belt. When the referee indicated he would award the contest to Braddock by foul, Braddock shrugged him off, insisting on continuing. His gracious gesture went without reward, and he lost a bloody ten-round decision.

Not quite three weeks later, his cut still not fully healed, Braddock stepped into the ring against Lou Scozza before a tiny crowd in San Francisco. He'd been forced to take the bout to earn money for his travel expenses home. He entered the ring with a plaster patch over the cut, which formed a clear, obvious target for Scozza. In the very first round, the two fighters clinched, and when they separated, blood began streaming from the re-opened wound. Braddock battled on, winning the first round, as well as the third and fourth, but in every round, Scozza targeted the cut and slammed punch after punch at the eye. At the end of the sixth, although the fight had been fought on even terms, referee Benny Wagner had no choice but to stop it. Braddock, "covered with gore and looked like a slaughterhouse attendant," according to the *San Francisco Chronicle*, had been beaten inside the distance for the first time in his career.

His West Coast trip had been a dismal flop.


On the day that Braddock was in California fighting Scozza, he could not do the one thing that millions of other poverty-stricken Americans were doing: vote for Franklin Delano Roosevelt. At about the same moment that Braddock was boarding a train to return home to Mae and the children in New Jersey, Roosevelt was being declared president-elect. His task could not have been more daunting: by the following spring almost 13,000,000 were unemployed and almost every bank was closed. America was hitting rock bottom.

Many boxers suffered. Jack Dempsey, a millionaire in 1929, was forced by 1931 to return to the ring and boxed well over 100 exhibitions over the next several years in any venue that would have him. Benny Leonard, who had retired a millionaire in 1925 to go on tour with a vaudeville troupe called the Marx Brothers, lost all of his money in the Crash, and came back for real, only to be battered by Jimmy McLarnin. Benny Bass, a terrific little featherweight who had amassed a decent amount of money from over 200 fights, was forced to declare bankruptcy. Former featherweight champion Johnny Dundee not only lost his money but was hit with a bill for back taxes.

One of the few fighters to buck the Depression was Enzo Fiermonte, a middleweight boxer of only fair ability, who met and "fell in love with" an older woman, Madeline Dick. She happened to be one of the country's richest women; she had been returning from her honeymoon when the ship she was in hit an iceberg, and her husband, John Jacob Astor, went down with the *Titanic*. She later married William K. Dick, an owner of the St. Regis Paper Company, but after a Reno divorce in 1933, she went to Miami to vacation. In one of the strangest love affairs of the 1930s, this Italian boxer, instead of suffering like the thousands of other young men and fighters, hit the jackpot. The two had a tumultuous affair, compounded by the fact that Fiermonte had a wife and child in Rome, and in one argument Enzo broke Madeline's arm. They married while she was confined to her bed in a New York hospital.

Braddock took off the rest of November and December, allowing his eye time to heal and taking advantage of the break to spend the holidays with his family. In January 1933 he was back on the road, hoping for a good payday to make up for any purses lost while he healed. The obligations of supporting a family were not suspended while waiting for stitches to be removed or broken bones to heal.

Gould got him a match in Chicago against a top light-heavyweight prospect, Martin Levandowski. Braddock traveled there alone, leaving Gould at home to save travel expenses. He would hire a local second to haul his spit bucket, but he was on his own when it came to fight-night strategy. On his arrival in the Windy City, the Illinois Boxing Commission met him with some disturbing news. They objected to him as an opponent for the hard-punching

Levandowski, who they considered too dangerous for the fading Jersey veteran. Before approving the match, the commissioners ordered Braddock to prove his fitness to fight by sparring before them with two fighters they had selected at a Chicago gym.

The fight's promoter, Joe Foley, attended the commission meeting. Foley, a former sports editor, had turned to promoting after his eyesight failed, and his lavender-tinted eyeglasses were a familiar ringside sight. He was told of Braddock's dismal appearance – shabby, unshaven, with a shaggy mane hanging over his collar – slipped the boxer a $5 bill, told him to get a shave and a haircut, and encouraged him to do his best to show he could still fight.

The next day, Braddock boxed four rounds for the commissioners, two apiece with rugged black journeymen Seal Harris and Larry Johnson. First up was Harris, a six-foot, five-inch behemoth who later served as a sparring partner for Joe Louis. Braddock waltzed around him, then put in two grueling rounds with the lighter Johnson. His solid performance gave the commissioners no choice but to sanction the Levandowski bout, but his excellent gym work did not impress the bookmakers, who installed Levandowski as a five-to-one favorite.

The odds were justified. Levandowski had reached the finals of the Olympic Trials in 1928, but entered with a badly cut ear, and in one of the preliminary matches it tore open again. In the final bout for a berth on the team, Levandowski caught a punch squarely on the same ear, which spurted blood, having been ripped nearly in half. The referee had no choice but to stop the bout on a technical knockout. The following year Levandowski won the National AAU light heavyweight title, and then turned pro. Going into the bout with Braddock, he had contested forty fights in three years, winning most by knockout. One of his few defeats came at the hands of the ubiquitous "Slapsie" Maxie Rosenbloom, who fought everywhere and everyone – he finished his career with 299 total fights, among the most ever recorded. Levandowski was looking to meet Rosenbloom in a rematch for the title.

As he had done before, and would famously do again, Braddock produced when the chips were down and no one gave him a chance. He stunned the Chicago crowd by flooring down Levandowski five times and winning a convincing ten-round decision. "Those knockout sensations are my meat," he told Gould afterwards.

Braddock had little time to celebrate the win in Chicago. Just a few days after the fight, Braddock's car skidded from the road; he broke two of his ribs and destroyed the car, likely the same one he had given Mae on their wedding day. On January 18, 1933, unaware of his injuries, Joe Gould caught wind that the main event scheduled for Madison Square Garden on January 20 had been cancelled. Hustling over to Jimmy Johnston's office, Gould sold Johnston on salvaging his card by matching Braddock against a stocky German heavyweight, Hans Birkie.

Gould then set out to track down Braddock and tell him. "I called him up and asked him did he know he was fighting in the Garden that night," Gould remembered. "[Braddock] said yes, he read it in the papers. That night when he got into the ring he told me he had a busted rib. I asked him why he didn't tell me about it before, and he said the reason he didn't was because he was afraid I would call off the fight."

Outweighed by twenty pounds, Braddock was mauled by the husky German. Birkie's choice of strategy could not have been worse; he directed nearly all of his punches to Braddock's midsection. Braddock was further handicapped when he injured his right hand on Birkie's head. At the end of ten torpid rounds, Birkie got the decision. "It was an emergency contest arranged with only two days' notice," wrote James P. Dawson of the *New York Times*, "but that doesn't explain a battle that was nothing so much as a slow-motion struggle between two mediocre heavyweights."

The same evening that Braddock was squaring off against Birkie, a few papers ran a small filler item from the news wires. Ernie Schaaf, severely ill with the flu, was resting comfortably in hospital in

Boston. He would be discharged a few days later to resume training for Primo Carnera.

By that point, the average fan didn't care much about Braddock or his career. The big name in boxing, Primo Carnera, had continued to win, and now seemed destined for a shot at reigning champion Jack Sharkey. Sharkey hadn't fought since beating Schmeling and figured to make a defense during the summer.

Carnera's scheduled contest against the "Blond Tiger," Ernie Schaaf, was advertised as an elimination bout. The winner would meet Sharkey for the title. Many observers thought it to be odd that Schaaf was in an elimination bout, since Sharkey was his manager. In order to assuage any concerns about back-room shenanigans, Jimmy Johnston announced that if Carnera won he would get the title shot, but that if Schaaf won, Sharkey would select some other opponent. Schaaf, therefore, had no real upside to the fight other than prestige and the purse. A title shot, the Holy Grail of every fighter, would have to wait for another day.

Madison Square Garden trembled from the stomping feet of the 20,000 fans that paid into the arena, a bumper crowd for such lean times. Jimmy Johnston nearly dislocated a shoulder patting himself on the back for his promotional skills and, even though Carnera's other fights often resulted in questionable knockouts, mostly this one would be fought *sans* hanky-panky. The bookies actually made Schaaf the seven-to-five favorite to knock off the lumbering Latin.

The referee, ex-boxer Billy Cavanaugh, had an impeccable reputation. He had earned his good name in over eighty professional bouts and his scientific approach to the sport, which led to his being hired as boxing instructor at West Point. By using Cavanaugh, Johnston meant to send a message that this fight would be a legitimate one.

Schaaf must have seen in the initial seconds of the first round that he had no chance of beating Carnera. Even if Carnera's early bouts had been "arranged," by this point he had learned how to box. He moved around the ring in a classic upright boxing posture, despite his bulk, and his arms were longer and bigger than any champion before or since. His left jab was nearly impossible to avoid, a telegraph pole driven by a piston.

Carnera used that jab constantly. For round after round, Schaaf would make an initial effort to get inside, but would be cruelly rebuffed. The best he could muster was an occasional hard left hand to Carnera's granite-like torso. By the fifth round, Schaaf's poor condition began to tell and the fight slowed to a crawl, punctuated by Carnera's jab and occasional attempts at power punching.

At the start of the thirteenth round, Carnera landed a light left jab on Schaaf, who backed away on wobbly legs. He reached down with his right hand as if looking for a chair, then sat on the canvas, from where he looked blankly across the ring at Carnera, who was too dumbfounded to move. Then Schaaf fell over on his side, face down on the canvas. Cavanaugh dutifully counted to ten.

The crowd could not believe that such a light punch had put Schaaf down. From all corners of the arena came cries of "Fake! Fake!" followed by beer bottles and other missiles.

Jack Sharkey, the world's champion, leapt through the ropes to Schaaf's side, lifted him and carried him to his corner. Both Sharkey and Johnny Buckley worked feverishly to rouse their fighter. When they could not do so, they carried him to his dressing room, where the commission doctor finally directed that the unconscious fighter be taken to the hospital. One of Schaaf's handlers rushed back to the ringside to report breathlessly the news that "the doc thinks he's got *conclusion* of the brain."

At hospital Schaaf's condition worsened, and doctors decided to operate in a last ditch effort to save his life. As they took him into the operating room, his mother was able briefly to rouse him.

"Honey, you are my sweetheart?" she asked.

"Yes mom," Ernie whispered.

"How are you?"

"I'm okay mom," he answered, then slipped once more into a coma.

Schaaf's mother spent the night at her son's side, praying for his recovery. Doctors worked on Schaaf over the next three hours, drilling into his skull in an effort to relieve the intracranial pressure caused by a hemorrhage.

At 4:10 a.m., Ernie Schaaf passed away. He was twenty-four years old. Mrs. Schaaf leaned over and kissed her son's finger.

"He's gone," she said. "My darling boy."

Jimmy Johnston, whose hide was as thick as tarpaulin, seemed truly overwhelmed. "It is the most terrible thing that has ever happened in boxing," he said later.

Schaaf's mother later telegrammed Primo Carnera:

Kindly be assured that I do not consider you in any way responsible for the death of my boy. I feel toward you like I would have wished your mother to have felt toward my Ernie if you had met with the same misfortune during your bout with him. I thank you for your offers of sympathy and for your kind expressions of admiration for Ernie.

The message from the dead fighter's mother moved Carnera to tears. "What can I say, I can't talk," he told reporters at his room in the Hotel Victoria. "It shows she has a heart like my own little mother in Italy. It hurts me here," he added tearfully while placing his had over his heart.

Schaaf's family had the body shipped from the city morgue to his mother's home in Sheldonville, Massachusetts, for a short wake. When his body was removed from the home for the funeral, a cortege of automobiles two miles long followed the hearse to St. Mary's Church, where the services were held. One of the eight pallbearers was Braddock's sparring partner and Schaaf's good friend, Jack McCarthy. Over 3,500 family and friends turned out for the funeral mass, including a Catholic priest sent by Primo Carnera. At the cemetery, a Navy firing squad sent up the traditional three volleys as Schaaf's coffin was lowered into the earth.

Detectives for the District Attorney's office made a show of questioning the major players involved in the fight, including Bill Duffy, Carnera's American agent, Mannie Seamon, one of his trainers, and referee Billy Cavanaugh. Medical reports issued a week after Schaaf's burial confirmed that his bout of flu had made him susceptible to otherwise non-damaging punches. "The deceased had a chronic or subacute meningo-encephalitis characterized by lymphocytic infiltrations around the blood vessels in the subarachnoid space. The meningo-encephalitis ... interfered with Schaaf's boxing skill so that he was less able to avoid blows."

It took George Trafton, a former Carnera opponent and hall-of-fame footballer, to cut through the medical gobbledygook and voice the view on why Schaaf really died. "Remember when Maxie Baer hit Ernie in the back of the head in the tenth round of their fight here last August?" asked Trafton. "That was the death punch. He never was the same."

Shortly after Schaaf's death, Braddock met young heavyweight contender Al Ettore in Philadelphia. Ettore, a popular red-headed slugger, just nineteen, was rapidly becoming a fan favorite in his hometown. Braddock couldn't do anything with the kid, as his injured hand had not recovered. In the fourth, the disgusted referee, Joe McGuigan, disqualified Braddock for lack of effort, unaware that he was trying to brave his way through the fight while injured. The Pennsylvania Boxing Commission took a dim view of Braddock's excuse, and suspended both him and Joe Gould for a year.

Three days later, on March 4, 1933, Franklin Delano Roosevelt took over as the nation's president. Many would remember a resonant phrase from his inaugural speech: "The only thing we have to fear is fear itself." It is likely that another, more existential part of his address did not resonate with Braddock: "Happiness lies not in the mere possession of money, it lies in the joy of achieving, in the thrill of creative effort." With his icebox empty and three hungry children to feed, Braddock no longer boxed for the joy of the sport. He fought, as do all prizefighters, for the money.

Gould planned several "out of town" bouts to try and rebuild Braddock's viability as a headline fighter in New York. Reaching out to his boxing contacts, he scoured for a promoter willing to take a chance on Braddock, who was now seen as an erratic, fading trial horse. Jack Tippett, a promoter in St. Louis, answered the call, and booked Braddock to meet Al Stillman at his club. In Stillman, Braddock once more would be facing a talented, younger fighter.

Stillman's professional career began in 1929 after a successful internship as an amateur. As with many fighters, to make a living on the reduced purses available during the Depression he fought often, cramming over seventy bouts in just four years. Stillman's punching power made his job slightly easier, as he often ended his night's work early. His record included fifty-five knockouts in seventy-two fights. Even with such a high kayo ratio, the quality of his opponents could not be quibbled with. Stillman had even dropped the iron-chinned Maxie Rosenbloom in a losing effort.

Braddock entered the ring an out-of-shape and flabby 182 pounds, and Stillman out-boxed, out-fought and out-thought him, circling at high speed while Braddock was limited to occasional slapping lefts to the body and looping overhand rights. Braddock's durability kept him in the contest as "Al's right hand, his money punch, bounced off Braddock's chin like sleet off a tin roof."

Braddock concentrated on Stillman's body with left hooks, and even though his left was not as powerful as his right, the rib shots eventually had Stillman wincing. With seconds to go in the ninth round of the scheduled ten, Stillman dropped his hands to protect his body. Braddock sprung his trap in that instant, whipping over a right hand that caught Stillman high on the head, dropping him in ring center. Stillman arose on shaky legs at the count of nine, just as the bell sounded.

The tenth saw a different Braddock in the ring. Cold, analytical and merciless, he now sidestepped when Stillman tried to circle away, cutting off the ring. Another right sent Stillman down for a nine count, then a left hook put him down a third time. Stillman again forced himself to his feet, but referee Walter Weisner stepped between the men, giving the fight to Braddock and saving Stillman from further punishment.

Stillman was heartbroken at the loss. "I was hit with a sucker punch," he moaned to the press. "I just couldn't get away from it and when that one hit me in the ninth round, everything went black. But I want another chance at Braddock."

Braddock had not been lucky at all; the knockout blow came as the result of carefully executed strategy. He explained that he used his left to "tease" Stillman into lowering his guard, giving him an opening for his right. The jubilant Braddock ignored the pain he felt in his bruised right hand and began agitating for a match against the ever-popular Maxie Rosenbloom. The win, though, did little for Braddock's bank-book; his percentage of the gross take was somewhere around $500.

The victory did show that Braddock, even at an advanced stage of his career could still reach down to pick up a big win. He had regained some of the credibility he had lost after the Birkie fight, and St. Louis became one of the few cities where he would be welcomed to fight. Promoter Joe Tipett immediately matched him against Martin Levandowski, whose loss to Braddock in Chicago was a source of embarrassment to the Polish warrior. Levandowski still harbored title ambitions and urgently needed to erase the Braddock loss on his record.

Braddock returned to St. Louis, again without Joe Gould, a few days before the rematch and trained at a public gymnasium to help build interest in the fight. As always, Braddock showed no discrimination in his approach to the game, hiring the two best sparring partners available, Dixie Shannon and Benny Deathpaine. Both were

African-American, though Deathpaine found it convenient to adver-tise himself as "Indian Benny." The work served Braddock well, as he entered the ring several pounds lighter and in better overall condi-tion than in the Stillman bout. He also talked up the fight, voicing his preference for a slugging match: "Those boxers always keep flicking left leads in your face, while with another puncher you have a chance to read his thoughts and bat him to the punch."

Once again, Braddock's purse would be in the neighborhood of $500 — not a very good neighborhood in which to be stuck – based on total attendance of 4,366 paying a total of $2206. And, once again, his brittle hands would fail him.

The bout itself was a virtual copy of the exciting match the two had fought in Chicago. Levandowski charged out of his corner from the start, performing as "the nearest thing to perpetual motion" for all ten rounds. Braddock also went for an early knockout, going punch-for-punch with his younger foe. In the second, he met the onrushing Levandowski at center ring, and shot home a right behind his jab, the classic one-two, which instantly caused Levandowski's left eye to swell shut.

A frantic exchange followed. Braddock launched a right uppercut that collided with Levandowski's elbow, sending waves of pain through Braddock's body. The punch, Braddock was sure, had broken his hand once more – and he still had eight rounds to fight against his young, determined opponent. Braddock's expression rarely gave much away in the ring, and now he drew on his years of experience to conceal his injury from Levandowski, the referee and the crowd. For the rest of the fight, most of his right-hand punches were bluffs and intentional misses. Nevertheless, Levandowski expended a lot of energy making sure he avoided what he thought was Braddock's deadly right.

When Levandowski managed to get past Braddock's left jab, he pounded the veteran's body with both hands. Several times his blows doubled up Braddock in pain, but always he roared back with punches of his own.

Levandowski had his best round in the ninth, landing numerous left hooks to Braddock's head. When he finally got through with a right, it ripped across Braddock's ear, nearly tearing it from his head, a wound eerily reminiscent of Levandowski's own injury in the 1928 Olympic finals. Dripping with blood, his broken hand throbbing beyond pain, Braddock still refused to buckle. At the end of the ten hard-fought, bloody rounds, he was still standing and still fighting back.

The crowd, judges, and ringside press all seemed to have differing views as to the winner. Judge Jim Solari scored four rounds for each fighter and two even, with fifty total points for each fighter. Judge Benny Kessler had the rounds even at five for each fighter, but had Levandowski in front fifty-one to forty-nine on the strength of the overwhelming number of punches he landed in the ninth round. Veteran referee Harry Kessler, the closest man to the action, made Levandowski an even bigger points winner, and so the majority decision went to him. By rounds, Kessler had tabbed it four rounds to Levandowski, two to Braddock, and four even.

Braddock had another close loss pinned to his record, but his reputation, in St. Louis at least, had stood the test, especially after news of his hand injury appeared in the press. In the next day's edition of the *Post-Dispatch*, St. Louis sportswriter W.J. McGooghan reckoned Braddock had won, and reported the results of the commission doctor's dressing room examination – Braddock had broken his right metacarpal. Fellow sportswriter Roy Smith described the ugly nature of the injury: "A lump the size of an egg stood out prominently when his glove was removed, leaving no doubt as to the damage done."

Astonishingly, recklessly, Braddock was back in St. Louis six weeks later, this time at the invitation of first-time promoter Barney McCarthy, who had seen his stirring local battles and noted the Jersey fighter's surging popularity. McCarthy rented the American Legion Post at Clifton Heights for a rematch against Al Stillman, seeking to capitalize on Braddock's seemingly miraculous come-from-behind victory in their previous bout. Stillman made the match-up especially viable, as in the interim he had fought a draw with the ever-active Maxie Rosenbloom.

Since word of his broken hand had played prominently in the press, many would-be paying customers stayed away, doubtful of Braddock's fitness to fight. He tried to offset any doubt about his physical condition by declaring that he had suffered only torn and bruised ligaments, not a break, assured the press that his hand was fine and said he had used it frequently in the previous two weeks of training.

Despite the natural appeal of the fight, the skepticism about Braddock coupled with McCarthy's unproven promotional skills killed the gate. On fight night, only 1784 customers showed up, paying a total of only $857. Braddock's share of the proceeds likely tallied under $200.

The second punch of the fight decided its outcome. Braddock landed a short right that caused Stillman to drop into a groggy genuflection, and fractured Braddock's hand once more. Clearly he had not recovered from the injury suffered in his prior fight.

Stillman got to his feet and got on his bicycle, backpedaling whenever Braddock tried to attack. Wilbur Wood, a legendary sportswriter for the *New York Sun*, happened to be in St. Louis and attended the tiny club show. He had seen Braddock fight at least twenty times, and so was astonished to see him begin throwing right hand punches in a "great arc over his head which landed on nothing but air." An effective right hand is thrown in a fairly straight line from the shoulder; looping punches are generally ineffective and easy to avoid.

This time, there was no fairytale finish. Braddock lost a unanimous decision. He returned to New Jersey, still looking for fights in order to earn money to support his family, but the years of boxing and repeated injuries now took their toll. He plodded his way through two desultory wins during the summer of 1933. In June, he scored over California heavyweight Les Kennedy in ten yawn-producing rounds; Kennedy had beaten Max Baer in 1929, but had won only infrequently after that. In July, Braddock outworked another Jersey trial horse, Chester Matan.

Before both of these fights, the desperate Braddock had cocaine injected into his hands to dull any pain. The "coking" of a fighter's hands was always a last ditch effort to prolong a fighter's career. The practice usually did more harm than good, as the boxer, insensitive to pain, would continue to throw and land punches, inflicting additional damage.

In late September, Gould found him a bout on the lowest rung of professional boxing, signing him to appear at a small club show in Mount Vernon, New York. Although just a few miles north of Madison Square Garden, Mt. Vernon was as far away from the big time as a fighter could get.

Proceeds from the promotion would go to the Home Relief Fund administered by the Mt. Vernon Police Department. President Roosevelt had promised prompt, vigorous action to restore the country's fortunes. During the heady first "hundred days" of his New Deal administration, Roosevelt presented two key pieces of legislation to Congress: the Federal Emergency Relief Act and the National Industrial Recovery Act, administered by the NRA. Once created by law, a logo depicting the NRA's blue eagle was plastered on products of every type – butter, clothes, indeed virtually anything sold in interstate commerce. The federal government now allocated to the states funds for distribution to the most needy families. The administration of this "home relief" fell to the state and local municipalities. The fight card would contribute to this fund for distribution to the poor.

The Mt. Vernon show brought together several ancient veterans of the game and a couple of younger fighters, none of whom were championship caliber. The star fighter on the card, Abe Feldman, had impressed the boxing writers as a potential contender on the basis of a decision win over former Braddock conqueror Hans Birkie. Undoubtedly, though, the big draw was an appearance by heavyweight champion Primo Carnera, who refereed the first two rounds of a preliminary fight. Carnera's attendance helped the promoters draw over 6,000 fans to a fairly low-level club show.

Against Feldman, Braddock looked like a completely shot fighter. Both men fought at a somnambulist's pace, with clinches outnumbering clean punches by a substantial margin. In the first round Braddock broke his "coked" hand on Feldman's head. He didn't just break it, he pulverized the bone. But Feldman was so inept that he was unable to take advantage and the fight deteriorated into a mauling, ugly display.

By the sixth round, the crowd had had enough and incessant jeers rang down on the fighters. Referee Cavanaugh, perhaps still unnerved by Schaaf's death, watched the fighters carefully – and was not pleased with what he saw. Finally, in the middle of the sixth round, he drew the biggest cheer of the night as he stopped the contest and ordered both men out of the ring for not trying.

In the dressing room, a disconsolate Braddock sobbed, "I'm all washed up, Joe," as trainer Doc Robb cut off his gloves.

Robb cut off the gloves and tape, and stepped back horrified. Even Joe Gould was speechless, stupefied by the ugliness of his injury. Braddock's hand was grotesquely misshapen and swollen. Sharp edges of bone could be seen pressing the underside of his flesh.

"Jim, no way all this damage was done tonight."

Braddock looked at the lump of bone and meat that was his hand and said simply, "It was a payday."

The promoter walked in, looked the trio over, and announced that the commission had held up Braddock's purse. He was out of the room before Gould could react. "Don't worry Jim, I'll get the dough," said Gould, and then he too was gone, leaving Braddock and Doc Robb alone in the dressing room.

Robb looked at the hand again. "Oh, Jim, this is bad," he said. "I gotta get something to bind this up."

Now Braddock was alone. Disqualified for being a bum. In the harsh light of the dressing room of the Mount Vernon Armory, he wept.

The door burst open and Gould and Robb re-entered. Gould was talking rapidly, but all Braddock heard was "suspension" and "holding up the purse."

Robb held up a broken picket from a white wooden fence. "I got this to use as a splint, I don't think the neighbors are gonna miss it."

*New champion Jim Braddock has his hands raised in victory after defeating Max Baer on June 13, 1935. Far right is trainer Whitey Bimstein. The Cinderella Man's upset win elevated him to a national symbol.*

# PART TWO

# Damon and Pythias

Damon and Pythias, two dear friends, lived in a land ruled by a hard and cruel king. One day a soldier overheard young Pythias speaking ill of the king and haled him to court. Pythias admitted that he believed the King to be cruel and wicked. The angry king immediately sentenced Pythias to death, but delayed the execution for two weeks, wishing Pythias to suffer while he awaited death.

Pythias asked the king's permission to go home to say farewell to his family, promising to return within two weeks for his execution. The king said "you may leave if a friend agrees to stay in your place. If you do not return, he shall be put to death in your stead."

At once Damon came forward and offered to stay in prison as a pledge for Pythias. Pursuant to his decree, the king allowed Pythias to leave and cast Damon into prison.

As the day for execution drew near, Damon's faith in his friend remained undiminished. "Pythias will be here if he can possibly do so," he told the king, "but I would be glad to die in his place. I have no wife and no children, and I love my friend so much that it is easier to die for him than to live without him."

Two weeks passed but Pythias did not return. Standing before the King for his execution, Damon declared, "Pythias is faithful and true. If he has not returned, surely it is through no fault of his."

At the moment Pythias ran into the courtyard, threw his arms around Damon's neck, and cried "Oh, my friend, thank the Gods I am not too late!" Upon seeing this, the calloused heart of the cruel king softened. With a wave of his hand, he set both of them free.

*Heavyweight champion Jack Sharkey and his challenger Primo Carnera shake on their forthcoming title bout as promoter Jimmy "Boy Bandit" Johnston cups their hands in his. Behind them are (from left) Johnny Buckley, Sharkey's manager, and "Big" Bill Duffy and Louis Soresi, handlers of Carnera.*

# CHAPTER 6

# The Oracle of Eighth Avenue

"I do the talking while you do the fighting."

—Jimmy Johnston

Arthur Flegenheimer served the healthiest beer in New York. If you bought your suds from him, he wouldn't kill you. His tax lawyers may have called him Mr. Flegenheimer, but his beer customers referred to him as Dutch Schultz.

The millionaires running Madison Square Garden valued their health, so, naturally, when they ordered the beer to celebrate hiring Jimmy Johnston as their new head of boxing, they reached out to Dutch, who dispatched a truckload of his best stuff from his Newark warehouse.

Ed O'Neil described Johnston accurately: "Black-haired, small, dapper, a dark derby perpetually cocked over one eye, Johnston is a dynamo, born and bred to the fight game ..." Indeed, by 1932, Johnston had been involved in boxing for over forty years. His business acumen, coupled with a brilliant mind for "ballyhoo," set him apart. "He is not likely to be outweighed by any of his competitors," one reporter opined, "for the man is shrewdness personified. He is so shrewd, in fact, that on more than one occasion he has been forced to slow down his mental processes less he outwit himself."

Jimmy Johnston was born in Liverpool, England, on November 28, 1875. He was always quick to add that he was born "of Irish parents." His father, an iron-moulder, moved the family to Hell's

Kitchen, which at that time was full of Irish immigrants who hated the English worse than the landlord. Because of Johnston's accent, "the neighbors' children hooted at his claim of being Irish, and lost no time in trying to convert him into a combination punching bag and human soccer ball but Jimmy was a tough little guy and the kids soon learned to steer clear of him," wrote his biographer, Marcus Griffin.

As a teenage boxer, Johnston apparently won a 115-pound amateur championship at the National Athletic Club in Brooklyn, and later boxed professionally on shows run by the wrestling champion, physical culturist and later sports administrator William Muldoon. His career, according to Johnston, ended with a devastating knockout by a future champion. "I fought Danny Daugherty, the bantamweight champion, in the Ice Palace at 106th and Lexington Avenue and lost in ten rounds. They stopped the bout. Patsy Haley whom you see refereeing at the Garden now and then, fought on that same night and was knocked out by Terry McGovern." Johnston's memory does not jibe with the facts. It is true that in March 1899, "Terrible" Terry McGovern knocked out Patsy Haley, but Johnston did not fight Danny Daugherty; the record shows he lost to Patsy Donahue of Philadelphia, it what may have been Donahue's only recorded fight.

Charlie "Handlebars" Harvey, then a manager specializing in British fighters, offered Johnston a job as an assistant. They worked together for years, managing such great boxers as Jim Driscoll, Owen Moran and Kid Lewis. When Harvey was appointed secretary to the newly formed New York State Athletic Commission in 1914, under the Frawley Law, he turned over his string of fighters to Jimmy Johnston.[1]

---

[1] After leaving the Commission, Harvey was forced to temporarily retire from boxing after an automobile accident "almost broke him into bits." Harvey's legs, shoulders, and arms, all suffered severe, permanent damage. Slowly Harvey regained the ability to walk, although now he was more often referred to as "crippled" than "mustachioed."

By then, Johnston had already begun to develop a reputation as a marketing genius. One of his most famous promotions involved a "Chinese lightweight" named Ah Chung. When Chung appeared in New York, the sportswriters had a field day with what was believed to be a classic Johnston put-on. Clearly Chung was not from China and spoke a sort of pigeon, imitation Chinese. But he proved popular and sold out St. Nick's Arena for his first fight, a kayo win. A few days later he appeared at Giants Stadium for a baseball game and drew more attention that the ballplayers. His short career came to a crashing halt, however, when Joe Gould's childhood friend, Benny Leonard, knocked him out in six rounds before a sold-out house. For years afterwards, Johnston was considered brilliant for having dressed up an Irishman named "Mickey Mulligan" and fobbed him off as Chinese. In fact, Ah Chung's real name was Harry Ah Chung and he *was* half Chinese. Before coming to New York, he had boxed just a couple of times in the sticks and was unknown upon his arrival.

Johnston also befriended an extremely influential man with a far-away look in his eye, the sportswriter Damon Runyon. The two became inseparable friends. Runyon wrote of his nightly excursions with Johnston:

> We considered ourselves a committee of two appointed to put the town to bed every night. Johnston owned a Stutz automobile. He drove it himself, and citizens seeing it coming would run for shelter, as Mr. Johnston drove it strictly on the bias.... The farthest south for us in those days was a Child's restaurant on West 34th Street where we would fortify ourselves with a gallon of coffee...we would then proceed in the Stutz through the "Roaring Forties," taking in each public station or cabaret that was the known haunt of any citizen likely to be aware of gossip or scandal, until by dawn we had reached our most northerly outpost, another Childs's restaurant on 125th Street in Harlem ... for 15 years running, our regularity at various ports of call were such that

failure to make any of them every night aroused comment. No, it didn't get us anything. Still, we always knew a lot of scandal.

Had Johnston and Runyon been roaring along Broadway January 15, 1916, and looked up at the marquee of the Hudson Theatre, they would have seen the opening of a new play, *The Cinderella Man.*

In 1915, Johnston began renting and running shows out of the old Madison Square Garden. His work there gave rise to another Johnston fable. It was said that before he took over, the staff had been terrorized by a number of infamous gangsters, including Gyp the Blood, Dago Frank, Whitey Lewis, and Lefty Louie. Among other things, this crew would sit in the working press section, perhaps leaving with an overcoat or two that wasn't theirs.

On the night of his first promotion, Johnston supposedly went up to Gyp the Blood, who was sitting in an unauthorized seat, and told him to leave. When Gyp refused to move, Johnston jerked the chair backward, throwing him to the ground. He kicked and punched the most dangerous killer in New York into unconsciousness, dragged him out and threw him in an alley. When Lefty Louie came to the aid of his partner, Johnston beat him up as well.

The gangsters appealed to Harry Perry, a cousin of the Tammany Hall political boss "Big Tim" Sullivan. Perry went to see Johnston on the night of a fight at Madison Square Garden. When he saw the thin, small, Johnston he looked at his men and shouted, "Is the fellow who's been kicking you around?" The politician began to laugh. "Beat it, you tramps," he ordered, "If you can't handle a little guy like this, it's a cinch I ain't gonna help you do it. Okay, Jimmy, from now on you won't have any trouble with my boys. I'm for you."

That story worked to Johnston's advantage in a number of ways. First, it showed him both fighting for the members of the press and the ticket holders who came to his events. Second, it showed anyone wanting to move in on him that he was a tough guy. There is only problem with it: Gyp the Blood, Dago Frank, Whitey Louis and Lefty Louie had been executed at Sing Sing at least a year before Johnston took over the Garden; indeed, the four murderers had been behind bars since September 1912 when they had been arrested after hiding out for months in a small apartment in the Brownsville section of Brooklyn. When the cops burst in on them, the four were sitting around a table drinking tea with their wives.

In February 1915, Johnston decided to install a new rule at the Garden that would bar spectators from smoking while a bout was in progress. He claimed that in recent fights, "smoke had become so dense that it impaired the work of the fighters and dimmed the view of those in the gallery and balcony." His edict was met with a roar of disapproval. "By telegraph, cable, telephone, letter, picture postal card, and wireless, a flood of protests poured in until Johnston realized that he was making himself about as popular as measles in a girls' boarding school," according to the *New York Times*. Watching boxing without smoking was viewed as absurd as "eating apple pie without cheese."

Johnston quickly revoked his ban. "I'm for the fans first, last, and at all times," he said, "and they can go as far as they like on the smoke thing." A happy consequence, of course, was that the newspapers were filled with stories about him, his fighters, and the Garden, for several days.

One of Johnston's more ingenious ideas was fully documented. In April 1915, Jess Willard beat Jack Johnson for the heavyweight championship of the world in Havana, Cuba. Moving pictures were taken but could not be imported into the United States because of a federal law that prevented the interstate transportation of fight films. Johnston thought he had a way around the federal law. He arranged to have the copy of the film sent from Cuba to Canada, where it was brought to the New York State border. Johnston and his crew traveled to the international boundary and set up a camera eight inches on the American side. The film was then projected across the border onto unexposed film on their side. An endless chain connected the two reels so that the films would move the same distance in the same time. The result was that an exact negative reproduction was taken on the American side of the positive film on the Canadian side. From this secondary negative, re-photographed by another camera, a positive film capable of public exhibition could be made and was made.

The head of the United States Customs Service at the Port of New York threatened to seize the film. Johnston brought suit first, seeking to restrain him, but a court ultimately made short shrift of Johnston's case: "The transaction is plainly within the mischief of the statute, but [Johnston] contends that the statute only prohibits the importation of something physical or corporeal, whereas nothing but rays of light were brought in on this occasion... We think that, when parties on each side of the boundary cooperate, by means of two plants connected together to transfer a prohibited picture from Canada to New York, they are carrying on foreign commerce and do cause the picture to be brought into the United States, within the meaning of the act."

On hearing the decision, Johnston threw off a classic one-liner: "Court decisions like that almost make a guy decide to give up thinking for a living."


Johnston also acquired a reputation as a man who could take a veteran fighter and rejuvenate his career. His first big "miracle" was the comeback of Mike McTigue, the veteran Irishman who was supposedly all washed up. Under Johnston's management, McTigue met several good fighters and eventually won a version of the light-heavyweight title, which he lost to Tommy Loughran.

The financial highlight of Johnston's promotional career, however, was his management of Phil Scott, the British heavyweight once referred to as "The Swooning Swan of Soho." By the time he and Scott parted ways, the pair had earned several hundred thousand dollars.

American sportswriters generally had a low opinion of British heavyweights, and Dan Parker of the *Daily Mirror* weighed in with the cynicism when reporting Scott's arrival in New York in the fall of 1927. "Phil Scott, the first vertical heavyweight England has produced since that ill-fated day when Joe Beckett assumed a horizontal position for the first time in South Hampton, arrived on our shores yesterday. Scott looks like a fighter. Whether he is or not we may soon find out."

Johnston announced that his charge would be fighting the rugged Basque Paulino Uzcudun, who had beaten Scott in 1925. But Uzcudun hadn't signed a contract for the bout, and refused to agree to it. Johnston gained great mileage in the press by claiming that the Spaniard had "run out" on "my Phillip."

Scott's first opponent in the United States was Knute Hansen, a Danish heavyweight. Curious fans packed the Garden to see the match between the two European fighters. Hansen knocked Scott out in two minutes and twenty-five seconds, knocking him down no fewer than six times. In the dressing room afterwards, the irrepressible Johnston claimed that Scott had been fouled and that the referee should have disqualified the Dane.

Johnston somehow managed to rehabilitate Scott with several more bouts, and shrewdly maneuvered him to near the top of the division. In November 1929, he ran into his pal Damon Runyon, who was helping promote the New York Americans' Christmas Fund card and was looking for a fighter to headline it. Johnston would have been happy to take $5,000 when Runyon surprised him with, "I'll give you a guarantee of $17,500. What is it, yes or no, right now?" Johnston quickly agreed and Scott was matched against a Norwegian, Otto von Porat. Porat "hit Phil with a straight left hand that was a foot low as the second round started and the ferocious fireman of Merrie Old England folded up and yelled for the nets," wrote Bill Corum in the *New York Evening Journal*. Referee Jack Dempsey awarded the fight to Scott by foul for the low blow. Scott now took on a new nickname: "Phainting Phil."

His next battle was against leading contender Jack Sharkey in Miami, before 30,000 fans. After a good first round, Sharkey knocked Scott down in the second. In the third, he drove a left hook to Scott's body, and the Englishman went down, claiming foul. A doctor examined Scott, saw no evidence of foul, and the referee ordered both men to resume fighting. Two more left hooks sent Scott down again, and once more he claimed he had been hit low. The referee had none of it, and declared Sharkey the knockout victor. Scott may have left the United States as a laughing stock, but for four fights for the Madison Square Garden Corporation, lasting less than fifteen rounds, he was paid over $400,000.

The man who paid Johnston such exorbitant sums for Scott's services was Garden head Tex Rickard, the greatest promoter in the sport's history and architect of the first "million dollar gate." In 1925, Rickard decided that a new Garden was needed, and he picked William F. Carey to built it, just two blocks from where Jim Braddock had been born. At the same time, Carey was appointed vice-president and treasurer of the Garden. He was a man who got things done: Carey had risen from a poor childhood to become a millionaire industrial leader both in the United States and throughout the world.

William Carey was born in 1878 in Hoosick Falls, the son of a stonemason. In 1894, with little money in his pocket, he left for Colorado to become a mule skinner in railroad construction camps. He was earning thirty cents per hour when he met Ocean Dailey, a college professor from Nebraska. They married in 1904.

Six weeks after their wedding, they left for the Canal Zone. Carey worked on the Panama Canal and became a general superintendent. He was instrumental in making possible the excavation of the Culebra Cut after many failures. After completing the canal, he returned to the States and went into business for himself as a railroad contractor. During World War I, he built a logging railroad in one-third the time the other contractors promised. The railroad carried the spruce logs needed for barracks lumber, making it quickly available and helping the War effort. Expanding from railroads to bridge construction throughout the country, Carey next turned to canals as well as other construction projects in China. He spent years below the equator in South America building railroads and bridges, and in 1924, his construction company built the Andes Mountain Railway for the Bolivian Government.

Upon Tex Rickard's death in January 1929, the Board of Directors turned to Carey to become president of the Garden. During his three-year tenure, he established a training camp in Hoosick Falls. Many in New York City felt it was too far away, but he insisted on the site. It brought many famous sportswriters to the village, as well as the outstanding boxers and trainers. Carey's construction company also built the Boston Gardens, of which he became a director.

In the spring of 1930, Jimmy Johnston's portfolio of fighters was frighteningly slim. One afternoon, Carey asked Johnston to meet him in his office.

"Concerning money?" asked Johnston.

"Maybe," replied Carey.

"Well, I'm for that. Let's go."

Carey laid out his thoughts to Johnston. Two small airports were being built in New York City by Carey's construction firm. The welter of forms and departments in the city's bureaucracy threatened to stall the projects. Carey wanted to use Johnston's political contacts to clear the way for the two airports. Carey's deal was sweet.

"You can name your own salary, and an office right here in Madison Square Garden is yours anytime you want it."

Johnston worked for Carey over the next year, while his brother, Charley Johnston, continued in the boxing business, managing several fighters. Johnston noticed that Tom McArdle, the Garden's matchmaker, was not using Charley's fighters for any of his cards, and spoke to Carey about it.

"Listen, Bill. Charley's fighters aren't champions or world beaters, but they're as good as any of those tramps Tom has fighting in the Garden week after week. His reason for refusing Charley work for his fighters goes back even further than you imagine. Tom was my glove boy during the old Fairmont days. He was jealous of me then and is now."

"I'll speak to him about putting some of your brother's fighters in," said Carey.

A few weeks later, Carey reported that McArdle had refused to use Charley's fighters. "He's the matchmaker and if he doesn't want to put them in, I'm not going to interfere," said Carey.

Angered by this, Johnston announced that he had decided to promote fights once more, and would compete directly with the Garden.

"Not only will I have Charley's boys working," he told Carey, "but several of the stars in your own stable."

"I think you're foolish to let this thing make an enemy of you, Jimmy," said Carey, "and I don't believe you can find a place to promote. The Garden has the ballparks tied up. That is, except for Ebbets Field, which isn't any good at all, because of its Brooklyn location."

"We'll see."

Carey extended his hand. "Then war is declared?"

"War," Johnston shot back.

Johnston left Carey's office and immediately formed the Dodgers A.C. to promote boxing in New York. He named Humbert Fugazy, who had promoted Braddock in his first year as a boxer, as matchmaker and leased the Ebbets Field ballpark. In April 1931, he signed Jack Sharkey and Primo Carnera to meet in a fifteen-round bout at Ebbets Field and began lobbying the State Athletic Commission to recognize it as a world championship fight. Surprisingly, the Commission agreed.

The Garden immediately instituted suit against Carnera to restrain him from violating its purported contract with the Italian.

The battle was on – and Jimmy Johnston never ducked a fight. He and the Garden were headed to court. "We have prepared vigorously to prosecute the suit for injunction and damages," said the Garden's president. "Papers in the action are now being prepared. Our suit will be started without delay." Johnston and Carnera's manager, Bill Duffy, were confident that they could break the Garden's contract because Carnera had signed it while he was under suspension in New York, and in April the Commission reinstated the giant, pointing out that "any contract signed for Carnera during his suspension was void in this state."

In May, Federal District Court Judge Knox ruled that the Garden was entitled to enforce its contract with Carnera and he would be barred from fighting Sharkey. Carey expressed satisfaction over the decision, the first round in his war with Jimmy Johnston. Still Johnston lobbied hard for the bout, even going so far as to announce that a portion of the proceeds would be donated to charity; he then petitioned the IRS to waive the twenty-five percent tax ordinarily imposed on all tickets priced over $3. Johnston was able to stage a Carnera bout in July – despite an unknown opponent, a decent crowd turned out to see him win in seven rounds – but not against Sharkey.

In August, Johnston promoted a light-heavyweight championship fight between Maxie Rosenbloom and Jimmy Slattery at Ebbets Field. It set a record low for receipts in modern championship fights. The net receipts from a paid attendance of 5,000 amounted to $9,552. After the officials were paid, $8,992 remained. Rosenbloom's share for winning the title amounted to $3,372, while Slattery received $1,124.

While Johnston's promotions were hurting the Garden, he wasn't exactly making fortunes himself. He and Carey held a peace meeting, and Johnston talked terms.

"You cost us plenty of money this past summer, Jimmy," said Carey. "The way I figure, you're a valuable man to us and worthwhile snaring for our organization. Those terms are all right. I have a three-year contract that should be filled in tomorrow, in line with your terms. Your office will be ready whenever you're set to move in."

"As long as my conditions and salary demands are acceptable to you, everything's agreed upon," said Johnston. "I'll be in tomorrow to sign the contracts."

"I think you'll be happy here, Johnston. Rest assured there'll be no interference ... I don't work that way."

"Say, I know how you work. It was damn tough fighting you. I'm just happy to be here as you are to have me."

"Shake," offered Carey, extending his right hand. Johnston took it.

"Bill," he said, "if you'd only given my brother Charley's fighters some work, this might never have happened."

"Personally," replied Carey, "I'm sort of glad it did."

In October 1932, Carey announced that he had made Johnston an offer to take over the management of boxing promotions at Madison Square Garden. And a few days later, Bill Carey threw a beefsteak dinner at the Madison Square Garden club to welcome their new head of boxing, the Boy Bandit of Broadway, Jimmy Johnston. A ticket scalper named Mike Jacobs was drafted to serve as bartender, and handed out foaming mugs of beer with one hand metaphorically cupped behind his ear. He was listening to everything.

Johnston soon settled into his office at the Garden. Painted on the door was the name "Thos. Tittimouse, Pekin, China," an in-joke between Johnston and his father. He hired a young secretary named Margie Reagan who got the job by telling Johnston she had worked for New York's beloved Catholic priest Father Duffy, who ministered out of Hell's Kitchen. "A damn lie she told too," Johnston said. "She never worked for Father Duffy in her life; but I figured anyone who could tell that big a lie could be invaluable."

The Carey and Johnston brain trust turned toward creative ways to improve the bottom line. The Garden Corporation needed to improve its cash flow, strained by the cost of building a massive outdoor boxing stadium in Long Island City, and until the facility opened in June 1932, cost cutting was in order. First, they decided to cut off charitable donations. In the early 1920s Mrs. William Randolph Hearst, wife of the formidable press baron, created a charity to distribute milk to needy children. For years, the Hearst Milk Fund for Babies received a percentage of the profits of major fights promoted by Madison Square Garden. Now, as the Depression deepened, Mrs. Hearst sought to have the Garden increase its donations. Jimmy Johnston refused. He and Bill Carey had come to resent the "bite" that contributions to the Milk Fund took out of their bottom line. When Hearst pressed him, Johnston cut off all donations to the Fund. With that one decision, Johnston set in motion the events that would eventually topple him from his cherished post at Madison Square Garden.

Mrs. Hearst began looking for a new promoter to sponsor her boxing events. Damon Runyon and two other top members of the Hearst sports staff recommended one Michael Strauss Jacobs, better known as Uncle Mike. Jacobs for years had run a profitable ticket-scalping agency out of his offices at the Mayflower Hotel. With the three Hearst sportswriters as secret shareholders, he formed the 20th Century Boxing Club and set out to take over boxing.

He wasn't the only one. In June 1933, Jimmy Johnston watched with interest as fight legend Jack Dempsey promoted the Max Baer versus Max Schmeling bout at Yankee Stadium. Dempsey was making his boldest move yet to control the destiny of the heavy-weight division.

Baer adorned his boxing trunks with the Star of David, telling the world how proud he was of his Jewish blood. It was common for boxers to play to their ethnic support – Jim Braddock often wore a shamrock embroidered on his shorts – but in truth, although Baer grew up respecting his Jewish ancestry, he was com-pletely unconcerned with religion. Trainer Ray Arcel was even adamant that Baer was not Jewish: "I seen him in the shower," he would quip. Now more than ever, however, Baer found it expedient to play up his "Jewish" blood. "It wasn't all show," said his brother Buddy. "Max believed he was going into battle with an arrogant symbol of the 'master race.' Max Schmeling was the first and only fighter Max Baer ever hated before meeting him."

Dan Parker wrote more cynically of Baer's motives. "Baer was only a 50 per cent Hebrew when he set out for New York. He became a 100 per cent when he arrived in Gotham and were it not for the fact that the Atlantic seaboard intervened, he might have kept right on traveling until he was at least 350 per cent Yiddle."

Even though some viewed this as a battle between the swastika and the Star of David, and despite rumblings of a boycott in the Jewish community, no real opposition to the Baer-Schmeling bout had coalesced. The horrors of the Nazi government's actions, and Schmeling's representation of that government, would not be so easily dismissed in the future, but in the summer of 1933 Schmeling was viewed as a pawn in a larger political game.

On fight night, June 8, an almost unbearable heatwave gripped the East Coast. Nevertheless, 56,000 fight fans made their way to the stadium for the fight. "As we walked [from] the dressing room the baked ground burned through the soles of our shoes, and slowly we were all bathed in perspiration," remembered Joe Jacobs, Schmeling's Jewish manager. "Baer had already jumped into the ring, and was laughing and kidding with the ringsiders. He had even stopped while walking down the aisle to autograph programs for the fans."

Baer, in superb condition, seemed to thrive in the summer heat. For nine rounds, he kept up a barrage of punches. Schmeling, effective in spots, slowly wilted in the heat. Westbrook Pegler described the crucial punch thrown by Baer in the tenth round: "A sucker's wallop suddenly arched through the atmosphere made milky by tobacco smoke and resin dust, and took Schmeling on the jaw with a squashy sound and a spray of moisture. Schmeling's neck seemed to snap. His body went limp, his legs spread and his arms fell as he swayed against the ropes. Baer's seconds, Ancil Hoffman and Mike Cantwell, howled insanely at him to go on punching."

Schmeling struggled to his feet at the count of nine. Baer attacked again. "Serious as a cyclone for perhaps the first time in his jolly old life, Baer sailed into his battered rival with a flurry of punches. Schmeling covered up, slid along the ropes in a desperate effort to escape but Baer was on top of him throwing his 203 pounds into every shot. A left doubled up Schmeling and a right sent him slumping against the post in neutral corner and that was the end."

The referee stepped in just as Baer was about to fire another shot at the defenseless Schmeling, who had turned his back to him. Jacobs was across the ring in an instant, with Max Machon at his heels. "Schmeling collapsed in our arms, and we carried him back to his corner, and it was several minutes before he really regained consciousness," said Jacobs.

A bewildered Schmeling tried to explain his defeat. "I was what you call – sluggish – yea, that is it, tonight I fight Baer. I cannot lift my arms. Everything is heavy. Nothing I do is right. But the next time, that is different."

In the dressing room, Baer held up a mirror to better inspect his battered face. "Boy," he chortled, "those fellows who wouldn't believe I have Jewish blood in me will be certain of it after they see this schnozzle. Well I guess June [his future wife] won't worry about it. She better not … for we are going to step out tonight."

Two weeks after Baer's stunning win, Bill Duffy's experiment in larceny won the heavyweight title when Primo Carnera flattened Jack Sharkey with an uppercut in round six. Carnera's gangster connections made many doubt the veracity of his kayo. Jimmy Breslin's description of the fight expressed the majority view:

> Sharkey went down in his face and never moved. Duffy leaped into the ring and Carnera held him high. They owned the biggest title

in sports. Duffy stood in the ring and would not let Carnera remove the gloves. "I want a commissioner," Duffy said. He kept pointing at the gloves. He wanted them inspected so that nobody would be able to claim he had put weights in those gloves, too. Finally, Bill Brown, a commissioner, came up the steps and into the ring. He looked at the gloves. "They're clean," Brown said.

Whether Bill Duffy actually rigged the bout will never be known. There is no direct proof that he did, though some sixty years later, in his last interview, Sharkey would tell this author, "Carnera couldn't have hit me in the ass with a handful of tacks if I didn't let him."

A few days later, William Carey resigned the presidency of Madison Square Garden. Johnston remained in charge of boxing and vice president of the Garden Corporation.


Max Baer was now the number one contender, and seemed head and shoulders above every other heavyweight. Yet even with his string of brutal wins, and Carnera's deficiencies as a boxer, some thought Baer's debauched lifestyle could prevent him winning the title. "The only obstacle to Baer's rise to the crown, should he and Carnera have it out this year, would not be Carnera but the American stage beauty," said one scribe.

The vicious nature of his victory over Schmeling also brought Baer to the attention of Hollywood filmmakers. MGM signed him to appear as "Steve Morgan" in a film entitled *The Prizefighter And The Lady*, with Walter Huston, Myrna Loy, Jean Harlow – and Primo Carnera. Jack Dempsey played a referee and there was also a role for "Mexican Spitfire" and all-around boxing fan Lupe Velez, while boxer Art Lasky, an uncredited stand-in for Primo Carnera, would play a large role in the Braddock story a year later. The picture, directed by W. S. Van Dyke, was an "A" film.

One of the many actresses that Baer spent time with on set was young Jean Harlow. He described her as a "happy, loveable girl." One day Harlow said to Baer, "You are always laughing, Max, you must like this work."

"Sure I like the work," Baer said, "and I will be laughing when I get into the ring with Carnera, but mostly I'm laughing to think that they are paying me to learn all about him."

The United Press reported that Jean Harlow had given Baer a "love bracelet." Max, ever the gentleman, said he would only marry Harlow if she got a divorce from Hal G. Rosson, her husband.[1] "I need a smart polished running mate like her," Baer said. "It is love at first sight. I think we'd get along just fine." *The Prize Fighter And The Lady* premiered simultaneously in New York and San Francisco in November 1933. It was fairly well received and became one of the big moneymakers in Hollywood that year.

While Baer was busy with his acting and stage performances, his manager, Ancil Hoffman, was negotiating for a title fight against Primo Carnera. The bout was scheduled for June 14, 1934, at Madison Square Garden's Long Island Bowl.

---

[1] In September, Baer and Dorothy had obtained a divorce. This time they would not be reconciled.

*In his darkest days, Braddock went back to manual labour in railway yards and on the Weehawken docks. In later years he manned a crane for a construction company. "What the hell," he would say, "I'm a working man."*

# CHAPTER 7

# The Corn is Green

Oh yesterday the cutting edge drank thirstily and deep,
The upland outlaws ringed us in and herded us as sheep,
They drove us from the stricken field and bayed us into keep;
But to-morrow, by the living God, we'll try the game again!

—John Masefield

The New York Boxing Commission released Jim Braddock's purse for the Abe Feldman bout only after he convinced them that he had actually broken his hand. But his recent string of poor performances led the Commission to suggest, strongly, that Braddock seek another line of work. The seriousness of this suggestion was confirmed just a few weeks later when German heavyweight Walter Neusel traveled to the United States for the first time, having been booked for his American debut at the Ridgewood Grove in Brooklyn. Neusel's representatives wanted a "safe" fight for him, but one against an opponent with at least some name recognition.

The ubiquitous Joe Gould saw his opportunity, quickly convincing the Germans that their best choice would be none other than James J. Braddock. To Gould's chagrin, the New York State Athletic Commission, still perturbed over Braddock's series of sub-par performances, rejected the match, leaving Braddock essentially barred from boxing. To add further insult, the Commission approved in his stead Les Kennedy, even though Kennedy, by now a perpetual loser, had lost to Braddock just four months prior. In the event Kennedy provided little opposition as Neusel battered him to a sixth-round stoppage.

Braddock sought work of the only kind he could get – hard physical labor on the Weehawken docks. Mae, pregnant with their third child, suffered as her husband sought to provide necessities for his family. "In order to make more money, there'd be times when he'd work all day and all night without a let-up – longshoreman by day, stevedore by night," she later remembered. "The days and nights when he didn't work, he couldn't really rest, for he was hunting for something to do and worrying when he couldn't find it."

Braddock contributed around the house as well. "On nights that he wasn't working as a longshoreman or stevedore, he'd tell me to go to my mother's house to visit while he remained home with the children." When Mae returned home, she'd find the children bathed and put to bed and sound asleep – and the kitchen floor washed and polished.

"He never talked much, but I know how he felt. He'd look so sad and discouraged and unhappy and he'd shake his head and say to me, 'You'll be thinking you made the mistake of your life when you married me.' I'd not let that go unanswered. I told him the truth – that I never had thought such a thing and never would."

That Christmas, at least, Braddock's family was together. Mae described how they passed the holiday. "I got a little bit of a twenty-five-cent tree and we trimmed it with a few tiny ornaments. Then I went down to the five-and-ten and bought all of the small toys I could afford – got some dolls and dishes and picture books, balls and little cars and other metal toys for the boys. It was a five-and-ten-cent Christmas, but I don't think they knew the difference. They acted as if they had a wonderful time."

Braddock, too, would recall the grim days during the winter of 1933-34. "I worked on the docks whenever there was any work to be had. On occasions I sweated through two straight eight-hour shifts of the hardest kind of labor. On other occasions I stood around all day waiting and hoping for a chance to work but things became tougher and tougher. Soon I was in debt to everybody."

The one thing that the Braddocks did was keep their children in good health, well fed, and happy. With three children under the age of four, an indispensable item for the household was milk. The day came, however, when the milkman cut off delivery for a $37 debt. Braddock, desperate and humiliated, set out to raise the money. With just a single dime in his pocket, he tramped the several miles from his home to the ferry docks on the Hudson River. There, he paid the four cents ferry fee, and with six cents left to his name, made his way to Manhattan. He walked through the neighborhood where he was born to Madison Square Garden on 49th Street. Joe Gould normally hung out in the afternoon in Jimmy Johnston's office, along with many other boxing managers, but Braddock could not bring himself to go upstairs. He sat in the first floor office of Garden press agent Francis Albertanti, quiet and withdrawn, and not even Albertanti's entreaties could bring him to speak.

Finally, Gould came in and Braddock told him the story. He needed $37 to pay his children's milk bill. Gould was tapped out himself and had recently hocked all of the furniture in his apartment to pay his rent. But he could never deny Braddock. Telling him to wait, he went up to Johnston's office, where he related the sad story to the other members of the boxing community. A hat was passed and Gould returned to Braddock and gave him the $37 he so badly needed. Braddock made the long return walk to the ferry, crossed over again into New Jersey, and walked home. That night, his children once again had cold milk with their dinner.

The fight game is always hungry for a heavyweight with a big punch. By early 1934, one name began to rise above the other contenders: John "Corn" Griffin. A soldier stationed at Fort Benning, Georgia, Griffin had used his furlough time to establish himself as one of the most exciting sluggers in the South. At just twenty-two years old, some viewed him as the second coming of Jack Dempsey. Veteran boxing observer "Pinkie Lou" Masters was especially high on Griffin. "Corn tears into his opponent at the sound of the bell," he wrote in *Ring*, "and, until someone drops, keeps punching away. He punches hard with either hand. He is always in the best of shape and he's sure to give his best." Griffin's reputation was based on the series of sensational knockouts over fighters with names like Battling Bozo and Mugs Kerr. Masters claimed he had had over 100 bouts, although the bulk of those are to this day undocumented.

Masters alerted old Charlie Harvey to Griffin's potential. Harvey saw in Griffin perhaps his last chance to manage a heavyweight champion, and promptly negotiated with Army officials in the hopes of securing his early release from service. Griffin, too, saw a major opportunity for himself if Handlebars took over his management. "I can truthfully say," Griffin told reporters, "that when [Harvey] takes me over, I will be a different Corn Griffin." He did not specify the exact nature of his change.

Harvey eventually "ransomed" Griffin from the Army by paying a reported $54. Not long afterwards, Griffin's hulking form appeared on Harvey's doorstep. The manager shook his head upon seeing the fresh tattoo on his new charge's forearm – Griffin's own name and address. At least he had made sure that he would not become just another boxer lost in the Big Apple.

Handlebars Harvey moved as quickly as his crippled body could carry him. Calling in a favor, he got Griffin a spot as one of Primo Carnera's sparring partners as the champion trained for his June 13 defense against Max Baer. As a member of Carnera's crew, Griffin was sure to be seen by the nation's top sportswriters who would be covering the "Ambling Alp's" camp. Harvey then approached Jimmy Johnston seeking to have Griffin appear on the Carnera-Baer undercard. Johnston, who always found time to assist his former mentor and lifelong friend, agreed to showcase Harvey's soldier boy in a special five-rounder as a warm-up to the title bout.

Griffin impressed the sportswriters covering Carnera's training camp. The first afternoon that Griffin sparred with Carnera, he looked like a million dollars. He was in and out and around the champion, jabbing, hooking, and ducking. Carnera couldn't touch him. He was also incredibly strong, and would push the 270-pound Italian giant around the ring day after day.

All Harvey needed was the proper opponent for his man's debut. He and Johnston began batting around a list of likely suspects. After running though several of the usual suspects, Harvey finally asked "How about Jim Braddock?" Johnston liked the idea and summoned Joe Gould to his office.

"Is that lemon of yours ready to be squeezed?" Johnston queried, before springing the name Corn Griffin on him.

Gould at first demurred, preferring a return match with Dynamite Jackson, Baer's sparring partner, who was also scheduled to fight on the undercard. Braddock had beaten Jackson on his California trip and Gould wanted an easier fight for Braddock's comeback.

The fiery Johnston exploded. "You have been hounding me for months to get a fight for your old warhorse! It is Griffin or no one." Gould capitulated, accepting an offer of $250. Then he rushed over to New Jersey to locate Braddock.

Braddock had worked a shift on the Jersey waterfront, arriving home after six in the evening. "I found him rolling out ash barrels," Gould recalled. "He hadn't been able to pay his rent, and the landlord had given him a job as janitor, and he and his wife and kids were living in two rooms in the basement." On seeing him, Gould blurted, "I got you a fight with a guy named Corn Muffins! Get yourself right in training."

Gould explained the sudden offer, this time getting the opponent's name right. "They want somebody for Griffin to lick tomorrow. They want you and will pay $250 for the job. Do you want it?"

Braddock accepted without hesitation. "I would have said yes if they wanted me to fight a gorilla," he later recalled. "No fooling, that $250 looked bigger to me than the big purses I had collected in other days. More than that, I felt in my bones it was the break I had been looking for so long."

But there was one hurdle Johnston, Gould and Harvey had over-looked. Braddock remained *persona non grata* with the New York authorities; indeed the New York State Athletic Commission refused to re-license him. Once more, Gould quickly figured the angles. He called Tim Mara, president of the New York Giants football team, whose son had just married the daughter of the chairman of the boxing commission at Gould's urging, Mara convinced his son's father-in-law to allow the fight.

As her husband left for the Garden Bowl on the afternoon of the fight, Mae Braddock stopped him at the door. She said nothing, but uncertainty showed in her hazel eyes. "What have we got to lose?" Jim finally said. "At least we'll have enough money to eat for a few days." Then, with his boxing trunks wrapped in that day's news-paper and a borrowed pair of boots slung over his shoulders, he set out to meet Corn Griffin in a five-round preliminary bout.

Jim Braddock's appearance as he walked to the ring caused comment among the pressmen. "I think I gave some of the boys who hadn't seen me in some time a surprise when I climbed into the ring," said Braddock later. "When I had been fighting Loughran and Slattery and those fellows I scaled around 175 pounds. That made me lanky and rangy. Well, with the lack of meals I hadn't put on more than five pounds in the meantime, but I was hard as nails. A fellow who works on the docks hustling freight hasn't much time to let fat accumulate on his frame."

Writer Jack Kofoed saw a different Braddock climbing the three narrow steps to the ring. "His work on the docks hardened him as most years of training could have done. Eight hours and more a day hauling heavy cases, running up and down gang-planks, made his muscles like iron and improved his wind."

The Jersey veteran stared at his daunting opponent. He had

never set eyes on Griffin before, and was impressed by what he saw: a honed, fired-up bundle of muscle, sinew and burning ambition. "He looked just as ferocious and fit as they said he was," said Braddock later.

Then the bell rang. Braddock quickly felt Griffin's contempt. "He was so sure ... so cockily sure. He knew he wouldn't have any trouble with me. And in the second round he landed a whizzing punch on the whiskers that knocked me down."

Braddock had been on the deck just once before, when Jack Stone dumped him in front of Mae and a gaggle of friends at the start of his career. This time he didn't panic. "I had eight years of fighting under my belt," he explained.

He took the count resting on one knee, nodding assurances to Joe Gould, who peered anxiously through the ropes. Braddock kept a poker face, but inside he was churning with emotion, doubt, and for once in his life, fear – fear not of pain but of failure. "It meant so much to me to win this fight. My wife and kids depended on me. I had to win. There was no foolishness about an honor or a championship. It was bread and meat and milk I was battling for ..., and the press agent who blurbed about a guy fighting for the wife and kiddies must have meant me."

He rose at the count of nine, his head clear, and kept his guard high. "I remember looking at Griffin, who a lot of people said was going to be the next champion. As I looked at Corn, I said to myself, 'This fellow is going to come at me with a left hook.'" Griffin came tearing in, wild to finish him. Some men are panic-stricken when dropped. It worked in reverse with Braddock. It made him cool and cautious.

"When he charged I let go the old Mary Ann, and Corn went down on his haunches, the most surprised man in the Bowl," Braddock would say. "He was sick and groggy ... and he didn't have experience enough to take a long count. He got up as fast as he could, and it was only the bell that saved him for the next round."

Griffin was still groggy at the start of the third. "He wasn't a boxer," Braddock observed. "All he knew was rush in and belt away at the other fellow. So at the start of what turned out to be the final round he was just a target; I clipped him off his feet, and he couldn't get up.

"Still rocky, I was standing there with my tongue out waiting for Joe Gould, my manager, to hit me in the face with a sponge full of ice water. Instead, he threw the sponge at Corn."

After the fight Braddock asked Gould, "What did you do that for?"

"Corn was in worse shape than you were," Gould answered.

Later, in the dressing room, Braddock asked how he had looked.

"Swell," Gould replied.

"Well," said Braddock, "I did that eating hash. Get me a few steaks and I'll knock these other guys stiff."

The win caused a minor sensation. "Joe Gould was the happiest man in the United States that night," said Braddock. "The clouds that had hung over us so long were blowing away. We were both convinced that I had hit my stride again. I had whacked Griffin hard without hurting my hand. We're going to be in the money again."

Both fighter and manager stuck around the arena for the heavyweight title fight. It was to be one of the most extraordinary in history.

Max Baer had exuded confidence leading up to his challenge. At a press conference in New York, he was asked who he thought the next heavyweight champion would be. "Every time I look into my crystal ball I see my own reflection," he answered. "Do I believe in crystal balls? Maybe not, but I do believe in balls, and I've got enough to beat anybody in the world."

Primo Carnera, too, believed he would win. Many critics dismissed Carnera, perhaps the least skilled champion in history, as a joke. But in his sessions with Bill Duffy and others, he had learned to box rather well, albeit mechanically. His huge size, strength and conditioning were enough to see him through most fights. To complement those attributes, he had added a decent left jab. Joe Louis, for one, would consider Carnera one of the better boxers that he faced.

Graham McNamee and Ford Bond handled the broadcasting duties for what was up to that time the largest worldwide radio event. Besides NBC's network, the fight was being broadcast to Italy and to South America by shortwave. Joe Humphries once more served as the ring announcer, and his famous "Quiet! Quiet please!" silenced the crowd and signaled that the bout was about to begin. As Referee Arthur Donovan gave his instructions, McNamee told the radio listeners, "Boy that man Carnera is big!" Moments later, one the wildest fights ever was underway.

Baer later described the outset. "We met in the center of the ring started right off throwing punches. Straight away Carnera nailed me, throwing fast and accurately. I threw a few swings and missed most of them, but all the time I was just waiting for Carnera to get away and give me a couple of clean shots at him."

The tense, even round suddenly exploded. Baer drove across an overhand, clubbing right and Carnera collapsed in sections, like a falling skyscraper. Commentator McNamee was yelling, barely able to keep up with the ferocious action: "Carnera is up ... He's down again! ... Baer drives a left and a right and a left and a right to Carnera's body." The round ended before Baer could do more damage.

In the second, Carnera went down three more times – with Baer falling on top of him. The sight of the two massive men tumbling to the canvas had a comical appearance to it, but inside the ring, despite playing to the crowd, Baer was fighting all out to take the crown. In the fourth round, Carnera jabbed Baer hard in the mouth. Baer dropped his hands and said, "That was a nice punch, Primo, try another one," and stuck out his chin. Carnera was too surprised to react.

The champion boxed competently through the middle rounds,

yet each time Baer landed a haymaker he looked shaky, and several of these single-shot bombs hurt or dropped him to the canvas. Yet Carnera kept going, and by the tenth Baer seemed to be tiring, when he suddenly unleashed two thunderous blows to Carnera's heart. The Italian's mouth dropped open in a gasp, and Baer knocked him to the floor again. By the round's end, Carnera had been reduced to a reeling, bloody hulk, with blood pouring from his torn mouth.

At the gong for the eleventh, Baer advanced "like a shot of lighting." He pounded Carnera to the canvas again, and again the giant forced himself to rise. "The man won't stay down," McNamee screamed. "This is a scrap, oh boy, oh boy." As Baer's onslaught continued, McNamee was fit to burst: "Carnera has fallen! Carnera has fallen again ... Talk about nerve, he'll fight until he's dead, that man!"

Baer advanced on Carnera again, and this time the champion turned and spoke to Arthur Donovan. After a moment, the referee stopped the fight and motioned Baer to his corner. It was over. Max Baer had done it; he had won the heavyweight championship of the world by "technical knockout." The only thing technical about it was the terminology.

Carnera left the ring a shambles, unable to speak through torn, swollen lips. Baer's manager, however, could barely wait to step up to the mike: "This is Ancil Hoffman speaking. I've got the greatest boxer in the world. Hurray!"


Corn Griffin never recovered from the beating he received that night, and would remain in awe of Jim Braddock's heart, if not his talent. "Braddock is no hell of a fighter any way you figure it, but he'll get up off of that floor until he wears you out," he rued.

Gould and Braddock both knew they could cash in on Jim's sensational win, and went in search of more paydays. Together they would haunt the halls of Madison Square Garden, looking for the next bout. Gould and his fighter sat together for hours at a time on the hard benches outside Jimmy Johnston's office, until the meager $250 they had earned was gone and both drifted off to try to earn a living. Gould, never one for heavy lifting, started hustling automobile radios, just then coming into high vogue. Braddock once more hung around the shape-up halls on the Weehawken waterfront. As the Garden's summer season drew to a close, his status became clear. Instead of a rebirth, his victory over Corn Griffin had been a goodbye to boxing.

Braddock discusses his perennial problem of hand injuries with the German heavyweight Max Schmeling (centre) and a physician. Despite broken fists threatening to end his career, the Cinderella Man put himself back into contention with sensational wins over ranked fighters including the talented John Henry Lewis (right).

# CHAPTER 8

# From Relief to Royalty

"If you have children, no matter how bad life is, you just can't give up and be sunk. And besides – no matter how hard life is – the children can put some joy and fun into it."

—Mae Braddock, June 20, 1935

Slowly, relentlessly, Jim Braddock's debts mounted. He fell behind on his rent, his electric bill, his milk bill. The creditors extended all the credit that they could, then began demanding payment.

Mae Braddock's nerves frayed as the cold winter dragged on. With little income, every crust of bread and grain of rice was precious. Once incident exemplified the tenuous grip she had on her family's well being. One morning, after cleaning the kitchen until it was spotless, she stepped out to the grocers for a moment, leaving the children playing in the apartment. When she returned, the children had emptied all the sugar, flour, coffee, tea, and oatmeal onto the floor and were busy "making a mountain." Without a word, she threw herself on the bed and cried until she fell asleep. When she awoke, she heard whispers and shuffling coming from the kitchen. Her husband and her brother were trying to clean silently so as not to wake her.

The Braddocks could no longer pay the rent on their small apartment. "Things got so bad, we had to move into a smaller apartment in the same building," remembered Mae. "There were four of us and two rooms and a kitchen. We had practically no money. One of our real friends, we shall never forget, was Doctor MacDonnell, who let his bill run and never once asked for money. About this time, my whole family was out of work too, and I was expecting another child. We were almost flat broke and without resources."

Mae's husband would come home half chilled to the bone after long hours shooting coal and other freight into the boats. One of his friends even had an ear frozen solid. "It hurt me for Jimmy's sake to think of him doing such back-breaking work, exposed to horrific weather. Yet, we are grateful for the little money he did make, although he was lucky to average twenty dollars weekly. As spring came along, the work fell off. Rose Marie, our little girl, was born in May, but for the kindness of Doctor MacDonnell, I do not know what we would have done. He arranged for all the expense."

Braddock rarely got more than two days work a week. He could no longer keep his family together. "Things got so bad we had to send the children away," recalled Mae. She went to stay at her mother's cottage in the Catskill Mountains, and when she returned, she found a different Braddock. "I found Jimmy grave and quiet, very discouraged. It was the first time I ever seen him jittering. If anyone spoke to him sudden or slammed a door, he would start as if a gun had been fired."

One day that September, while Braddock was looking for work, men came to disconnect his gas and electric service. Mae pleaded with them, but to no avail. When Braddock came home and saw his darkened apartment, his face turned gray.

"I'll be back in a minute or two," he told Mae, then turned on his heel and left. He came back a short time later with several candles. They sat in silence, eating questionable bread by candlelight. Mae thought back to her wedding breakfast of 1,500 people. Where were they now?

As Mae cleared the table, she suddenly heard sobbing from the dark corner where her husband was sitting. "He had broken down completely," Mae would write years later. "I went to him. I put my arms around him and kissed him. I told him I loved him, would stick to him through anything; and finally he pulled me in his arms. Something about it thrilled me, even in the grief and tragedy of that moment. Something told me we'd win, that a man like Jimmy would find a way; all in the world he needed was a break and if there had been any distance between our hearts, they came together that night."

That night, for the sake of their children, the Braddocks decided to apply for welfare relief. Braddock would have to apply at the local police station. It must have galled him to know that "old friend" Harry Buesser, who had helped to drive his taxi cab company into bankruptcy, headed North Bergen's Relief Commission.

Braddock became one of 600,000 in New Jersey to obtain relief at that time. The agency also arranged to have milk delivered for their children. In all, the Braddocks would receive $6.40 a week.

Just a few months after his stirring win over Corn Griffin, Braddock was boxing's forgotten man. He had gone from headline to bread-line, while other boxers began to take center stage. In October 1934, Steve Hamas followed a win over Max Schmeling with a disputed win over Art Lasky. The Lasky-Hamas bout had a couple of immediate consequences. First, the New York City Boxing Commission adopted a fifteen-round minimum for championship elimination matches.

"In this way, we can eliminate dissatisfaction over the decisions in important matches and at the same time satisfy ourselves on the matter of whether a challenger is physically equipped to travel the full championship distance," explained the commission chairman. "In bouts of eight, ten, or twelve rounds it is difficult to provide a satisfactory trial."

Second, the commission directed Jimmy Johnston to hold a "round robin" tournament among available heavyweight contenders to select a leading contender for Baer's title. The winner would meet Baer for the title in June. The entrants would be Art Lasky, Steve Hamas, Max Schmeling, and Primo Carnera. Charlie Harvey immediately objected to Hamas's inclusion, believing his fighter had earned a straight title shot by virtue of his victories over Lasky and Schmeling. It was arguments as usual.

Facing another Christmas with no money, Braddock turned once more to his chosen profession, boxing. Since no promoter would hire him, he undertook to promote himself in a bout against another Jersey heavyweight, Steve Dudas. On October 24, Braddock signed to meet Dudas in an eight-round bout on November 23. The bout would be held at Columbia Park under the auspices of the North Bergen Social and Athletic Club. Braddock had no great affection for Dudas, who had beaten his good friend Pat Sullivan the year before in an amateur fight. In slightly more than a year as a professional, Dudas had fought no fewer than twenty-two times, losing just once. As his reputation grew in north New Jersey, perhaps a little jealousy crept into the mind of the veteran fighter.

Just a few days after agreeing to fight Dudas, his club threw him a "benefit." Obviously, Braddock's friends knew what difficulties he was facing financially.

Meanwhile, Jimmy Johnston was putting together a show that would feature Slapsie Maxie Rosenbloom defending his light-heavyweight title against Bob Olin. Johnston intended to showcase an impressive Californian light-heavyweight, John Henry Lewis, in his East Coast debut in the semi-final bout, which spoke volumes about his approach to promotions. In an article for *Ring*, Johnston had written, "Pleasing the public is our biggest job and we cannot hope to overcome depression by putting one over on John Q. Public." That meant featuring fighters of all races and colors, black, white, or in the case of Ah Chung, an artificial yellow. In John

Henry Lewis, he was featuring a great fighter who happened to be black. After several other top light-heavyweights declined to meet Lewis, Johnston reached out to Gould, offering him $700 to have Braddock step in at the last moment. Braddock cancelled the Dudas bout and accepted the offer.

Johnston's workload threatened to overwhelm him that November. Besides arranging the Rosenbloom-Olin bout, he needed to stage the round robin to select Baer's challenger. The Boy Bandit turned his efforts to trying to sign Hamas and Lasky to a rematch, predicting a sell-out of the Garden at $7.50 ringside. As was the norm, Johnston offered to pay Hamas a percentage of the gate.

Then Walter Rothenberg, a promoter based in Holland, offered Harvey a flat $25,000 to have Hamas meet Schmeling in Germany. "Money for old bottles," said Harvey, and began packing his bags for the trip. If Hamas was going to fight for Johnston, Charlie Harvey wanted it to be against Baer and for the title. "We licked Lasky according to the decision rendered in the Garden, and we want no more of him," old Handlebars told Johnston, accepting the German offer.

Lasky, though, was willing to fight whomever the Garden set up in front of him. Charlie Harvey sought an opinion from the New York State Attorney General as to the validity of the Garden's contracts. On November 15, 1934, on the eve of the Braddock-Lewis fight, the Attorney General declared the Garden's multi-bout contracts with its fighters to be void. This meant the contracts, as written, were binding for one bout only. Hamas and Carnera immediately became free agents, while Baer, the champion, was tied in to just one more bout.

On hearing of the ruling, Johnston exploded. "The Attorney General is talking through his hat," he shouted. "Who does he think he is, head of the United States Supreme Court?" Johnston turned to his secretary: "Margie, get my lawyer on the wire!" Then he dashed into his private office and slammed the door.

Against John Henry Lewis, Braddock fought like a young man.

He immediately engaged his opponent, fighting him on the inside. Lewis attempted a series of hooks, but Braddock blocked each one and countered to the body. John Henry's sheer athleticism still allowed him to out-hustle Braddock on the inside in the early rounds, but Braddock slipped punches cleverly without excess movement; his rust was gone and his reflexes were working well. When Lewis jabbed, Braddock parried with his right and countered with his own jab.

Most of Lewis's work focused on the body – and this may have cost him the fight. In three separate rounds, his punches strayed below the belt, and referee Arthur Donovan awarded those rounds to Braddock because of the fouls. In the ninth, Lewis slammed a left hook to Braddock's face, splitting his right eye and bringing blood that dripped for the rest of the fight, but not enough to force a stoppage.

The bout had been close, but Braddock's harder punches carried the day, and he was awarded the decision against one of the best young prospects of the day. Many of the nation's top sportswriters took issue with the Braddock victory; at least ten wrote that Lewis deserved the win. All agreed, though, that it was the best fight of the night, with fast action and hard punching throughout. The dispute over the verdict was just one of a series that week, including the decision in the main event that deprived Maxie Rosenbloom of his light-heavyweight title. For some reason the New York Commission's solution was to ask the legislature to amend the boxing rules so that the referee's vote would count the same as the two judges'. At that time, the referee made the casting vote only if the two judges disagreed.

Shortly after Braddock's win over Lewis, Johnston offered the bigger Joe Louis a fight against Braddock at the Garden on December 14. Louis declined. Johnston did not know that the "Brown Bomber" and his managers were already negotiating with Uncle Mike Jacobs for a long-term contract.

Braddock's two victories in 1934, over Griffin and Lewis, although months apart, brought him back to the fringes of the game's upper echelon. In its year-end rankings, the venerable *Ring* magazine broke the contenders into three groups. As champion, Baer, of course, was sole member of group one. *Ring* identified Baer's leading contenders as Carnera, Hamas, and Lasky, in that order. The third tier included King Levinsky, Patsy Perroni, Joe Louis, Natie Brown, and Walter Neusel. Braddock was ranked ninth in this third group. In all, even with his wins over Griffin and Lewis, fourteen other fighters ranked ahead of Braddock.

For all its influence, *Ring* was essentially the province of one man, Nat Fleischer, the Johnny Appleseed of boxing, who shouted the sport's virtues across the globe. The nation's top sportswriters also issued annual rankings through a poll conducted among sportswriters by Wilbur Wood of the *New York Sun*. In those rankings, Max Baer received 100 percent of the votes for the best heavyweight. Steve Hamas, Max Schmeling, Art Lasky and Primo Carnera came next. A rising phenomenon called Joe Louis, with just twelve fights under his belt, ranked number ten. Braddock was one of twenty-seven heavyweights who received at least one vote. His comeback obviously had taken the sportswriters by surprise and several weren't sure how or where to rank him. A number of votes even named him as one of the top light-heavyweights, and he was ranked tenth in that division.

The dangerman on the list was Joe Louis. In signing the black sharecropper's son to an exclusive promotional contract, Mike Jacobs had caught lightning in a bottle. Several people would claim credit for alerting Jacobs to Louis. Reporters with grudges against Jimmy Johnston would even write that the Boy Bandit had blown his own deal with the fighter and his Chicago managers by making racial remarks and suggesting that Louis would need to "lose a few"; instead they were introduced to Jacobs by fellow Chicagoans Sam Pian and Art Winch, who managed welterweight star Barney Ross. Whatever the truth, Jacobs now had the machine to cement the Garden's grip on boxing.

At the time Jacobs became aware of Louis, he had been a professional for fewer than six months, but had already cracked the top ten. A 1934 National Golden Gloves winner, he had marched through a succession of progressively tougher professional opponents with a destructive capacity not seen since the days of the young Jack Dempsey. Louis had an aura that terrorized his opponents even before his punches paralyzed them. His talent was limitless, and race seemed the only possible bar to his ambitions.

Meanwhile, the madcap champion continued to earn money with a series of tough exhibition fights. In December, about 16,000 spectators showed up at Chicago Stadium to see him box King Levinsky. Exhibitions were meant to be easy, but as in most of his, Baer fought without headgear and with six-ounce gloves, which in some states were actually two ounces *under* the regulation size.

In the days leading up to the show, Baer cheerfully signed autographs for fans and clowned in the ring during workouts. In sparring sessions, he was also boxing better than he ever had. He seemed very relaxed in the ring, was picking off jabs with his right hand, and was actually jabbing with consistency. His reflexes, too, seemed fine-tuned.

Baer had fought Levinsky twice before and had not seriously hurt him on either occasion. This time he posed and mugged in the early moments of the first round, and generally seemed to be having a good time. Levinsky circled warily, then tried two hard rights that barely missed Baer's jaw. A moment before the bell ending the round, Levinsky slammed home a hard right hand to Baer's head. Max seemed angry.

Baer returned to his corner, refused to sit down and chatted with his corner men. At the bell for the second round, he stayed in the corner, his arms draped across over the top rope, and waited for Levinsky to advance. Levinsky walked to ring center and motioned for Baer to come to him, shouting something while he did so.

It was a colossal error. Baer's expression changed and he charged.

He was now the killer, not the clown. He hammered Levinsky to the ropes with a series of savage, overhead rights, then threw a short, terrible left hook that knocked Levinsky flat on his back. He was counted out at just fifty-three seconds of the second round.

What had caused Baer to snap into berserker mode? Sportswriter George Gallati reported that Levinsky said, "Come on and fight [expletive deleted]." It was this unrepeated epithet that caused Baer to lose his temper. Gallati also recorded Baer's only wisecrack of the night. As he was leaving the ring, he remarked, "Fancy that fellow laughing at me."

For his three minutes and fifty-three seconds' work, Baer earned $9,000.

After witnessing that devastating display of punching power, Jimmy Johnston visited Baer's dressing room to congratulate him. The champ, still pumped from his exhilarating performance, was in no mood to be flattered. His ill feeling towards Johnston and the Garden spilled out in front of the delighted reporters packed into the dressing room, and Johnston, for once, was forced to remain silent in the face of a virulent diatribe. "You say I'm not doing anything to help the fight game," Baer began. "You are the one ruining the fight game. You go around knocking everybody and everything. You're the smart guy. Five years ago when I wanted to come back against Jimmy Braddock, who turned things down on the bout? You said Braddock was washed up." Johnston did not have time to protest that he had not been at the Garden's helm at that time. "Now you have Braddock matched with Art Lasky. Is it because you have a piece of Lasky?"

Johnston for once was speechless, while Baer was on a roll. "Listen Jimmy, you may have the fighters, the officials, and the politicians on your side. But you don't have these." Max held up the taped fists that had just pulverized Levinsky. "I have these and I'll use them to beat the living daylights out of every fighter you have tied up."

Not willing to continue such a one-sided discussion in public, Johnston left without a word. The exchange showed that the relationship between the Garden and Baer had soured irrevocably. Baer was certain to sign with a new promoter after his contractual obligations were satisfied – if not before.

In February, Baer flew to California to fight in a benefit for Elisa Camilli, Frankie Campbell's widow. At her side was Francis Camilli, Jr., born three months after his father's death. Ancil Hoffman told the press that Baer would fight ranked heavyweight Stanley Poreda in a four-round bout using six-ounce gloves. Poreda had wins over Primo Carnera and Tommy Loughran to his credit, and Donn Shields, chief inspector for the California State Athletic Commission, interpreted that the conditions of the bout meant that Baer's title would be at risk. "They've agreed to a fight, not an exhibition," said Shields. "Baer could lose his title by knockout. It's a pretty large order, of course."

Baer donated his services, and all of the proceeds would go to Campbell's widow. On the night of the fight, over 10,000 paid $15,000 at San Francisco's Dreamland Auditorium to see the champion. The official program to the bout stated in stark, black letters, "Not An Exhibition." Apparently neither Baer nor Poreda read the program. Baer, solemn prior to the bell, began clowning almost immediately, and pulled every stunt out of his well-stocked bag of tricks. He mugged, he grinned, he stuck out his chin, he pretended to stagger.

"The playboy champion could obviously have knocked out his opponent at any stage of the fight if he chose," reported the Associated Press, "but he preferred to play it being groggy himself and demonstrating the little of everything he had in the way of swings and clowning."

In the last round, Baer turned to business and sent Poreda down for a count of nine. The champ left the ring with a bloody nose, and a small part of his conscience eased.[1]

---

[1] Campbell's widow would face another tragedy. Her son entered West Point at age 21. In February 1952, Francis Camilli, Jr. and 20 other West Point cadets died in a plane crash while training in Arizona.

★

Jimmy Johnston needed to rehabilitate Art Lasky as a viable contender after his slim victory over Steve Hamas. Since Hamas was refusing a rematch, Johnston selected Jim Braddock as a foil for Lasky, scheduling a bout between the two for February 1, 1935. Shortly before the fight, however, Lasky reported a severe case of the flu, and it was postponed until March.

Braddock had trained studiously and was frustrated at the postponement. Plus, the $4,100 would come in very handy – the small stipend afforded by the Relief Agency was barely able to keep the family from starving. "I whipped myself into condition for the bout on February the first," said Braddock. "Then, almost at the last minute, the match was postponed. Some said Art had hurt his hand. Others that the gate had fallen below expectation and that a little high-pressure publicity was needed before we actually fought. The setback was disappointing, because I needed the money and because I would have to go through the training grind again."

In the interim, Max Schmeling caused an upset by stopping Steve Hamas in their rematch. Schmeling's manager, Joe Jacobs, described the end of that bout: "In the eighth round Hamas took worst punishment. His teeth were broken; his mouth gashed, widening cuts opened under and over both eyes, and down he went and only his fighting heart dragged him to his feet again."

The Lasky-Braddock bout now took on added significance. When the odds managers set the price on the Lasky-Braddock bout, they made the bigger Lasky a five-to-one favorite. "There it is," said Joe Gould when he heard the odds. "Five-to-one again. Those gamblers will never learn."

Braddock was philosophical. "Even if Lasky beat me, I had gone through the worst of my financial problems. I had cleaned up my debts, and the match would bring in $4,000 more. That would carry the family along until I could find a better job."

On March 22, 1935, the man they had all written off stepped into the ring against the top contender, Art Lasky. Lasky would be trying to pin a Grimm ending on Braddock's fairytale comeback.

Braddock proceeded to fight the fight of his life. On the outside, he used head movement to slip one punch after another. On the inside, he bulled Lasky to the ropes with body punches. At every turn, Braddock sought to control the bout and to show that he would not be pushed around. In round two, he popped a series of jabs at Lasky, as if to convince the youngster that he should treat his elders with respect. Braddock's masterful left shocked the ringsiders, who were used to seeing him as a right-hand counter puncher. Braddock's work with the tie hook on thousands of railroad ties was paying unexpected dividends.

But Lasky was a tough, resilient foe, and the first half of the bout was fought at a terrific pace. In the fifth, coming out of a clinch, Braddock clipped Lasky with a left hook, then repeated the move a moment later. During a third clinch, Braddock threw the left just as the referee called break. The ref immediately called a foul, turned to the judges and took the round away from Braddock.

At their home in New Jersey, the stress had Mae on the verge of nervous collapse. "I shall never forget that Lasky fight, for that was another crisis, Jimmy's definite comeback. No one knew that he had been on relief; no one knew that he had been living on hash and the cheapest food possible." Mae had a hard time discounting a premonition that Lasky would disable or kill her husband. Each blow described by the radio announcer seemed to confirm her dark fears. Mae switched off the radio. Alone in their basement apartment, she heard the sounds of the broadcast seeping down from the apartments above. Stressed, desperate, and terrified for her husband's safety, she finally broke and ran running into the street to escape.

But even there she heard the sounds of the fight as each house and apartment she ran past had tuned in the commentary. Unable to escape, Mae yielded, returned to her room, and switched on the radio just as the fight was entering the eighth round.

"I fell down on my knees and prayed. What an ordeal it was.

Round for round, the suspense continued. Any moment he might be killed. I was afraid of his broken hand, afraid of everything. He had not been eating properly – how on earth would he be able to last out the fifteen rounds?"

In that eighth round, Lasky sought to attack Braddock's body on three separate occasions, looking to weaken the older fighter. "Kill the body and the head will die," was an old boxing adage passed round from trainer to trainer, gym to gym. Braddock repelled Lasky each time with crisp right hands to his prodigious nose, and near the end of the round he even opened a cut over Lasky's left eye with a slashing blow. Astonishingly, at halfway through the fight the veteran was matching his bigger, younger foe punch for punch. But this bout was under championship conditions, over fifteen rounds, and seven long, grueling rounds lay ahead.

Mae listened intently through to the end of the fight. Suddenly, it was over. Time seemed to stop as she awaited the verdict. "Then, all at once – like a stroke of lightning – I heard the announcer say that Jimmy had won. Believe me, I almost went crazy."

Jim Braddock beat Art Lasky by a unanimous decision. He had marshaled a lifetime of experience, and a courage that was in-born and indomitable, to eventually dominate one of the best heavy-weights in the world. He was, well and truly, back.

*Knockout*, a West Coast boxing newspaper, came up with a reason for Lasky's poor showing: "Lasky allowed a ham doctor to shoot his sore hands with something that was supposed to fix up the mitten so it would not hurt him. The doc filled the needle with barley water, or something equally as ineffective and Art took an awful licking, thereby eliminating himself from the heavyweight picture."[2] If true, it was something Braddock could readily empathize with.

[2] By September 1935, Art Lasky was a $4 a day laborer in California, but he had invested $40,000 of his ring earnings in an annuity that he would begin collecting when he turned forty in 1948 – or so he thought. Shortly after his fortieth birthday, Lasky discovered that his brother-manager Maurice had pilfered the funds. The brothers litigated for years afterwards.

Slowly, inexorably, Jimmy Johnston's grand scheme was crumbling. Hamas was out of the round robin, Schmeling was proving to be a tough negotiator, and Primo Carnera's manager, Louis Soresi, refused to match the former champion with Braddock unless the Garden posted a $50,000 guarantee to assure that the winner would be matched with Baer for the title. Johnston refused, conceding that he planned to match Baer against Schmeling.

Mike Jacobs saw an opportunity and pounced. Before any real negotiations with Johnston could take place, Jacobs dealt a death-blow to the heavyweight tournament by signing Carnera to meet Joe Louis that June. Johnston was running out of options.

Even after the Lasky fight, most believed Schmeling remained a better draw than Braddock, but the German seemed unwilling to leave Berlin. With the deadline for setting up a June title bout fast approaching, the New York State boxing commissioners held a closed-door meeting with Braddock on March 26, 1935. "The commissioners asked me if I thought I had a good chance with Baer," Braddock told the *New York Times* afterwards, "and I told them I thought I had. I not only have a good right but I have developed a good left and I never felt so well before in my life."

Braddock's humble but confident demeanor convinced the commissioners, who did not have much of an alternative. Shortly thereafter, to the surprise of the New York press, the commission named James J. Braddock the number one challenger to Max Baer's world heavyweight title. But the commission left a little wiggle room for the Garden, which clearly preferred Schmeling for the title fight, as he would be, they assumed, a more formidable opponent and a bigger draw. Accordingly, the commission directed Johnston to contact Schmeling and offer him a fight with Braddock. If Schmeling agreed, the winner would meet Baer. At that point, Johnston still believed he could get the German to agree to terms for a Baer fight without the need for an interim bout with

Braddock. He even threatened to promote the fight outside of New York State if forced to by the commission.

The news of Braddock's ascension to top contender reached Max Baer in California, whose reaction was reported by the Associated Press. "That's the biggest laugh I've had in months," said Baer. "The New York Commission says that Braddock is the number one challenger. And I suppose that makes it official. They call me a clown but I couldn't pull anything as funny as that if I sat up five nights a week."

Baer spent money at a prodigious rate and needed a lucrative fight for his first defense. The exhibitions he had been fighting did little for his bottom line, although they did keep his name before the public. And Baer believed that a fight with Braddock would be a financial and artistic flop. He did not expect any paying customers to attend what he viewed as an easy knockout win for him. Like Johnston, Baer believed that a rematch with Max Schmeling would draw a bigger gate and a larger purse for both fighters. Baer finished his interview with another broadside against the New York Commission. "I suppose this fellow [Commissioner] Bill Brown is serious about sponsoring Braddock as the commission's leading contender ... I'm supposed to be a dumb fighter, but if I couldn't make up better matches than what the New York Commission tries to cook up, I'd go back to milking cows."

Baer's manager, Ancil Hoffman, warned Johnston not to name Braddock as the designated challenger. "What's the idea of dragging [Braddock] out now?" asked Hoffman, rhetorically. "Braddock's victory over Lasky meant nothing. I saw a bum beat Lasky." He even threatened to break Baer's association with the Garden. "If they don't name a logical contender by April 15, our contract is off and we'll fight anybody we want to." Baer and his management were looking past any June defense to the result of the Carnera-Louis bout, as a win by Louis would likely set up a million-dollar gate in the Fall.

Nevertheless, with time running out to select an opponent for

Baer, Jimmy Johnston signed Braddock to meet the champion. Johnston and the rest of the Garden's organization then began preparing for an exit from boxing promotion. The expected win for Baer, who would then be a free agent, would leave the Garden without a major boxer under contract. Associated Press reporter Ed Neil had good sources both at the Garden and the 20th Century Sporting Club, headed by Mike Jacobs, and revealed that former Garden head Bill Carey had signed on as president of the Jacobs organization. Moreover, Carey had been negotiating with Garden officials and had reached a tentative deal. After Baer's victory, the Garden would cease promoting fights for its own account. In turn, the 20th Century Sporting Club would lease the Garden for its own promotions, guaranteeing a certain amount for rental plus a share of the profits. Coupled with his existing leases on Yankee Stadium and the Polo Grounds, the Garden's exit would give Uncle Mike a monopoly in the sport's most important city.

Now all Max Baer had to do was beat Jimmy Braddock.

*Ring magazine highlights the forthcoming big fight between Max Baer and Jim Braddock. Most reporters deemed it a foregone conclusion.*

CHAPTER 9

# Homicide Hall

"Good evening friends, here's where your worries end!"

—Al Jolson, April 13, 1935

In April 1935, Al Jolson, the nation's most popular entertainer, broadcast the first episode of his new radio variety show, *Shell Chateau*. Jolson loved boxing and boxers. He had a reserved seat at the weekly fights at the Hollywood Bowl (as did, among others, the Mexican actress Lupe Velez, who was often heard shouting, "Give it to *heem!*"). Jolson also invested in fighters, the most successful being the stupendous three-division champion Henry Armstrong. For his premiere show, Jolson got Max Baer to appear. Max brought along his brother, Buddy, who was a better singer than a boxer.

A week later, when Braddock officially signed to be Baer's challenger, Jolson invited the Jersey veteran onto his show. Braddock didn't say much, but he did hit the speed bag for a few moments. He was paid $300, and through NBC's nationwide system, the country was introduced to Braddock and his story. It was a melodrama with which so many listeners could identify; the ordinary, blue-collar guy who pulls himself back from penury with nothing more than his fists and his heart. A legend was beginning to form.

Ever the ham, Baer decided to appear in his own thirteen-episode radio show, beginning April 29. The show, entitled *Lucky Smith*, starred Baer as a detective, Peggy La Centra as his assistant, and sportscasters Ford Bond and Graham McNamee as the rest of the cast. Since Baer ostensibly was in training, WEAF made arrangements to broadcast the show directly from his camp in New Jersey. Gillette Razor Company sponsored the show and hosted several contests, including one that gave away ringside tickets and travel expenses to the Braddock-Baer fight. Tens of thousands of entries flooded Gillette's offices. A second contest sought a name for Max Baer's dog. Hardly ideal preparation for a title bout, it reflected Baer's *laissez faire* attitude and blithe overconfidence.

Sportswriters began searching for a "hook" in an attempt to build up what many perceived as a mismatch. More than one referred to Braddock as exemplifying the Horatio Alger ideal, but it was Damon Runyon, as so often, who coined the phrase that stuck[1]. Braddock's story, he wrote, was akin to a fairytale. Perhaps recalling the play (and movie) of the same name, he called Braddock a "Cinderella Man." The name quickly took hold, though the boxer himself detested it.

On May 9, Johnston got a call that threatened to turn white his "suspiciously" black hair: Max Baer had been shot at his training camp. It soon emerged that Baer had been joking around on the set of his radio program, had picked up a gun and accidentally fired it, discharging a paper wad into his chest. A blank can still do substantial damage; indeed, the ricochet knocked his co-star to the ground. Max suffered a severe burn on his chest. Even though Baer wound up in the hospital for a short time, the sportswriters generally regarded the incident as a joke.

One photo of Baer's co-star, Peggy La Centra, was captioned, "The shot from a blank cartridge pistol that was heard around the world (press agents hope) as it burned the formidable bosom of Max Baer also seared the face of Peg La Centra, winsome blond shown above..."

---

[1] Runyon is also credited with the nicknames for Jack "Manassa Mauler" Dempsey, Mickey "Toy Bulldog" Walker and Primo "Ambling Alp" Carnera, among others.

Writing for the *Times*, John Kieran observed, "If a wad of paper could bring him down, just think what Jersey James would do to him with good quality leather." Kieran also reported that Braddock was "concerned" that Baer should be injured before their fights. Braddock supposedly suggested "the Boxing Commission should send a man to Asbury to take the pins out of Baer's fancy shirts when they come back from the laundry."

As the bout drew near, Braddock's training camp in the Catskills attracted curious members of the press. Harry Grayson found the challenger sitting on a rubbing table in a philosophical mood. "Funny racket this," mused Braddock. "Bum one day, headliner the next, and then back to the coffee pots." Yet his confidence was strong and rising. "There isn't a chance of Baer getting rid of me in the early going, when I expect it to be toughest for me," he said. "I am confident that I'll be the boss after the first few rounds."

Braddock's years of experience in the ring allowed him to make some perceptive observations about Baer's style, points overlooked by all of the "experts." "Max won't have any time to clown this trip. His antics won't fool me, and I won't stand still and watch them like Carnera. I know why Baer clowns. He's resting when he does it, and the way to stop it is to keep on top of him."

Braddock's thoughts now spilled out, revealing in stark, personal terms the level of determination he would bring to the ring. "This is the most important event of my life, and after coming this far, I'm not going to be ruled out for not trying against Baer. I'll either step from the ring champion or be carried out of the ring feet first."

Mae Braddock chilled when she read those words. Her fears deepened about the fight and its potential for disaster. She also had to deal with another problem; the rough and tumble of local city politics was about to draw her husband into the center of a controversy he could well do without. Braddock's old friend and taxicab competitor Harry Buesser had a falling out with North

Bergen Mayor Julius Reich, and Buesser took a leave of absence from his position as Municipal Relief Director for North Bergen to assist in a campaign to unseat Reich.

On April 29, at the same moment that Braddock, Gould, and Johnston were setting up the Catskill training camp, Mayor Reich was giving a campaign speech at a meeting of the Woodcliff Democratic Club. Reich attacked Buesser, claiming that he had mismanaged the relief agency. Furthermore, he claimed that Braddock had abused the system through his connections to Buesser. "Even today," Reich told the crowd, "milk was delivered to his door by the city which is supporting Braddock's children."

When Mae read the story in the newspaper the next day, she felt "humiliated and miserable." And when Braddock phoned her from camp, she couldn't bring herself to mention it. "What I hated so much," she later wrote, "was to have my friends know what we had gone through. I was so embarrassed I didn't go out of the apartment for an entire week; I was too ashamed to show my face, even though now I don't care who knows it. I cried that whole week; and, on top of that I couldn't be hopeful that Jimmy would defeat Baer."

Buesser angrily denied Reich's charges. Braddock had received relief, he conceded, but had been removed from the relief rolls in March, at the time of the Lasky fight. The North Bergen Social and Athletic Club weighed in, issuing a statement condemning Reich for engaging in "petty politics." "May we again call to mind that Jim was down," wrote John Sullivan the club's president, "but he took full advantage of his opportunities and it looks as if that relief was a sad chapter of his life. Too bad Mr. Reich found it necessary to unfold it to the public."

Reporters rushed to Braddock's camp to ask if it was true that the heavyweight challenger, pictured always as a young athlete rolling in wealth, actually had been on relief?

Braddock did not duck the question. "Sure I was," he said. "I'm not ashamed of it either. I didn't mind for myself but I couldn't let the kids starve."

Braddock's poverty was soon detailed in the press. Until the Lewis fight the previous November, "He hadn't even an overcoat to wear," said one paper. "The few times he came around the fight lanes his hair was overhanging his collar." The family's descent into their basement apartment, the struggle to pay for the children's milk, every embarrassing detail, was recorded in articles syndicated across the nation. Braddock held his head high throughout, asking only that it be reported, "As soon as I was paid off for the Lasky fight, I gave $300 to the Relief Fund of Union City. That covered the $240 I got all told when we were on relief. It was the only fair thing to do. I couldn't let the kids go hungry. I'm not ashamed."

An editorial cartoonist for the *Hudson Dispatch* weighed into the controversy. Across three columns of its Saturday paper, the *Dispatch* published a cartoon that depicted Braddock standing, hands above his head, while a small pudgy man in a three-piece suit with the word "Right" written across his chest delivered a punch squarely below Braddock's belt. Word balloons emitting from the crowd all contained the same word: "Foul!"

Buesser continued his counterattack. "The acquisitions of the mayor are false and malicious. The individual he speaks of was, it is true, on relief at one time but the charge that he is on relief now, was on relief in April, is untrue. I can state to the mayor here publicly that I can understand that in politics almost anything goes, but that it was unfair of him to bring in some of the unfortunate who were on relief."

Buesser's rival mayoral candidate, Paul Cullem, also went on the attack. "When things sink to such a low level that the sad chapter of a man's life is uncovered, showing that he had to go on relief, I say it is time to go to work on the individual responsible for bringing out such a thing." Candidate Cullem rode the anti-Reich backlash to victory in the election two weeks later.

Interest in the fight picked up as word spread about Braddock's ordeal. Thousands of letters and telegrams from around the country poured into Braddock's camp. His story touched the hearts of many Americans, and gave them hope. Jimmy Braddock had come back: why not them?

Soon tales appeared about the "new" left hand that Braddock had developed during his time on the docks. "Braddock obtained work at $5 a day on the New York Central Railroad Docks at Weehawken," wrote Harry Grayson. "The current challenger transferred ties from the lighters to gondola cars. This work is done with a longshoreman's hook, and, his right hand being in a cast, Braddock did his hooking with his left." It is probably true that repeatedly swinging a tie hook with his left hand and lifting heavy bales and other objects contributed to his overall physical condition, but his brother-in-law Bill Fox believed that it was probably more "mental than anything else."

More importantly, Braddock was working harder than he ever had to prepare himself. Even when he hurt several ribs, one of his trainers constructed a padded corset that allowed him to keep training – covered by a heavy sweatshirt – without the press learning of his injury. After one particularly vicious sparring session, Joe Gould predicted, "Jimmy will enter the ring in great shape – if he lives through the workouts." Thereafter, some reporters began datelining their stories "Homicide Hall, NY."

Gould exuded confidence in his fighter. "Jimmy does not fear Baer, and that is a point in his favor, especially when you consider that the last few men to face the champion seemed to have too much respect for him. To Jimmy it's just another fight. In my experience" – and here he turned metaphysical – "I have found that the toughest game is the game of life, and when a man can do in that game what Jim has done, what does a fight mean, or a punch on the chin?"

Braddock too was confident. "Baer is a swinger, and swingers have never given me much trouble," he told a reporter. When reminded of Baer's literally lethal punching power, Braddock remained unintimidated, and chillingly matter-of-fact.

"I'll either step from the ring as champion or be carried out feet first."

Baer had absolutely no doubt that he would win, and win easily. Three days before the championship contest, English reporter Trevor Wignall visited his training camp. He encountered the champion taking a cold shower singing, and drinking from a bottle of beer.

"I need this," Baer said, "to put back what I lost over in that lousy ring."

Baer postured for the English writer. "Look at me," he ordered, expanding his chest and stretching his muscles. "Ever seen anybody in better condition?" Wignall agreed he hadn't, but, "I caused him to frown a little when I mentioned that the shine on his body and the rippling of his biceps were no evidence that his stamina and judgment were all they could be."

Baer's arrogance was evident in interview after interview. "Boys," he told *Knockout*, "if Jimmy Braddock beats me when we clash I am through with the ring. I will never pull on another glove. I really mean it and if you think I am spoofing one will get you ten."

With training completed, Braddock commenced a tour through his own past. One day, Gould took him to visit Joe Jeanette at his Union City gymnasium, a small nod of recognition to Jeanette's early tutelage. The next day, Braddock stopped to see Judge Robert Kincaid, who had deftly deflected the serious assault charges leveled against the fighter in the wake of his early morning brawl at police headquarters. Judge Kincaid interrupted a trial to greet him. He then held a quick mock proceedings pursuant to which he "sentenced" Braddock to win the title.

The day before the fight, the head of the New York Commission directed Gould to post $5,000 to guarantee that Braddock would show up at the fight. The incensed manager refused in the strongest terms. "Are you crazy," he asked. "If you're worried about Braddock showing up, I'll leave him here in your custody. You can lock him up until Thursday night and guarantee his appearance." No guarantee was required.

Yet despite Braddock's growing popularity, the odds were overwhelming in Baer's favor – as high as ten-to-one, long odds indeed for a two-horse race. The overwhelming number of the press agreed with Associated Press sports editor Allen Gould when he wrote, "The champion will have the speed and the power to achieve his objective, an early knockout." When press agent Francis Albertanti prepared a mimeographed biography of the challenger, the odiferous blue sheets remained on his desk; none of the reporters wanted them.

Damon Runyon, who had seen a lot of fights, was one of the few who conceded the possibility that Braddock could beat the odds. "A fast clever boxer could always make Braddock look futile," Runyon wrote, "but Baer hardly rates as either fast or clever. [Braddock] is more difficult to hit than many observers think, and has a style all of his own that is somewhat deceiving."

Some reporters began playing up the notion of a "jinx" on the Long Island Bowl, where the fight would be held. Since its opening, the Bowl had become known as the "Graveyard of Champions" because no reigning champion ever successfully defended his title there. Now a series of "coincidences" seemed to point the way to a Braddock victory. "James Braddock" had thirteen letters (it was now convenient to leave out the middle initial); the fight would be held on the thirteenth of the month; Baer was the thirteenth heavyweight champion since John L. Sullivan (actually he was fourteenth, but nobody bothered to check the list). It was all a bit of fun, and helped maintain interest in a bout many considered a mismatch.

During the 1928 presidential campaign, the Republicans equated a vote for Herbert Hoover with a chicken in every pot and a car in every garage. Hoover's chicken must have been a cat with nine lives, because it reappeared in 1935 to take down the National Industrial Recovery Act, one of the cornerstones of Roosevelt's New Deal. In 1934, the Schecter Poultry Company of Brooklyn had been convicted of violating certain provisions of the Live Poultry Code of the NRA. Appeal of the conviction reached the Supreme Court in 1935. On May 27, Chief Justice Charles Evans Hughes announced the unanimous decision of the court: the NRA was unconstitutional.

But in the narrow span of its life, it afforded millions new hope – and one of those millions, James J. Braddock, was about to fight for the heavyweight championship of the world.[2]

---

[2] Braddock is often said to have received day-labor employment through the Federal Works Progress Administration (WPA). The WPA, however, wasn't created until May 6, 1935, when Braddock was already deep in training for Baer.Braddock is often said to have received day-labor employment through the Federal Works Progress Administration (WPA). The WPA, however, wasn't created until May 6, 1935, when Braddock was already deep in training for Baer.

*Jim Braddock takes the fight to champion Max Baer in their historic clash in Long Island City, New York, in June 1935.*

# CHAPTER 10

# Bringing Home a Turtle

"I think they had an idea – and a hope – that the 'title' everyone told them daddy was bringing home would be small enough so that they could tie a string to it and trundle it about. I heard them telling Rose Marie that if there was a little title, she could have it, and they'd have the big one."

—Mae Braddock

Shortly before ten p.m. on June 13, 1935, Con Ed, New York City's largest provider of electricity, saw a massive surge in demand. Within moments, Con Ed was called upon to satisfy an additional 274,000 kilowatts over its normal supply. In home after home, radios were being switched on and tuned in to the big fight.

NBC Radio carried the bout for a nationwide hookup; in New York it broadcast on both of its stations, WEAF and WJZ, the red and blue networks. The broadcast team comprised Graham McNamee and Ford Bond. McNamee, often referred to as the "father of sports broadcasting" would serve as the blow-by-blow announcer; Bond would provide analysis in the one minute between rounds.

Mae Braddock decided to try to listen to the broadcast at the home of her parents. A couple of reporters and a photographer would spend the evening with her. Mae chatted with them before the fight. "Jimmy came home for some cooking," she told one, "and stayed around awhile before going back to the Mayflower

Hotel in New York." Her nervous manner belied the confidence she had in her husband. "That Maxie clowns," she said, "but Jimmy will knock off the clowning out of him." Braddock's brothers barely gave the champion a chance.

After all three of her children were asleep, Mae slipped away to Saint Joseph's Church, intending to light a candle. When she entered, she was astonished to see the pews packed with her friends and neighbors, who had gathered to pray for the Braddocks. Mae later admitted that she prayed "my husband shouldn't be killed. It was nice to know that if he didn't win, it wouldn't be because I didn't pray."

The A train from Manhattan bulged with the flow of fans headed toward Long Island City. The fighters would have perfect weather for the bout; "The sky was a cheap postcard smudge of red, purple, and blue," observed one reporter. A little man furiously pacing around the stadium barely noticed it. For all his confidence, Joe Gould's nerves had threatened to overtake him, and to discharge some of his kinetic energy, he walked the perimeter of the stadium three times before the fight.

At the ringside, word circulated to a surprised press corps that boxing's foremost referee, Arthur Donovan, would be shelved for the bout in favor of diminutive Johnny McAvoy. As with so many other characters that touched upon Braddock's life, McAvoy had long been a colorful presence around New York. Born in Brooklyn, by age thirteen the diminutive McAvoy was one of Maspeth's top steeplechase jockeys, piloting such famous jumpers as Rodman, Maggie Richards, Ligerio, and Austerlitz. At the same time, he dabbled as a professional fighter, until a kayo loss convinced him to turn to refereeing.

The selection of McAvoy over Arthur Donovan pleased both Baer and Braddock. Braddock believed the smallish, aging McAvoy would let him clinch on the inside if necessary. Baer, happy with anyone besides Donovan, figured that McAvoy wouldn't have the strength to prevent him from the type of wrestling and roughhouse tactics that made the Carnera fight as ludicrous as it was memorable.

Shortly after ten p.m., the fighters began making their way to the ring. Baer entered first, once again wearing the robe he had worn in his film, *The Prizefighter and the Lady*, with his character's name, Steve Morgan, embroidered on the back. Braddock entered a few moments later; Jack Kofoed watched him walk past. "Braddock brushed against me as he came to the walls. His face was white as a layer of snow on a cold-pile. His eyes were narrowed, his lips were tight. Everybody thought he looked scared to death. It was not fright, it was concentration. He was so intensely set on the business lying ahead, he hadn't a thought for anything else."

After greeting Baer and the crowd, Braddock sat in his corner. Doc Robb laced on his gloves.

Al Frazen gave the introductions on the drop-down microphone, which also carried to the radio audience. Frazen's clipped cadence silenced the crowd.

"Main bout. Fifteen rounds for the heavyweight championship of the world. Introducing the world's heavyweight champion from Livermore, California, Max Baer."

Baer waved to the crowd in his typically off-hand way as Frazen continued his introductions.

"His opponent, the man who in the last year, made the greatest comeback in ring history, James J. Braddock of Jersey City ... Weights, Baer, 209½, Braddock, 191¾ ... referee, Johnny McAvoy."

After the brief pre-fight instructions, the two boxers returned to their corners, and radio announcer Graham McNamee picked up the action. "And there's the bell for the first round. The boys walk out, Braddock circles around Baer, and Braddock shoots a right to the body."

So often the first punch of a fight is like the first kiss in a love affair, and this one was no different. Braddock was committed; Baer was screwing around.

A focused Braddock surged towards the champion who, somewhat startled, backed up, watching his foe warily. Braddock flicked a left then tried a hard overhand right that missed – Baer saw that Braddock had thrown the punch with bad intentions. Baer sneered at this attempt, but before he could retaliate, Braddock closed on him, throwing a left-right-left combination to the body.

Baer fought the second in the same lazy way, not trying to do much scoring while Braddock continued to slam home hard jabs when he was within range. In the third round the slow pace caused the crowd to start booing. Cinderella Man or not, the fight crowd wanted more action. Braddock moved inside one of Baer's ponderous swings and unleashed a series of left hooks to the body, punctuated by a right to Baer's face. Baer shook off the blow and retaliated with a hard right of his own, then swung a left to the jaw and then chopped a right into Braddock's face. Braddock replied with a sharp right to Baer's head, followed by a left and a right to the body.

Through the first four rounds, Baer had not done much, fighting on the inside more than usual. His best punches were usually launched from long range, so his in-fighting strategy was a puzzle. In the fifth round the crowd again began to call for hotter action, and Baer launched his first sustained assault, punching in combination. Braddock continued to circle, avoiding most of the punches. He stepped smartly forward to slip one overhand right and Baer backhanded him across the face – a foul. The apoplectic Gould nearly climbed the ropes, but referee McAvoy motioned him back and warned Baer to "knock off the cheap shots."

Braddock continued to circle to his right, away from Baer's awesome Sunday punch. Baer followed, trying to cut off the ring, but the challenger remained elusive, and the best Baer could muster was an occasional looping punch to his ribs. Before anyone realized it, Braddock had banked six of the first seven rounds.

Baer seemed unconcerned, still believing he was going to knock out Braddock. Braddock's cornerman, Whitey Bimstein, had other ideas. "This big dope is still trying to knock you out," he told his panting fighter at the end of round seven. "You're no sucker; let him keep trying those haymakers. You can go under, around, you can play fast and loose. Just be sure he misses. You can pile up points with your jab and a once-in-a-while right hand. It ought to be a piece of cake."

Baer continued to play to the crowd in the eighth round, pawing at long range, but Braddock pumped in two hard jabs to make him blink. As Baer wound up to throw a left hook, Braddock stepped inside with a hard right to the face, a thudding blow. Baer stumbled back, apparently groggy, his legs wobbly – and the crowd rose in unison.

Then it became clear – it was just one of Baer's "Leon Errol" routines. The punch hadn't hurt him badly, and he was mugging for the crowd. Braddock, unimpressed, settled back and continued to box. At times he appeared to be tiptoeing the champion, but he was sticking to the strategy.

Baer altered his fight plan. Unable to land his overhand right – he even shouted to reporters that his hands had "gone bad" – he began to throw more left hooks. He knew his body punching would eventually weaken the veteran, and mixed his left hooks to the ribcage with lefts to the head, trying to drive Braddock into the path of his right. In the clinches, Baer never threw fewer than three slashing uppercuts, snapping Braddock's head upwards. Clearly, he was counting on wearing down the older man.

It seemed to be working. Braddock looked tired at the start of the twelfth – then caught his second wind. A rush of adrenalin gave him renewed energy, and suddenly he upped the tempo. He was going to make his stand and take back control of the fight.

Baer pressed but Braddock stopped him dead with solid jabs and crosses. Again they went in close now, both swinging fiercely to the body, each attempting to deflate the other. The fight had reached its most crucial point. Baer worked over Braddock's torso, his blows thudding into ribs and organs, while Braddock pounded away at his large, shaggy head.

The bell rang. As Braddock relaxed, Baer slammed another half a dozen punches at his body, at the same time the referee was separating them. Gould vaulted over the ropes and was in the mix, and the referee gave the round to Braddock on a foul.

As the thirteenth round opened, Mae, gripping the arms of her chair in front of the radio, blurted, "Let's hope it's lucky," then sat back, silently listening with her hands clenched in her lap.

Braddock connected with a series of uppercuts to Baer's jaw, but took more punishment to the body. As round fourteen opened, it was clear that Baer would be trying for a knockout. Braddock beat a tattoo on Baer's face with his left, looking for an opening as the champion became increasingly desperate. Suddenly he saw a gap and let loose a long right haymaker, but missed.

McNamee picked up the fight as it entered the final round. "They come out for the fifteenth round. This is the finish." The fighters shook hands, then Braddock took the initiative, slamming a left to Baer's nose the way he might smack a naughty dog. He moved close to Baer, safe from his long swings, and the pair went punch for punch on the inside for the rest of the round.

McNamee's voice was shrill as he counted off the seconds to the final bell. "And Braddock comes in with a left to Max's jaw. Max pounds right as they're in close, Max pounds his right six times, seven times into the side of Braddock's body. Max is following Braddock now. Max puts over a hard left to the side of the jaw and Braddock is forced to go away."

Baer lashed seven consecutive rights to Braddock's side and finally slung over a hard left hook to his head, but the challenger took them all and came back, leaning in and hitting to the body. Baer was now desperate for the knockout, and cracked over a right to the jaw that clearly hurt his opponent. He quickly followed up with a left uppercut but the bell rang, ending the fight. It was too little, too late.

Baer congratulated Braddock immediately; he knew he had lost. "Well, you're the new champion, Jim. I hope you make a lot of dough out of it."

Braddock, too stunned to answer, grunted noncommittally and walked to his corner.

"The decision will be with us in just a moment…and here it is. Listen! … 'The winner and *new* heavyweight champion…'"

McNamee forced his way through the tumult to speak to Braddock, the champion. Moments later, in New Jersey, Mae heard her husband's voice crackle through the radio: "It was a great fight and Max is a great fella. And I'm glad to be champeen of the world."

Eventually the bedlam of the ringside gave way to the comparative calm of the dressing room, where radio commentator McNamee continued his interview with the remarkable new champ.

"I am glad to say a few words as the new heavyweight champeen on the world. It was a great fight," said Braddock.

"What were you thinking about during the scrap, did you have any special thing in mind or were you just fighting?"

"I was thinking of the wife and kiddies and I was out there to win for them, to bring the title home. We told the kids I was gonna bring them home the title and they always kept asking me for it, so I had to live up to it and bring it home. They sure will be tickled!"

"What are you going to do tomorrow?" asked McNamee.

"I'm gonna go see the kids first of all." Braddock thought for a moment, and then added, "And then go in and collect the dough."

Mae laughed as she heard this. She finally began to relax. Then Max Baer came on the radio.

The fallen champion remained sanguine in his dressing room. "If you ever see me pull on another glove, I'll buy you a steam yacht," Baer told the *New York Times* reporter. Then he lit a cigarette, which earned him a $5,000 endorsement fee from Chesterfield, and asked for a bottle of beer.

"I have no alibis to offer," he continued between sips. "Jimmy won and no better fellow deserves a break. He didn't hurt me in the fight, but my trouble was that I couldn't hurt him."

Baer held up his bruised and swollen right hand. "That hand, none too good to start with, went completely in the fifth round and the left, you may not believe it, went in the third."

Baer then said a few words to Tommy Manning over NBC's hook-up: "Hello mother and dad. I want to tell you all and the folks too, I had a grand time out there. Of course I lost the title, but they come and go, you know. But I'm glad and really happy to see Jimmy happy...he'll appreciate it more than I did, I guess, and he needs it more. After all, he's got a family and he's married. Of course, I might have a family around the country too, but I don't know it!"

Madison Square Garden press agent Tex Sullivan later recalled this risqué comment. "Remember, this was 1935 and that kind of talk on radio stirred a lot of feedback. People wrote in to the station complaining about his loose talk and some even said that they were glad he had lost because he was an immoral man."

Baer's loss, coupled with his saucy outburst, indeed had one indirect effect: NBC promptly cancelled his detective show, *Lucky Smith*. Tens of thousands of listeners were deprived of learning the winning entry in the contest to name Baer's dog: "Livermore, the Gay Blade."

At the Fox home in New Jersey, the telephone rang. It was Jim. "What did you think of the fight, Mae?" he asked, still breathing hard.

"I do not know what to think. I am crazy, darling ... I am crazy. I cannot think!"

"Then get dressed. Come to the hotel."

Jim himself did not have time to fully dress before his delirious handlers pulled him out of the dressing room and whisked him to his Manhattan hotel suite. Within the hour, Mae was at her husband's side, as well-wishers crowded the suite.

Joe Gould was in overdrive. The entire room throbbed with his peripatetic energy as he regaled the crowd with an incessant monologue about Braddock's past, present, and future.

By three a.m. Braddock, resting on the bed, could barely keep his eyes open. "Is it alright if I go to sleep?" he asked no one in particular. Mae, at his side, promised to take him away for a rest, but he couldn't sleep. Telegrams, hundreds of them, were being brought into the room and he read them lying on the bed.

One was from Maxie Rosenbloom: "Congratulations, Jimmy. Now that you are champion maybe I can get a crack at the heavyweight title which I could not do when the great lover was the champion. Although I beat you once and can do it again, I hope you will show the world you are a real fighting champion and fight me this summer. Regards and good luck – until we meet in the ring. Maxie Rosenbloom."

Braddock plucked another from the pile and read it silently. It was from Ernie Schaaf's mother, congratulating him.

"Hey Joe," the champion called to Gould. "Do you think we can go up and see Ernie's mom?"


The next day, Braddock and Gould made a triumphant appearance at Jack Dempsey's restaurant. The old champion met them at the door with hand extended. "Well, Jim," Dempsey saluted, "you did it. More power to you." Braddock just smiled and asked, "How about some sandwiches or something?" Dempsey quickly had a table for twenty set up for Braddock and his soon expanding entourage. While Braddock devoured a platter of sandwiches and a pitcher of beer, Gould regaled all within earshot with plans, offers, and visions of sugarplums. Braddock then stopped at a pet store on his way home and purchased three small turtles.

On June 19, Gould slipped off to New Jersey to pay a bill. A day later, the head of the New Jersey Emergency Relief Administration issued a statement: "Yesterday Mr. Gould called at my office and handed me $367.24 in cash ... I have notified the North Hudson relief authorities to credit Mr. Braddock's account, indicating that he paid back all relief given in his case."

# PART THREE

# An Epigram of Gaius Lucilius

Onesimus the boxer sought the prophet Olympus wishing to learn if he would be living to an old age. Olympus answered: "Yes, if you give up the ring now. But if you continue to box, Saturn is your horoscope."

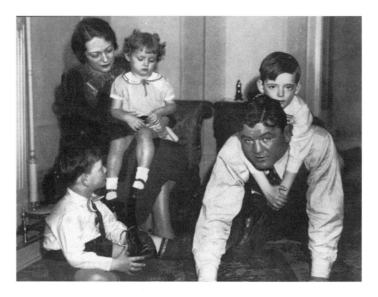

*Braddock clowning around with his wife Mae and children Jay, Howard and Rose Marie. Mae feared the worst every time he fought, but it was his desire to provide for his family that drove the fighter on.*

CHAPTER 11

# The Champion in Repose

"There is only one direction in which the heavyweight champion can move – that's down."

—James J. Braddock, December 1935

A champion's life is fodder for the unquenchable maw of the popular media. Immediately following Braddock's win over Baer, "biographies" of the Cinderella Man appeared in several newspapers and magazines, most regurgitating the official biography that Francis Albertanti had compiled and circulated during the training camp at Loch Sheldrake. The new champion's good friend, cartoonist and sportswriter Ludwig "Lud" Shabazian, churned out a somewhat white-washed book on Braddock's escape from the breadlines, *Relief to Royalty*, a title that Braddock himself approved since he hated the appellation "Cinderella Man" that Damon Runyon had bestowed upon him.

Suddenly all of the members of Braddock's family were fair game for the press. "The Braddocks are a versatile family," reported one feature. "Jimmy's dad is a night watchman on a Hoboken dock. One brother is an assistant yardmaster, another is a milkman, another a ferry boat worker and a fourth a bookkeeper in a brewery. It took Jimmy three months to get up enough courage to speak to the girl who is now Mrs. Braddock."

In a series of interviews and by-lined articles, Mae told the nation every intimate detail of their struggle: "We had been on home relief up to a few months ago. Things got so bad that we actually had to send two of our children away, one to the home of Jim's parents and one to my own mother's home. Our bread basket was empty; there was no work, and we simply couldn't afford to feed them the right kind of food on the $24 monthly we received from home relief."

Her dreams were laid out for national examination. "She dreamed a small house with white ruffled curtains, a copper moon over some slim, black trees, and other suggestions which lyric writers make in song," cooed one female reporter.

Her Cinderella Man was now in demand for boxing exhibitions, vaudeville appearances, radio shows and motion pictures. He even got an agent to handle his appearances, signing with the William Morris Agency. The same day he signed, Joe Gould appeared at the Jersey ERA office and gave $367.24 to cancel the note that Jim had given just after the Lasky fight. Jim Braddock became just one of a handful of people who repaid the money that had been given to them through home relief.

When Gypsy Rose Lee tried to recruit him to appear in one of her movies, Mae nixed the deal. "Uncle Jimmy was a good-looking guy and Aunt Mae could get real jealous," Braddock's niece, Ruth Boughton, later told the *Albany Times-Union*.

Braddock's work in print advertising was erratic to say the least. One of the few ads he was featured in was for something called Kelpamalt Tablets. These were credited with allowing Braddock to gain extra weight in training: "This new mineral concentrate from the sea gets right down and corrects the real underlying cause of skinniness – iodine starved glands."

But Braddock was not able to capitalize on his renown immediately. Nor could he go on tour. Mae, overwhelmed by the stress, needed to be cared for first. In a later interview with Hy Hurwitz, she told what had happened, without shame or adornment:

"When I first knew it," declared Mrs. Braddock, "I was dazed. Reporters kept asking me how it felt to be the wife of the heavyweight champion, and I don't even remember what I answered. Not until lately when the first excitement departed have I actually known what it was all about.

"The rush of photographers and interviewers for a full week left me in a highly nervous condition. At night in bed I used to see the glare of flashlights. If I only had myself to consider it wouldn't have been bad, but the cameramen wanted my three youngsters in so many poses they almost drove me nuts."

Mrs. Braddock collapsed from this ordeal. She had to spend three weeks in the mountains to recuperate. Jimmy had a chance to go on a vaudeville tour immediately after annexing the title, but when Mrs. Braddock became sick he canceled the engagement in favor of staying with the frau.

By August, Mae was well enough for Braddock to resume his exhibition schedule. On his first trip after her illness, he took her with him to Boston, where he was invited to serve as guest referee at the world wrestling title match between Dan O'Mahony, a young Irishman, and champion Ed John George. "Danno," from County Cork, had been a private in the Irish Free State Army before turning to the ring. His record going into the George match was a reported sixty-two consecutive victories. George's title claim was rather thin, as he was recognized only in certain parts of New England and the Canadian province of Quebec, but the Irish in the Boston area wanted to see Danno challenge for a title and they would see him do just that.

Braddock, Mae, and Gould passed a pleasant week in Boston prior to the match. Paul Dowser, the match promoter, made sure Braddock's Irish ancestry was highlighted for the press as O'Mahony was vying to become the first native-born Irishman to win the title. Dowser's efforts paid off when the match attracted over 40,000 to Braves Field, a record attendance.

The match itself followed the classic wrestling script, with the guest referee playing a crucial role. After ninety minutes of chest thumping and assorted maneuvers, George tossed Danno over the top rope and into the ringside seats. Under the controlling "championship rules," Danno had twenty seconds to return to the ring. He scrambled back at the count of eight. George once more tossed him into the seats. As Braddock tolled off the count, Danno made his way back to the ring, getting one foot inside the bottom rope at the count of nineteen.

George, playing his part correctly, acted as if he believed that Danno had been counted out. Danno sprang upon his surprised foe and tossed him over the ropes. Braddock this time counted to twenty, giving the Irishman the championship. Of course no good wrestling bout could end without a brawl. George's trainer, Frank Dellano, immediately attacked Braddock and "floored" him with a right to the jaw, to the delight of the spectators. A general brawl ensued, Braddock decking several tough guys in the fray. When several soda bottles were tossed into the ring, the cops finally were called in to restore order.

A few weeks later a midtown theater in New York saw good box office receipts showing full-length pictures of the wrestling bout. The referee was advertised as "doing more punching than he did against Baer."

In mid-August, Braddock made a triumphant return to Jersey City, boxing in an outdoor stadium against three different opponents: Jules Veigh, George Nicholson, and Tom Patrick. Clearly, Braddock held no grudges; Patrick had caused his only stoppage loss when he butted him in 1932. Not only was the stadium filled, but also the surrounding rooftops were packed with people who could see into the arena and watch the exhibitions.

That Fall, Braddock traveled to the Pacific Northwest with sparring partner Jack McCarthy. The Seattle fans were the first to get a glimpse of Braddock, and saw that the championship had swelled more than his bank balance; his boat line was expanding as well.

Braddock's troupe moved on to Oregon for exhibitions in Portland and Marshfield. On arriving in Marshfield, Joe Gould found all of the hotel rooms in town booked due to an upcoming college football game. The trio checked into a room with a single bed. Gould, who was not feeling well, stayed in the hotel room as Braddock and McCarthy went to the exhibition. The next morning, Gould awoke to find Braddock sleeping on the bare floor next to him. "Can you imagine that?" Gould told a Braddock biographer. "The champion of the world sleeping on a bare floor, and me in the only bed! Can you imagine Tunney, Dempsey, Baer, or anyone else doing that?"

"Oh Joe, you have done it for me," chimed in Braddock, who had been listening to Gould's story.

Braddock's popularity was at an all-time high. When he agreed to give a speech and referee a few boxing matches at the Boys' Athletic League in Hell's Kitchen, only a block from where he had been born, advance word ran through the old neighborhood, and over 1,000 boys and girls lined up along Tenth Avenue, hoping for the chance to meet the world's champion – their champion.

When Braddock was spotted entering the facility, the crowd rolled past police into the auditorium, rushing the champion and beseeching him for autographs. The yelling turned to pushing and for a moment the crowd threatened to turn into a mob as Braddock's coat was ripped and his hat snatched by one admiring fan. Finally, with the assistance of the League's director, Braddock escaped into a private office. On the streets of Hell's Kitchen, at least, Braddock was the "local boy who done good." While plotting his escape from the building, Braddock told a reporter he had decided to defend against Joe Louis, not Max Schmeling, in June.

The constant stream of interviews, appearances, newsreels and plain gossip had laid bare the Jim Braddock story – at least as honed by his press agent, Francis Albertanti. It took a Huck Finn quality of ruddy cheeks, boisterous rough-and-tumbles and high-spirited childhood pranks.

Braddock had attended St. Joseph's Parochial school, and his schoolyard fights were examined with great interest. Of course, at that time at least, just about any Catholic School playground had as many good fights a season as the Garden did. In one of his, Braddock was said to have landed a haymaker on a boy named Elmer Furlong. In virtually every expiation of Braddock's childhood, poor Elmer was knocked out again and again.

Braddock's "hobo" days – with his "best pal Marty McGann" – also became a staple of the story. Apparently, Braddock had hopped a few rails in his youth, "once getting as far as Chicago" or "Washingtonville, NY," depending on the teller. A fight with Braddock's brother, Joe, over a sweater supposedly sparked his interest in boxing. And, finally, at one of brother Joe's bouts, Braddock was convinced by Harry Buesser to box under the assumed name of Jimmy Ryan.

Braddock's career was depicted as one where he frequently overcomes incredible odds, and the actual betting odds for each fight were often given. This core story, stripped down to its basics, was presented over and over again to the public in the popular media.

One of the most popular comic strips of Depression-era America centered around the trials and tribulations of the good hearted, hard punching heavyweight boxer Joe Palooka, created by cartoonist Ham Fisher in 1932. Palooka's adventures began appearing on radio in 1934, the same year the character made its debut in pictures. Jimmy Durante played Palooka's manager, Nobby Wash, Joe Gould's *doppelganger* in all respects except the schnozzle and the bar mitzvah.

One of the most famous single pages in comic strip history is a *Joe Palooka* strip published on December 22, 1935, just months after Braddock won the title, and obviously influenced by the desperate conditions of the Braddock family.

In the first panel, a tough-looking mug in a peak cap stealthily climbs through an open window on Christmas Eve. He is surprised as a young, tow-haired boy sits up in bed and asks innocently, "Are youse Santee Claus?" The man attempts to silence the boy, telling him, "Yes, I'm Santee Claus. Shhh, keep quiet kid...." The man then tries to leave, but the boy entreats him to stay.

"Oh please, Santee Claus, won't you talk to me for a minute. I think youse are the nicest man in the world. I love you."

On hearing those words, the man confesses – he is not "Santee Claus," but had intended to burglarize the boy's home. "I guess I'm pretty low, going out on this night to steal, sonny, but I was desperate."

Moved by the man's sad story, the boy insists that he take an armful of presents for his own children. As the man leaves, young Palooka tells him, "I'm gonna say my prayers over again and ask God for a job for you."

The last panel reveals Palooka's mother telling the tale at Christmas dinner. The boy of the story was a young Joe Palooka.

The notion that the heavyweight champion of the world could turn a man from a life of crime was not limited to the Sunday funny pages. Just a few months after the Palooka morality tale appeared, Braddock received a letter from Johnny McGrath, an inmate at the Iowa State Penitentiary. McGrath had completed two years of a ten-year prison sentence. His crime was worthy of Victor Hugo: he had broken into a café and stolen a bottle of beer. McGrath had grown up in northern New Jersey and knew the champion slightly. When the other inmates laughed at him when he claimed to know the champion, McGrath wrote asking for an autographed photograph. Braddock sent the picture, and followed that up with a personal appeal for clemency to Iowa's governor, Clyde Harry. Braddock also wrote to the State Parole Board, promising to employ McGrath in his "publicity department" at no less than $35 a week and to supervise his "social activities." Mainly on strength of Braddock's efforts, the Parole Board released McGrath. "There's one guy who won't go back on a pal," McGrath told the press. "I'm still off liquor now and I got my religion back."

In September 1936, Braddock's story began appearing before its widest audience yet – the millions who read the funny pages. From the last Sunday in September, 1936 through May 1937, Braddock's life played out each week in a cartoon "topper" to *Joe Palooka*. Ham Fisher, who peppered the strip with his own personal knowledge of Braddock, codified each "fact" of Braddock's early life in comic strip form. For example, the last panel of the first installment depicted the newborn Braddock snuggled next to his adoring mother. Braddock's father, workman's cap in hand, points to his young son and exclaims, apparently in a British accent, "He's a bloke of a lad, let's name him James J. after the great Jeffries."

Fisher whitewashed Braddock's hard-bitten youth. "Knowing Jim well," he wrote, "it's hard to believe the quiet gentlemanly Braddock of today was always ready for a street fight. Let me assure you, there is not a vicious bone in him."[1]

Each Sunday for several months, Braddock's hard life became a four-color strip cartoon. Once more, poor Elmer Furlong was knocked out on the playground of St. Joseph's school; Braddock descended into Freddie Huber's cellar to begin learning the rudiments of boxing from Barney Doyle; Joe Gould appeared with Harry Galfund in tow, to take over as Braddock's manager; while Braddock's string of wins over Latzo, Griffith, and Slattery and his loss against Loughran were all detailed. (Gould: "Keep away from that @#!!*#@ left of his!")

His timid courtship of Mae was dramatized – "Like Joe Palooka the shy Braddock (afraid of no man living) had taken three years to work up enough nerve to ask Mae Fox to go to a movie with him" – and even his days as bartender in a "social club" were depicted.

During the 1930s, millions read the Sunday funnies, but tens of millions more listened daily to the radio, the medium of the masses. Radio was interactive, in a sense, since a person's imagination was required to truly enjoy a radio drama. On December 1,

---

[1] On first meeting Fisher, Braddock asked Gould, "Is he Irish, too?" "Nah, he's Jewish," Gould responded.

1936, a dramatized version of Braddock's life story began being broadcast over the WJZ network. Pulp writer Jack Kofoed collaborated with columnist and actress Stella Unger on the script and Braddock played himself on the program, which ran for fifteen minutes, three times a week. Unfortunately, no recordings of this show have surfaced. From its title, though – *My Fight For Life* – it is fairly certain that the well-worn story was rehashed once again.

After so many years of struggle, Braddock's view of the title was understandably pragmatic: "Once you get the title you may as well think straight. There is nothing else to win. The only thing a guy can do is cash in as much as he can while he's hot. Everybody is going to be licked some day."

Gould's outlook was the same: "[W]e're in the saddle now and we can say whom we'll fight. We want the guy who will draw the biggest gate." That person, he was sure, was Joe Louis.

Braddock's timetable, however, was derailed when in June 1936, Max Schmeling knocked out Joe Louis in an upset that rivaled Braddock's win over Baer. Louis had been touted as an unbeatable "superman," but Schmeling had spotted that the tyro dropped his left slightly after throwing a jab, and punished him consistently with right hand counter-punches, eventually chopping down his young foe. Schmeling became the number one contender, and half-hearted negotiations with him began. With no viable option, Braddock signed to fight him in September 1936.

Louis rebounded in August by stopping the comeback of former champion Jack Sharkey in just three rounds. The thousands that crowded Yankee Stadium, coupled with his win, demonstrated that Joe's drawing power had quickly recovered. His physical prowess, coupled with renewed dedication to training, was also superb. Over fifty years after, Sharkey could still remember the relentless pressure his opponent applied. "He was unstoppable," said Sharkey.

Joe Gould obviously counted the tickets sold at Yankee Stadium that night and calculated what a Louis bout with Braddock would be worth. The next day, he cancelled the Schmeling bout, alleging that Braddock's left hand was badly bruised; Braddock was suffering also from arthritis, blood poisoning, and a "sub-acute rheumatic condition in his elbows." For good measure one sports writer added rickets, mumps, and measles, and other assorted ailments.

Schmeling compounded his problems by proposing an exhibition tour through the southern states; he wanted to spend the winter in warm-weather states. The Anti-Nazi League, however, portrayed the proposed tour as an effort to capitalize on racism and his support among southerners because of his victory over Louis. Films of him knocking out the young black man had met with cheers in the south, and the League asserted that his personal appearance there "would serve to further widen the breach between the races and make pro-Nazi propaganda."

*Ring* magazine weighed in on the proposed boycott:

A few weeks ago ... the non-sectarian anti-Nazi stepped into the picture with the news that a national boycott campaign was being started against Schmeling and the promoters and all those interested that they would do anything within their power to prevent this match from taking place. Such a move would prove financially disastrous to those who contemplate the promotion. Whether it would materialize or not, we are not in a position to say. The fact is the boycott is underway and is seriously hampering the promotion. Ordinarily, the Braddock-Schmeling bout figures to draw between $400,000.00 and the $500,000.00 mark. With the expected bombshell over their heads, it is doubtful if the coming match would reach half that amount, and that is why the promoters are very much worried.

As the champion's idle period stretched into 1937, some journalists began reporting Braddock once again was in dire financial straits, earning by some estimates less as champion than any since John L.

Sullivan. Previous champions had reaped fortunes through exhibitions, vaudeville, theater, advertising, and other ventures, but not Braddock, and certain reporters wrote that he owed Mike Jacobs as much as $50,000 to repay money advanced by the promoter.

By some calculations, a Louis fight would net Braddock no more than $60,000. Braddock very rarely did more than allude to his finances in the press, but these repeated stories compelled him to speak. He explained that he was not indebted for the astronomical sums attributed to him. The Louis fight, he assured all, would provide him with what his entire life had been about – security for his wife and children. What the press didn't know was that Joe Gould was negotiating a secret deal to provide just that. But first, he needed to break with the Garden.

"Uncle" Mike Jacobs, who rose from scalping tickets to become the most powerful promoter in the game through his 20<sup>th</sup> Century Sporting Club and his control of heavyweight star Joe Louis.

# CHAPTER 12

# A Shadow Across the Throne

When fortitude swells, loyalty, bounty, friendship, and fidelity may be found.

—Sir Thomas Browne, *Christian Morals*

Joe Gould decided he needed Braddock to face Joe Louis in order to get the biggest payday for his fighter. He began exploring ways to dodge out of the Garden contract they had signed, exploring all angles, testing all weaknesses. Braddock had signed several extensions, and Gould's brother Samuel, a lawyer, began to review them for an out. On February 1, his intention to break with the Garden became irrevocable when he announced that Braddock would box two exhibitions for Mike Jacobs at New York's Hippodrome. The exhibitions never came off, but the Garden was on notice.

"We're holding our fort," said Jimmy Johnston, for the Garden. "We know our legal rights, and will stop any Louis-Braddock fight until Schmeling has had his chance June 3."

"We're going to fight Louis in Chicago, positively, contract or no contract," shouted Gould. He then contemplated a "no decision" bout between Louis and Braddock. Max "Boo Boo" Hoff, a notorious East Coast gangster, said he would promote the bout at Atlantic City. "Our contract with the Garden – the one we have now – doesn't [prohibit] a Louis fight at Atlantic City," said Gould. "I've had five lawyers look it over and that's what they tell me." But the proposed bout never got past the planning stage.

One last effort was made to explore the possibility of a Schmeling fight. Whether Braddock or Joe Gould even knew of the efforts are unknown, but in January 1937, political boss Frank Hague, Jersey City's "king of hanky panky," sought to obtain an agreement to a Braddock-Schmeling fight in Berlin. Hague had one of his men meet and negotiate with representatives of the German government for the fight. His efforts were not undertaken solely to benefit Braddock. Instead, Hague wanted to leverage his involvement in the fight to gain a foothold in the optical supplies market. Hague's man in Germany proposed that a Dutch company be used to handle the financial transactions for the bout. Hague and his cronies would use any money "left over" in the Dutch firm's coffers to market the lucrative optical supplies to consumers in the United States.

Hague's man played hardball with the Germans, threatening to scuttle any arrangement between Braddock and Schmeling if they did not accept terms. The American Consul General in Berlin became aware of the scheme, and recorded that Adolf Hitler supported the deal. Hague's scheme to control a profitable market failed, however, when Braddock signed to meet Joe Louis.


At exactly 12:07 on Friday, February 19, 1937, speculation about Jim Braddock's first title challenger was put to an end. Before a throng of 200 reporters crammed into the Roosevelt Room at Chicago's LaSalle Hotel, Braddock put pen to paper to fight Joe Louis the following June 22. Braddock's end of the purse was said to be "the greater of $500,000 or fifty percent of the gross." Louis had to be content with taking seventeen-and-a-half percent of the same pot.

Joe Foley, the blind promoter with the lavender-tinted spectacles who had aided Braddock with a $5 bill when he had appeared before the Commission in 1932, would promote the fight. Mike Jacobs partnered him, as a way of satisfying certain Chicago "interests" while at the same time leaving a buffer between him and the

New York Commission. Jacobs knew he would need to deal with New York and did not want to alienate them permanently.

Joe Gould was recognized as the prime mover behind the scuttling of Schmeling as an opponent. It was said that Gould had the "same philosophy as that of the penniless father who throws a brick through a bakery window to get bread for his children. He does not care what anyone says about him, so long as Braddock is in the money again."

What was certainly not disclosed, at least not at the time, was a side deal Gould had extracted from Jacobs. In addition to a percentage of the fight gate, Braddock and Gould would be entitled to ten percent of the profits earned by Uncle Mike in all his future world heavyweight title promotions for the next ten years. Jacobs, Gould and Braddock kept this agreement secret, since it exuded a little more than a whiff of impropriety.

When gossip in the press began leaking bits and pieces of the deal, Mike Jacobs tried to put it to rest, telling *Daily News* sports editor Jimmy Powers that "there is absolutely no truth to the rumor that Joe Gould, Owney Madden or Big Frenchie [DeMange, Madden's partner] were given a piece of Louis in return for a chance at Braddock." Technically, this was true. Braddock and Gould would be getting a piece of Jacobs, not Louis.

Before returning to New York the following day, Braddock revealed his schedule: "Now that the business with Louis is on the line I will go from New York to Wisconsin for six weeks and do all the rough work preliminary to a fight, such as sawing wood, chopping trees, and with a little boxing thrown in. Then I will hit Chicago in about ten weeks to begin earnest work." Schmeling and the Germans were livid. Max even sought anointment as world heavyweight champion by Europe's International Boxing Union and the British Board of Boxing Control, an effort that met near universal ridicule.

Despite Schmeling's anger, most of the press in the United States at least viewed Braddock's selection of Louis for his first defense to be a wise move. Hype Igoe expressed the majority view in *Ring* magazine: "In my opinion, Braddock's run-out, if it is considered to be so, plucked the heavyweight situation out of the doldrums. A meeting between Braddock and Schmeling in New York would have been a beautiful floperoo. Had Braddock been forced to go through with this battle, perhaps his last and only chance to earn that annuity to which he is entitled, he wouldn't have got himself out of hock much less set himself up in ease and comfort for all time."

That was not a view shared by the officers at Madison Square Garden. When word of Braddock's agreement to fight Louis reached the president, Colonel John Reed Kilpatrick, he quickly issued a call to arms: "It's now up to our attorneys. This is warfare, you know, and it's not customary to disclose gun positions in advance of executing an attack."

Jimmy Johnston was less reticent about revealing his thoughts. "Reports indicate your willingness to participate in holding the Braddock-Louis boxing bout in Chicago this spring must have been made aware by newspapers of our existing contract with Braddock calling for Braddock-Schmeling bout," he wired Illinois Commission chairman Joe Triner.

"Such contracts prohibit Braddock from entering into a boxing match with Joe Louis and from defending his world heavyweight championship title except under our auspices. Any action which may design or aid to permit Braddock to enter into a boxing contest with Louis or to defend his title unless under our auspices will constitute interference by you with our contract with him. We shall hold you responsible for any damages occurring by reason of such interference and shall take such action against you being advisable to protect our interests.

"Boxing has already suffered far too much from action of this kind and we are surprised that you individually as a boxing commissioner of the important State of Illinois should be involved in an attempt to break contract rather than insist that it would be lived up to."

Triner, delighting in his chance to put the screws to Johnston, lit up the wires with his response, copied, of course, to the local press: "Our commission has approached Braddock-Louis bout for Chicago June 22 STOP I have legal advice to effect that this bout and its date does not interfere with your contract calling for Braddock-Schmeling bout to be held in New York June 3 STOP Neither as an individual nor as commissioner have I at any time had any thought of interfering with your contract."

But a small majority in the Illinois legislature threatened to force the fight out of Chicago. The legislators passed a bill limiting the top ticket price to $10. "If this bill becomes law," said Joe Foley, "it will drive the fight out of Chicago … we couldn't stage the fight at ten dollars tops."

On hearing of the bill's passage, Gould quickly began exploring the possibility of reactivating the Schmeling negotiations. Schmeling had thrown up his hands at a potential deal and boarded a trans-Atlantic liner for Germany. Gould contacted him by ship-to-shore phone but the fighter declined to enter into new negotiations, claiming that he needed to confer with his promoters in Germany. Undeterred, Gould sent out a floater in the press, indicating he would reconsider the Louis fight if Schmeling's backers upped their offer to a $400,000 purse for Braddock.

The bill on ticket prices failed to become law, but the swirling rumors about whether the fight would go ahead slowed ticket sales once more. Nor were the Garden officials prone to slumbering on their rights. Before Braddock set up his training camp, he took a three-week vacation to Florida with Mae. Meanwhile, the Garden's attorneys prepared legal papers that would seek to restrain Braddock from fighting Louis – or anyone else – without the Garden's participation.

Since Braddock was in Florida, the Garden's attorneys filed suit in circuit court in Miami, then sent a deputy sheriff to serve Braddock with the papers. Twice the sheriff attempted to find him, but both times the champion eluded service, and Joe Gould refused to disclose his whereabouts; perhaps for the first time in his life, Gould kept his mouth shut.

It soon became clear that Braddock was in fact no longer in Florida, and the attorneys returned to New York. They filed their second attempt at suing Braddock in New Jersey Federal District Court, headquartered in Newark, but Braddock remained elusive. One sheriff thought he had nailed the champion, only to find he had served a Braddock look-alike who called himself Gunboat Williams, but who was probably Braddock's sparring partner and *doppelganger* Jack McCarthy.

The press had a field day reporting the Keystone Cop-like antics of the Garden's process servers when, on March 29, Braddock showed up at the Newark courthouse and accepted the papers. After receiving the papers, he explained for reporters how he had evaded service.

"I was at the racetrack in Miami last Monday when I heard they were looking for me," the champion said. "I called home and my wife told me they were outside the door, so I had her pack my bags and give them to a friend who met me on the other side of town and drove me to Savannah, Georgia. I got on the train and came right here to Newark. All the time the Garden people thought I was in Chicago, I was right at home."

Braddock would have to "show cause" in court why he should be permitted to fight Louis instead of Schmeling. Gould and Braddock were confident of a legal victory. Gould's brother, Samuel, was a prominent attorney. He had reviewed the contract with the Garden and found it contained several fatal flaws. A few days later, Braddock boarded the 20th Century Limited at New York for Chicago to open his training camp.

In May, Braddock's team won the first round in the legal battle when Federal Judge Guy Fake ruled that Braddock was free to fight Louis. The Garden swiftly appealed. Unless they prevailed, there would be no way that Johnston and the Garden could stop the Louis-Braddock fight. Schmeling himself returned to New York in late May, intent on helping to prevent it. He considered the title chance to be rightfully his.

On June 1, 1937, the New York State Athletic Commission met to decide on the penalties it would impose on Braddock if he failed to show up for the Schmeling fight. The Commission set fines for Braddock and Gould at $1,000 each, and its chairman announced that it would suspend any boxer meeting Braddock before the champion went through with his contract to defend the title against Schmeling – which meant that Louis would be suspended in New York.

Once more, Schmeling's frustration led to anger. "Who cares about being suspended in New York?" he moaned. "Is that a punishment for a world champion who chickens out? The whole decision is a joke. The championship, it is a joke. And your commission is a bigger joke."

The New York Commission wired its decision to Chicago, which responded: "We will not recognize the suspension of champion Jim Braddock and the action of the New York Commission will not interfere with the fight between Braddock and Joe Louis at Comiskey Park, June 22, as our Commission is concerned."

On June 3, Schmeling went through the ludicrous charade of weighing in for what would be called the "phantom fight." This would be the German's most one-sided contest; Braddock, of course, would not be participating. That evening, several intrepid reporters hopped the A train at Grand Central and made the fifteen-minute trip out to the Bowl's stop in Long Island City. They encountered nothing more than the forlorn sounds of a hurdy-gurdy from a children's circus on the grounds. The episode was closed. Schmeling would have to await the outcome of the bout in Chicago.

In his autobiography, Schmeling would write, "Let me make it clear that Joe Louis had nothing to do with it. He and I were both pawns in a game between other more powerful players." Left unsaid by the bitter German was the identity of those players, a couple of New York Jews who controlled the fight game at that time: Joe Gould and Mike Jacobs.

On June 10, 1937, with the fight less than two weeks away, the United States Court of Appeals for the Third Circuit refused to overturn Judge Fake's denial of the Garden's petition to enjoin the fight in Chicago. The last legal obstacle to a Braddock-Louis championship bout had been removed.

Notified by telephone within moments of the Third Circuit's 2-1 ruling in his favor, Braddock whooped for joy. "Now I have only one more to win and I will do that on June 22," he said. "Now my worries are over. I can settle into the battles of my training camp grind with no further mental handicaps. The fight with Louis isn't worrying me a bit. I am confident I shall finish him before the end of the eighth round."

Throughout his training camp reporters asked Braddock to describe what he expected to do to repel Louis. Braddock expressed variations on one theme: he would punch Louis and then see the results. "I saw the [Bob] Pastor-Louis fight," observed Braddock. "Pastor ran like a thief. I wouldn't be guilty of fighting like that. Remember I'm Irish and I like to mix it a little myself. Louis is no palooka. I know that. He has power, he can punch and I'll guarantee he'll be too busy to get set for any right hand at me."

When asked about possible strategy, Braddock responded testily: "I'm not worried about [Joe] now. Why should I? After all I have been fighting for twelve years and I think I know all the answers. Why not ask Joe Louis how he is going to fight me? Joe can't pull anything on me. He isn't smart enough. I can out fight him, out box him, out step him, out think him, in fact, I can beat him doing anything so why worry? ... What I aim to do is beat the stuffing out of Louis, and come back here and whip Max Schmeling."

Despite the champion's fighting talk, most observers saw the coronation of Joe Louis as a foregone conclusion. Yet few would be rooting against the good-natured Braddock with much fervor. Sparring partner George Nicholson, now in Joe Louis's camp, continued to speak highly of his former employer. "There is no discrimination with Jim," said Nicholson, an African-American. "When I was training with him in 1936 for that Schmeling fight that never come off, he put rocks in my bed just like anybody else."

Lester Rodney, a Louis supporter who wrote for *The Daily Worker*, viewed Braddock as a hard-working boxer deserving of some respect:

Braddock isn't such a bad guy either. You know about his story. A ring veteran who hit bottom and fought his way back to the top. A longshoreman who proudly carries his union card. A guy who tasted the bitterness of New Jersey's "experimental" relief and saw his wife and kids go a bit hungry once in a while and a guy who refused to fight the Nazi Schmeling when the fans boycotted the affair.

These sentiments would be echoed in thousands of newspaper articles filed from both training camps.

Braddock set up camp at Pinewood, near the Golfmore Hotel on the shores of Lake Michigan. His training, while hard and productive, had none of the gloomy intensity normally associated with the preparations for a world heavyweight title fight. The reporters, a hard-bitten bunch, noted the difference. Even Joe Gould took advantage of the relaxed attitude at Braddock's camp to have some fun himself. When *Ring* editor Nat Fleischer arrived, Gould greeted him carrying a box of cigars.

"Nat, do you know where Mike Jacobs is?" Gould asked.

"I left him a while ago," replied Fleischer. "He'll be back in about an hour."

"Well, I can't wait. Will you give him this box of cigars he asked me to buy for him?"

Fleischer took the box – and jumped as a terrific electric shock crossed through his hands. Gould had rigged the box with a strong battery and made the world's largest joy buzzer.

That afternoon Fleischer joined in the laughter as Gould pulled the same stunt on Maxie Roesch, one of Braddock's sparring partners. Gould had such a good time shocking visitors to the camp that he soon graduated to rigging an "electric chair" with even stronger batteries. Fleischer claimed that Gould's chair was so powerful it felt like the "real thing."

The stern, overly serious Fleischer made the perfect foil for a stunt pulled by Jimmy Cannon a few days later. Fleischer had spent a long day hustling to appear on several different radio programs. At four in the morning, a telephone call woke the *Ring* boss.

"Is this you Mr. Fleischer?" a voice asked. "This is the National Broadcasting Company. We just received word from New York that we are to put on a British broadcast from our local headquarters at 5:30 this morning and we cannot locate Clem McCarthy, our master of ceremonies. We hate to trouble you at this time of the night but would appreciate it if you would help us out of a predicament by preparing the program and doing the announcing."

This appeal to Fleischer's vanity had the desired effect. He quickly showered, dressed and began getting ready to leave his hotel when another call came in. McCarthy had been located and Fleischer would not be needed. The next morning at breakfast Fleischer related his sad tale.

"Gee, they could have gotten me," laughed Jimmy Cannon. "I was in the lobby all night. We had a swell time here."

It finally dawned on Fleischer that Cannon had been behind the calls. Fleischer took little solace when he learned that Cannon had called half of the reporters staying at the hotel with similar concocted emergencies.

The sophomoric giddiness that pervaded the press corps spread to Braddock's camp. On June 14, the third anniversary of his victory over Corn Griffin, Braddock was in a particularly playful mood. He passed the day by playing a few rounds of golf, jogging, and playing practical jokes on his sparring partners. That night after all workouts were over, he and his sparring partners, dressed in their pajamas, paraded from the Pinewood camp to the Golfmore Hotel. Braddock, followed by his own private parade, marched through the lobby and the kitchen, with his sparring partners banging on pots and dishpans.

On a chilly evening a few days later, Braddock broke up several of the folding chairs to use as fuel in the fireplace. He had the relaxed air of a champion comfortable in his own skin, and his hard work and obvious conditioning was starting to make the experts take a second look at his chances.

Reports from the challenger's camp varied from day to day. Certainly, Louis, the younger, stronger fighter, would be favored. Yet, as the press analyzed every aspect of the Brown Bomber's training, some began to convince themselves that the Jersey veteran had a good chance. Often, Louis would be hit by looping right hands, the same punch that Schmeling had used to chop up and finally stop him. Yet, as soon as one report would circulate about Louis losing something off his punches, he would flatten a series of sparring partners before an astonished press.

In reality, both fighters were conditioning themselves at the pace best suited to them, not the critics. Come fight night, both would be in peak condition. It was for the reporters to trot out the clichés: youth against experience; man against boy; black against white. It would be, all said and done, a fight for the heavyweight championship of the world.

Sid Mercer, of the *New York American*, spoke to Braddock two days before the fight. With the Lindbergh kidnap trial still fresh in the memory, Mercer was fishing for a story angle. "Do you mean to say you have no bodyguards and aren't afraid of being kidnapped on the eve of the fight?" he asked.

"No need of that stuff around here," Braddock said. "Who'd want to kidnap me anyway? I ain't got a bean. After the fight, maybe that'll be different."

On his last day at the training camp, Braddock showed complete confidence in his ability. Holding out his hands in front of him, he said, "I've gone into the ring with these cracked for $150. I've had this nose of mine broken and a rib busted for a couple of hundred dollars. Do you think, with a price of $400,000 or more staring me in the face, that fighting Joe Louis, or a couple of Joe Louis's, means anything to me?"

Louis's trainer had his own, typically unsentimental, view. "Braddock will have to be a great fighter if he can whip Joe," said Jack Blackburn. "A great fighter, not a pretty good fighter, is going to beat Joe."

As the boxers broke camp, press agent Francis Albertanti concocted a parting shot at the challenger: "An hour before Joe Louis left Kenosha, Wis., for Chicago and his battle with Champion Jim Braddock, he received a package by special messenger at his training quarters. Joe and his handlers crowded around as Jack Blackburn unwrapped the parcel. It was a phonograph record entitled, 'You Can't Take That Away From Me,' and on a card was the name: 'James J. Braddock.'"

As Braddock finished his final workout, he muttered to Jimmy Cannon: "Well, it's all over but the clam bake."

Left: *Braddock sensationally floors challenger Joe Louis in the first round of their title bout in Chicago in June 1937. But Louis came back to knock out the brave champion in round eight (below), the only time he was ever counted out.*

# CHAPTER 13

# The Clam Bake

Reader, have you ever seen a fight? If not, you have a pleasure to come ...

—William Hazlitt, 1822

A team of carpenters descended on the White Sox clubhouse, partitioning it into two dressing rooms large enough for the fighters. Having dismantled the ring he used at Yankee Stadium for the Louis-Schmeling bout, Mike Jacobs had it reassembled in Chicago over the second-base bag.

Mae Braddock traveled to Chicago a few days before the fight. As usual, she would not attend, but she wanted to be near her husband before, and with him after, the contest.

Braddock's pre-fight comments revealed a somber but confident champion. "No use planning a fight in advance," he told reporter Howard Roberts. "I'll know what to do when I get in there and see what Joe's going to do. I will retain my title by knockout within eight rounds."

Louis was similarly terse with the press: "One round or fifteen, but one's nicer. It's my fight. I'll go get it."

Fans streamed to Chicago from all over the country. Special trains were run into the city, which quickly filled with the fight crowd. Those without tickets scrambled to acquire them. One mother wrote her daughter, desperate to get a good seat for the fight.

Dear Daughter Enclose $11.00 go immediately and purchase me a
$11 ticket ... do not trust this to no one but please attend to this
personally for I am depending on you to get me located near the
ring as $11.00 will permit.... With love I am your loving Mother
Dear p.s. this ticket is for Louis-Braddock, fight

Radio announcer Clem McCarthy presented a special remote
broadcast from in front of the Morrison Hotel to get the view of
the "man on the street." Virtually everyone he stopped had an
opinion, most picking Braddock, the clear sentimental favorite. In
short order, McCarthy spoke to people from, among other places,
Iowa, Toronto, New York, Memphis, Ohio, Washington, and Cork,
Ireland. "Always bet on the champion," one speaker advised.
Several proffered "no opinion," asking only for a good fight and
that the "best man win." Although the contest had great racial significance – if he won, Louis would be the first black heavyweight
champion since Jack Johnson – only one speaker raised the issue of
color. Braddock would win, spat out a man from Memphis, "if he
gets a good blow on that nigger." McCarthy ended the broadcast
moments later.

On the eve of the fight, the *Chicago Daily News* polled thirty-
eight sportswriters and boxing experts. Twenty-seven picked Louis
to win. As in all such "objective" polls, the subjective views of the
participants were obvious. Former champion Jack Johnson made
clear his jealousy of Louis, sneering, "Louis was hit with more
rights in that Schmeling fight than I caught all my life." The prickly
Westbrook Pegler offered his opinion despite admitting he had not
visited the training camp of either fighter – "it is not a question of
which is the better man but which is worse and that if there were
any justice in this cruel world the contest would be called off to
spare the customers unnecessary punishment."

On the afternoon of the fight, Illinois Commissioner George
Getz conducted the weigh-in before 2,000 fans, reporters, and officials at the Auditorium Theater. Amid the hum of cameras and the

brisk flash of countless speed graphics, Braddock pushed the beam to 197 pounds even, while Louis weighed just one-quarter pound more, the closest match up in the heavyweight boxing history, at least in terms of weight.

Louis sported a three-day stubble of beard, perhaps attempting to invoke the feral look of former champion Jack Dempsey.

"Say Joe," said Braddock, pointing to his face, "you need a shave." Louis glumly shook his head, his efforts at ferocity immediately deflated.

Gould did his best to nettle the challenger. "Hey Joe!" he shouted, "What's the matter? You are so small today, you worrying?" Louis glared at the champion's diminutive manager. "Well," Gould continued, unabated, "You got plenty to worry about tonight."

Tough Joe Triner cut Gould off to review the commission's rules of the fighters. During Triner's presentation, Gould made a few more attempts to rile Louis but the challenger kept his customary poker face. He seemed more amused than annoyed at Gould's transparent tactics.

When Triner had finished, a radio reporter caught Braddock's last words to the public before stepping into the ring: "I'm in shape. Joe's in shape. There'll be a helluva fight out there tonight."


By early evening, with the bout scheduled for ten p.m., the roads leading to Comiskey Park began to fill with the early arrivals. Approximately 60,000 fans eventually filed into the arena. Movie and radio stars studded the ringside audience. Spectators stood on seats and craned their necks to get a view of Al Jolson, James Cagney, Jack Benny, George Burns and Gracie Allen, Cab Calloway, Bing Crosby, Clark Gable, George Raft, Bojangles Robinson, Edward G. Robinson, and Mae West.

And, of course, the old guard of the boxing community turned out. A tumultuous roar greeted Jack Dempsey's introduction. Giant Jess Willard, fat and happy, took his turn in the ring. Gene

Tunney, Battling Nelson, Willie Ritchie, and many other former champions saluted the crowd. Notable by his absence was Jack Johnson; some said that "certain parties" were looking for him in Chicago and he wisely decided to stay in New York.

Braddock entered the ring once the ceremonies were over, with his corner team of Gould, Whitey Bimstein, Ray Arcel and the long-serving Doc Robb. His Kelly-green satin robe shimmered under the staccato flash of the ringside photographers. Louis joined him moments later, resplendent in a robe of navy blue trimmed with turkey red. One of the commissioners handed up a set of boxing gloves specially made for the fight. Each man's seconds carefully laced up the gloves.

The announcer spoke into the open mike, beseeching that "regardless of race, religion or creed, the highest ideals of sportsmanship be respected upon this night, and everybody present – and over the world – respect the code 'may the best man win.'"

Referee Tommy Thomas called the fighters to ring center, where his instructions were also heard over the open microphone. He sent the fighters to their respective corners after entreating the boys, "Shake hands and come out fighting."


Braddock stepped out briskly at the sound of the bell. Once in range, he let fly a right-hand punch that Louis avoided. Louis landed a left, and Braddock stepped back, not wanting to mix it with hit potent foe. Louis came in hard, and just seconds into the fight the champion was being forced to give ground. Louis snapped out his short, vicious jab – once, twice, three times. He pressed Braddock to the ropes. The titleholder, a veteran of eighty-five fights, rarely fought with his back on the ropes, but against the stalking Louis, he seemed powerless to escape.

And then he knocked Louis to the floor.

"I didn't hit him very hard," Braddock would later recall. "I couldn't. You see, he came at me pretty hard and got me back against the ropes. We banged away there for a while, and then I saw that his hands are straight out, his head was down like a man doing a dead man's float. I couldn't draw my right back far on account of the ropes, so I hit him with a short right-hook."

The roar of the astonished crowd drowned any count the referee had begun as Louis dripped to his haunches, then rolled over on the mat. In a single motion he was up and on his feet, backing away from Braddock.

"He got up so quick I guess I was surprised, for he was over in the corner by the time I took after him and right there's where I lost the fight, I guess. I swung as hard as I could for his chin, but the punch went by his head. Gee, I missed a lot. I stepped back and tried it again but I hit him on the chest or something."

In those few moments, the fight was won and lost.

Louis regained his composure at the interval, and thirty seconds into the next round he cut Braddock over the left eye. Braddock hit back with another crunching right hand, and when Louis tried to retaliate, deftly picked off the punches. Louis seemed understandably over-anxious and missed a left hook coming in. On the inside, Braddock ripped two uppercuts that jolted Joe's head back. The bell sounded, and Braddock had won the first two rounds on all scorecards.

In the third, Braddock tried to keep control of the pace but Louis was beginning to let fire. A right to Braddock's left eye brought more blood. Both landed hard punches, then sparred for openings in mid-ring. The deadly challenger had stopped nineteen opponents inside the first three rounds, but Braddock was hanging tough. "Whenever there was a rally," a reporter wrote, "it was always Braddock who came back first; he fought with the solid fatalism of a man foredoomed but ever hopeful."

Braddock came out for the fourth on his toes. Louis continued to move forward, and his punches were now doing damage. His punch combinations were crisp, clean and precise, and a triple left hook stole the otherwise slow round. In the fifth, Braddock snapped a left jab and brought blood from his challenger's nose, but Louis brushed the blood away and dug a thunderous punch to Braddock's body, stopping him in his tracks.

In Louis's corner after the fifth, wily Jack Blackburn realized that Braddock had begun to fade. "Pour it on him a little now," he advised. "Be careful and don't shoot all you've got, let him have a little."

In the sixth round, Louis hurt Braddock with two rights to the jaw, followed by a flurry to the body and head. Braddock staggered, and once more blood ran from several cuts on his face. Two crushing right hands sent his body slack for a moment, and he almost fell, forcing himself upright as the battering continued. Another sledgehammer right tore Braddock's top lip, and red spurted furiously from the cut. Yet Braddock willed himself to throw punches, and had Louis backing off at the bell.

It was obvious to all that the fight had turned irrevocably in Joe's favor. Gould scrambled up the steps to the ring as Braddock staggered to his corner. "How do you feel Jim?" he asked.

"I've never felt worse in my life," said Braddock, honest as ever.

"I'm going to stop the fight," Gould said, reaching for the bloody towel, the classic sign of surrender. Braddock saw his motion from the corner of his eye.

"If you do," he croaked, "I'll never speak to you again." Braddock forced his words through torn and swollen lips, "I'm the champion, if I'm going to lose I'll lose it on the deck."

No further words were exchanged. Instead, cuts man Ray Arcel worked furiously to staunch the flow of blood from Braddock's face.

"Braddock took punishment that seemed beyond human endurance," wrote ringside reporter Davis J. Walsh. "Even as the crowd gasped in pity, he shook his crimson head and advanced on the jabbing challenger. Occasionally, a left or right would crash through the Negro's guard but almost invariably, Louis would counter, set him back on his heels and follow through with a ripping blow."

The end was in sight. Braddock, still coming forward, was slowly being punched to a standstill. "What Braddock saw through the red mist was a weaving brown figure, full of fury, whose fists jolted with power to stop the heart of an ordinary fighter," wrote Henry McLemore. Still the champion's seconds worked furiously at the end of the seventh, trying to keep their man going. "What a heart he had," remembered Whitey Bimstein, who would go on to train numerous champions. "You'll never find a gamer fighter. He was game to the last punch."

By the eighth round, everyone in the stadium knew that Braddock was on the verge of a knockout. Everyone, that is, except for Braddock himself.

"I was still figuring, in the eighth, that if I could straighten up his hit with a left-hook I could cross over with my right and nail him," Braddock would later tell Bob Considine. "Well I missed with that left, and it must have thrown me off balance, because I was half leaning toward him when he nailed me."

The sound of the short right that landed on the side of Braddock's face resounded throughout the stadium. "I never saw that knockout punch. Never even felt it," Braddock said afterwards. "All I knew was ... well ... I was swinging my arms, and then a kind of darkness. The last thing I remember was when I swung a left hook at Joe's face. It missed like a lot of others I threw at him."

Braddock collapsed to the mat, "his body trembling a little then becoming still as a stone while his title was washing away in the pool of blood alighting on the gray canvas."

British boxing writer Peter Wilson called it "the hardest single punch I have ever seen one man land on another." America's Grantland Rice agreed: "It was one of the most terrific single punches I have ever seen delivered in the ring. Braddock had to be carried to his corner with blood pouring from half a dozen open wounds. His head was hanging to one side, there was no glint of life left in his half opened eyes."

Across the nation, radio listeners heard broadcaster Clem

McCarthy pick up the count. "The count is two!" McCarthy shouted. "Two! Three! Four! Five! Six! Seven! Eight! Nine! Ten! A new world's champion! Joe Louis is the new world's champion!"

Sharp-eyed Bob Considine picked out one detail that, in retrospect, may be the exact moment that the age of fan-as-moron began. Considine spotted a young man vault into the ring as Tommy Thomas brought down his arm at the count of ten. The man – with slicked-back hair and a wild look – knelt at Braddock's side "shaking the insensate champion." Under one arm was an autograph book – he wanted Braddock's signature. Thankfully, a cop finally grabbed him and "gave him the heave ho."

For the first and only time in his life, Jim Braddock had been counted out.


Columnist Jimmy Cannon managed to rush to the dressing room before even Louis or his entourage. He was there in time to see Louis burst into the room, "snorting a scarlet mist," elated at winning the title, but showing the effects of the difficult bout himself. Louis took Cannon's hand as he hopped onto the rubbing table. "That man hit me on the jaw, Jimmy!" Louis said incredulously. Within moments, the new champion's cheerful demeanor changed, his eyes narrowing in a faraway stare. He had remembered unfinished business. "Just give me one more shot at Schmeling," he murmured, "Just one more."

On Braddock's side of the plywood wall dividing the clubhouse, Ray Arcel and Whitey Bimstein tried to tape their fighter's face together. Someone asked Gould if Braddock was finished as a fighter.

"Why should he be?" snapped Gould. "He can lick any of those other guys. Give him two more fights and he can come back against Joe Louis too. I'd be lying if I said I wanted this guy back again in September, but Jimmy can fight him with two bats under his belt."

As Gould spoke, he looked at his fighter, who lay motionless and speechless on a massage table. Whitey Bimstein slowly cut the laces off of his boxing gloves, while Arcel continued to tend the many cuts and bruises on his face.

Turning back to the reporters, Gould spoke more softly now. "But I don't take any credit away from Louis. I'm tickled to death he's a champion and so is Jim. Louis has done more for this fight game than any other fighter who ever lived, and that goes for Dempsey too."

After a half hour, Braddock was finally lucid enough to speak. Several reporters approached the devastated Cinderella Man to ask the standard post-fight questions. "Give me a couple of fights and I'll knock this guy's brains out," Braddock answered. "I forgot to duck," he added, without prompting.

Gould could not refrain from giving his true opinion: "Let's stop kidding ourselves, Joe is the best, fastest, hardest punching heavy-weight champion ever. You can toss all of your John L's, Fitzes and Dempseys in the wastebasket."


Chicago's Southside lit up with a noisy but orderly celebration. Hundreds of proud Louis supporters poured into the Eighth Avenue Regiment Armory, where the party carried into the morning hours. Celebrants of both races packed the Club DeLisa, a former speakeasy turned jazz club and the self-proclaimed "Harlem of Chicago" run by Chicago tough guy Mike DeLisa.

In New York the celebration was no less boisterous. Moments after Louis had been declared champion, boisterous revelers "spilled out of doorways, spewed from windows, streamed out of alleys, shouting, laughing and chanting 'we got a champeen! We got a champeen now!'" Ten thousand "happy colored folk" and even certain intrepid "white people" gathered on Seventh Avenue in an impromptu parade, led by one young man draped with the flag of Ethiopia.

The following day Braddock received seven reporters at the hotel suite where he and Mae would stay for several days while he recuperated before returning to New Jersey. "I never knew what hit me," he said of the punch that dropped him. "I didn't see the punch start and I didn't feel it land. Perhaps it was just as well – I guess I got a break. Don't let anybody tell you that Louis can't slam 'em home ... his left jabs had me dizzy. They were the things that beat me."

Braddock even admitted that he had foreseen the fight's end. "I knew in the fifth round that my number was up and I couldn't raise my hands. I figured I couldn't last much longer, so I went out and gambled – and I lost." Braddock's thoughts turned once more to his three children, and he told Jack Miley, "It's going to be tough to explain to the kids what happened to my 'turtle.' I guess I'll tell them it died of old age!"

In later years, when asked to describe how it felt to be punched by Joe Louis, Braddock would answer, "If I had electric bulbs on my toes they would have lit up." He also took to describing his brutal loss to Louis using an extended metaphor for comic effect:

Immediately after taking off I ran into a dark cloud. Well the sailing wasn't so rough for a while until suddenly, I ran into a storm – a storm of leather – and I was hit with a bolt of lightning. I had to make a forced landing and put in for repairs. Well, I got repaired that night – I got twenty-two stitches in my face.

In New York, even the boxing commission had to face reality, and its chairman duly issued a statement: "This Board does hereby recognize Joe Louis as the World's Heavyweight Champion, on the strength of his knockout victory over James J. Braddock last week. We cannot suspend notice for his having floored Braddock, for the former is not duly licensed with this body. However, should Louis make application for permission to box in this state, he will not be accorded such permission until he promises to make the first defense of his championship against Max Schmeling ... and Braddock will remain under suspension in this state indefinitely."

*Tommy Farr, the rugged heavyweight from the Welsh valleys, who gave Joe Louis a torrid fifteen rounds and then lost a disputed decision to Braddock in the ex-champ's final fight.*

CHAPTER 14

# Doing the Big Apple

"Doc, watch me do the Big Apple!"
—Jim Braddock, January 21, 1938

During the winter of 1937-1938, a vivacious up-tempo dance whistled through New York City dance halls, having been carried north from its origins in a synagogue-turned-juke-joint in Columbia, South Carolina. The "Big Apple" was a species of foxtrot, characterized by frenzied twists and twirls that ended in an irrelevant shout of "Praise Allah!" Some said the dance reflected the slowly blossoming optimism accompanying Roosevelt's second term. For somebody such as Jim Braddock, it represented no more than the carefree joy of other nonsensical dances favored by the young, such as the Charleston of his own boyhood.

In 1937, though, Braddock was far removed from the limitless potential of his youth during the Roaring Twenties. Real life had intervened. Now, he was a husband to a high-strung, devoted wife and father to three sweet, rambunctious children. Years of toil in the brutal vineyards of professional boxing had consumed his youth. Just thirty-two, he looked ten years older. "There is no profession as dangerous as boxing," Braddock said, "and there is no profession which forces so much denial. It is not a game for weaklings, and those who survive deserve whatever they earn. They have paid for it in lost youth that was wasted away in stuffy gyms and sweat rooms. They have paid for it in parties they could not attend, sweets they could not eat, water they could not drink. It is a hard game." Braddock had made that observation at age twenty-two.

Against all odds, the Cinderella Man had survived – and no one would say he did not deserve what he had earned. Happily, his labor had been rewarded – the beating administered by Joe Louis had come with a "bushel of berries." Unlike the callow boy of 1929, Braddock would invest those proceeds for his family's long-term benefit.

As always, the paramount concern was family. Braddock's first large expenditure addressed one of Mae's chief desires – to have a permanent home for her husband and children. In August, Jim purchased a small, nine-room house with a two-car garage at Park Avenue and Thirty-Fourth Street, North Bergen, New Jersey. The brick house, occupying a plot fifty by 100 feet, sold for $25,000. Braddock paid cash. He would live there for the rest of his life.

He invested also in a real estate holding company incorporated by Joe Gould's lawyer brother, Sam, headquartered at his Newark office. Joe and Braddock put money into a small trucking company, which paid them each roughly $150 a week.

In the immediate aftermath of his brutal loss to Louis, Braddock had insisted that he would fight again. ("I guess the poor guy hasn't come to yet," Jack Kearns had said.) However, few believed he would make the effort to come back. It was up to Joe Gould to convince the naysayers otherwise. Braddock had meant what he said. While his boxer recuperated, Gould kept Braddock's name in the press.

In August, as Joe Louis prepared for his first defense against the British Empire Heavyweight Champion, Tommy Farr, Gould announced that Braddock had been matched with Max Baer for a return bout at Madison Square Garden that Fall. Promoter Uncle Mike Jacobs dutifully placed the fight on the Garden schedule. In September, Jacobs called it off. Nobody seemed to care.

Tommy Farr, a tough Welshman from the mining village of Tonypandy, took the great Louis fifteen rounds in a close fight, and several respected commentators – and Farr himself – actually felt that he deserved the victory. Mike Jacobs could not offer him an immediate return, and the Brown Bomber was already booked to meet a couple of other fighters before a long-awaited clash with Max Schmeling in June. Nevertheless, Jacobs wanted to keep Farr busy pending his next big match.

Jim Braddock saw Farr as the perfect choice for his comeback. For the first time in their long relationship, he went to Gould with a demand for a fight: "Get me Tommy Farr." Then he paid $1,000 to the New York Boxing Commission to discharge the fine levied against him for failing to go through with the Schmeling fight. Restored to the good graces of the commission, he retreated to his training camp at Loch Sheldrake.

Braddock went into camp a man fighting for his legacy more than his wallet, and worked as hard as he ever had in preparing for Farr. Once again, his lead sparring partners were old friends Jack McCarthy and George Nicholson. Braddock held no grudge against Nicholson for his work with Joe Louis.

A frequent visitor to Braddock's sparring sessions was a young ballplayer who was rapidly becoming one of baseball's biggest stars, Yankee centerfielder Joe DiMaggio. In fact Joe Gould and DiMaggio became inseparable during the winter and spring of 1938, to the consternation of officials of Major League baseball. DiMaggio's contract with the Yankees had expired, and many believed Gould was behind his negotiations for a raise "somewhere near" the $36,000 Lou Gehrig was receiving.

Long hours of roadwork and gym preparation paid off for Braddock, who weighed in at a rock-hard 199½ pounds. In sparring, his legs looked solid and his timing was impeccable. Newsreel footage showed Braddock purposely avoiding punches by just inches, leaving himself in perfect position to counterpunch. He needed to be in top shape to have a chance with the aggressive, arrogant Farr.

The day before the fight Braddock mused for reporters while taking a rubdown from Doc Robb, "Now that I've lost the title, it seems like a great weight has been lifted, no more banquets, parties, and affairs to attend. People don't ask me out as much as before. I'm just another fighter now – and I think a better one than I was last summer."


New York fight fans are notorious for last minute ticket purchases. Walk-up sales at fight venues typically total over fifty percent. Bad weather, therefore, can badly dent attendance. The evening of the Braddock fight, an ugly snowstorm ripped along Manhattan Island. Its fierce, biting wind cut through the air, taking not a few fedoras with it.

Yet at the turnstiles of Madison Square Garden, the ticket takers were shocked. Despite the brutal, inclement weather, lines of buyers waited patiently in the cold. New York's fight fans were heading to the Garden to see old man Braddock one last time. The joint was a sell-out: 17,369 fans with wet cold feet gathered for the return of the Cinderella Man.

As had become his custom, Braddock arrived early. For a time he sat alone in his dressing room, preparing mentally for the challenge ahead. Joe Gould, Doc Robb, and Whitey Bimstein would work his corner. Robb spent extra care taping Braddock's brittle hands, until at last the call came for him to make his way to the ring.

Braddock entered first, gracefully ducking through the ropes and taking three small bows to different sides of the arena. He wore black trunks which had a tiny green shamrock sewn on to the right thigh. He sat in his corner awaiting a commission official to bring his gloves to the ring.

As he waited, the two-to-one betting favorite Tommy Farr entered and walked directly across the canvas to Braddock's corner, where the two shook hands. Farr returned to his corner, sat heavily on his stool, and his trainer began lacing on the approved gloves. The fight was moments away.

Harry Balogh's introduction was spare. He gave the fighters' names, weights (Braddock 199½, Farr 207), and then the pair was called to ring center for final instruction from referee Johnny McAvoy.

Farr began with several swings at Braddock's midsection. Braddock stuck a jab at his opponent, and the fight was on. In the first two rounds, Braddock controlled his distance well, jabbing at Farr's head and body. When Farr got inside, Braddock was able to tie him up and push him off. Surprisingly, Braddock seemed much the much stronger of the two, as Farr couldn't move him at all in the clinches.

In the third, the Welshman, who fought out of a semi-crouch, continued to drive chopping lefts and rights to the body. Braddock countered mainly with uppercuts. Farr dug two hard hooks at Braddock's abdomen. Quickly, referee Johnny McAvoy pushed the two apart, ruling that one punch had been below the belt. He awarded Braddock the round on a foul. "They were fair punches," Farr asserted, but McAvoy had the final word and waved the fighters together.

Farr increased his punch output after that. He began to edge ahead of his more methodical, one-paced opponent. The sixth, seventh, and especially the eight went in Farr's favor, as he battered Braddock's body and "left red welts on his ribs."

The Associated Press reported that going into the ninth round, practically every scorecard at ringside had Farr well ahead. Doc Robb slapped Braddock's thighs, trying to rouse his fighter, while Gould looked on, small and pale in the glare of the overhead lights.

"Go to town Jim," Gould whispered as the bell for the ninth round sounded. "Tag him a few, maybe there won't be a tenth."

A tired Braddock looked over at his anxious corner men and tried to reassure them.

"Doc, watch me do the Big Apple," he said as the bell for round nine echoed through the arena.

Braddock came out to ring center bouncing on tired legs, but ready for Farr's renewed assault. "When Farr put his head down and came in like a wet mop, I shifted, and used a right upper cut," he later said. "I hooked with the left and then the right. Tommy wondered what on earth had happened, because I'm pretty sure he figured me finished at the end of the eighth."

Braddock dominated the round, and continued his near-miraculous performance in the tenth round, pushing Farr off and slamming home lefts and rights. With forty-five seconds left in the round, a three-punch combination – left hook, right hand, and left hook – hurled Farr to the ropes. It was all Braddock.

"The tenth and the last round was the real thriller. It was even more one-sided than the ninth. I don't know how many times I hit Farr, but it was plenty. As I battered him around for the latter part of the round, I wondered whether or not he would have been knocked out had the fight been twelve rounds long."

Announcer Balogh studied the cards of the judges, then reached for the overhead microphone: "The winner, Braddock!" The crowd at the packed Garden erupted with tumultuous applause for the Jersey veteran. Braddock walked over to Farr's corner, hand outstretched.

"Hard luck, Tommy,"

A livid Farr, rather than take Braddock's hand, turned his back and stormed out of the ring, kicking his water bucket into the crowd. He ran to his dressing room, bringing boos and jeers from crowd and press alike.

At that moment, radio announcer Sam Taub reached Farr's corner. Ignoring Farr's gaffe, he interviewed Braddock across the top rope. "I thought I had it all the way," Braddock practically shouted. Then he too made his way from the ring.

In his dressing room, Farr seethed. "I'm no bloody actor," he later recalled. "I thought I got the worst of a raw decision and I still think so. That fight meant about $200,000 to me in contracts which I had signed – and all lost on that decision. I didn't want to see anybody at that time."

The scoring revealed that Braddock had been awarded the win on the narrowest of margins. Judge LeCron scored it six rounds to

Braddock, four to Farr. Judge Lynch scored it six to four for Farr. Lynch, who would drop dead of a heart attack in front of the Garden just two days later, was unrepentant. "It was one of the few times I was in a minority" was all he would say.

The deciding vote was up to the referee Johnny McAvoy, who tabbed five rounds for Farr, five rounds for Braddock, which normally would have resulted in a draw verdict. New York's rules at that time, however, allowed for a tiebreaker based on supplemental points. McAvoy awarded Braddock extra points for his inspirational showing in the final two rounds.

In his last professional fight, Jim Braddock had won a split decision.

Surrounded by well-wishers, including his pal Joe DiMaggio, Braddock admitted in the dressing room that he had "shot the works" in those two rounds in a desperate effort to win, and couldn't have gone much further.

Gould strutted. It had all been part of the strategy, he told the pressmen. "Well, Jim and I have been together for a long time. I never kid him and he never kids me. At the end of the seventh round I asked him how he felt and he said 'fine.' From the beginning I had in mind a strong finish. I knew Farr couldn't hurt him, and I knew Jim's legs were none too strong. I knew also that a strong finish frequently saves a bad fight – and this figured to be a bad one. So I said to Jim at the end of the seventh, 'Take it easy again this round and I'll turn you loose in the ninth and tenth.' Jim wanted to start winning in the eighth. Some of the customers were beginning to boo, and this disturbed him. But I wasn't sure he could go through three rounds at top speed so I held him back. I knew he could mess up Farr plenty with only two rounds to go, because he told me he felt all right. Realizing now he just went through the motions in the eighth. He couldn't wait for the bell to stop at ninth. When it did sound – did you ever see such an old guy look better?"

The next day, champion Joe Louis had some kind words about Braddock's performance. "Braddock fought a smart fight last night," he said. "He didn't wear himself out in the early rounds and had plenty to spare at the finish. Against me, he started wading in right from the start. Braddock seemed faster and he was punching nicely all through the fight against Farr."

Braddock received about $22,000. By February, a film of the fight was being shown at theaters nationwide, and Braddock's loyalty to Gould's old gangster friends became clear. The credits opened with a shot of an American flag flapping briskly from an unseen breeze.

Above the title in bold letters appeared the words "Copyright Bill Duffy."

*Inseparable pals Joe Gould and Jim Braddock whiled away their post-fight years "playing two-handed pinochle" and watching the fights, searching for a young heavyweight to guide to the title.*

CHAPTER 15

# Back to the Coffee Pots

"Being hit on the chin isn't so bad; it's what you do afterwards that makes the difference."

—James J. Braddock

Fight fans bickered for days about the result of the Braddock-Farr contest. The closeness of the ballot made a rematch a near certainty. Braddock's purse for a rematch, it was said, would surely be around $50,000.

Instead, ten days after beating Tommy Farr, Jim Braddock retired from boxing.

"I won my last fight," Braddock told reporters, "and think I could beat most of the outstanding contenders for the heavyweight championship, but I have spent fifteen years in the game, and in fairness to everyone, especially to my wife and children, I believe it is time to withdraw."

He penned a farewell to boxing that appeared in an obscure pulp magazine, *Blue Ribbon Sports*. Honest as ever, Braddock conceded that one reason he was retiring as an active fighter was that, "frankly, I do not think I could beat Joe Louis.... While I might tag him for a finisher, the odds would be against me doing so, and it is reasonable to suppose that he wouldn't pick and pick and hook and cross as he did in our other meeting after getting up from the floor."

More importantly, Braddock stated he did not want to risk a

defeat that could injure him or disappoint his fans, family or friends. Fittingly, the plain-speaking Braddock employed a metaphor of home and family to explain the end of his boxing career: When a man builds a house, he stops when the house is finished, and it is finished only when he cannot improve it anymore. "The house that I have built," he said, "is not the greatest that any boxer has built, but it is finished. There is nothing that I could do to improve it."

Nat Fleischer of *Ring* lauded the former champion:

James J. Braddock has hung up the gloves. One of the most likeable characters in the history of boxing has retired from competition. To Braddock go nothing but well-wishes ... and so I say good luck, and goodbye as a fighter and the world is more the richer for him having been in it ... The Braddocks are only too few and far between in boxing.

Fight scribe Eddie Borden was similarly effusive:

Jim Braddock put himself into the memory of every fighting man the hard way. He made the grade on the up-climb, and bowed out in much the same way.

Jim Braddock's stature as the hero of the underdog was secure. By bowing out at the right time, he never became a punchbag for younger men, as so many ex-champs do. He knew when it was time go, but he would remain involved with boxing. He and Gould would manage fighters – their first under contract was none other than Tommy Farr. (Farr: "Joe Gould has the reputation of being, and is in fact, one of the shrewdest managers in the world ... in every regard he served me well.") They would also follow the lead of many former champions and open a bar. Gould and Braddock spent the better part of February preparing Inn Braddock's Corner for its opening. Gould told reporters he had spent $6,000 decorating the joint with a boxing motif. The bar was twenty-two-feet square, with ring posts at all four corners and the ropes stretched just above the heads of the customers.

Tommy Farr, however, never could get over his controversial loss to Braddock. One night, he went to Braddock's restaurant and shouted at Jim, "Why don't you admit I beat you?" Braddock glared back across the bar. Finally, he answered quietly, "Let's go outside and settle it once and for all." Gould quickly broke up the imminent battle. For years after their impromptu meeting, Braddock regretted that he had not "settled" matters with Farr.

Braddock's restaurant had a short life. It opened in February, but by July Braddock had the company file for bankruptcy protection, listing assets of $99,000 and liabilities of $32,000. The slow, hot summer had made clear that the bar would not be able to stay open and pay its liabilities. At least in this instance, Braddock wisely pulled the plug on a bad business deal. With luck, in liquidation he would walk away breaking even.

With the failure of Inn Braddock's Corner, the veteran ex-boxer even contemplated a ring comeback. Gould went so far as to announce that he would meet Tommy Farr in a fiteen-round bout in London. One reporter thought Braddock's comeback to be inspired, because in England, "second-rate fighters, at least judged by American standards, are as numerous, and fully as agile, as old-age pension advocates." Like so many other trial balloons floated by Gould to the press, the idea fizzled out.

According to *New Yorker* feature writer A.J.Liebling, who loved boxing and the characters it furnished, Gould and Braddock whiled away much of their time playing "two-handed pinochle" in Gould's "office" at the Mayflower Hotel. "Walls of the room are covered with photographs of Gould, inscribed 'To my dear pal, Jim Braddock,' and of the former heavyweight champion, autographed 'To my dear pal, Joe Gould.' Most of the pictures autographed by Gould show Gould posed between large game fish in Florida or signing contracts with promoters. The Braddock pictures mostly show Jim knocking somebody out, although there are a few of him shaking hands with eminent statesmen." The pair, wrote Liebling, "have a habit of discovering young heavyweights, whom they stake to meals and boxing lessons."

Yankee centerfielder Joe DiMaggio spent so much time with Joe Gould, appearing with him nightly at Toots Shor's and other New York gathering places, that reports surfaced of Gould secretly managing DiMaggio in an arrangement whereby the ballplayer paid him twelve percent of his gross earnings, including his baseball club salary. Two percent of that amount allegedly went to Jim Braddock.

"Baseball authorities are resolutely opposed to either indirect mingling of baseball with boxing or horseracing," explained James Dawson of the *New York Times*. The Yankees would not negotiate with DiMaggio, so he finally accepted their offer of $25,000 flat. When DiMaggio started working out on his own prior to joining the club, Gould was there to share the spotlight. He actually shagged fly balls for DiMaggio, alongside his latest fighter, Popeye Woods.


Henry McLemore broke the story about Braddock's ten percent kicker from Mike Jacobs's future title promotions with a classic lead: "This is a story about a man fed by the hand that bit him." McLemore had some of the details wrong – he incorrectly reported that Braddock got ten per cent of what Louis was paid, rather than a percentage of the promoter's net – but the impact was the same. A faint aroma of backroom dealing followed Gould and Braddock thereafter. McLemore further reported that Braddock earned about $100,000 from Joe's first eight defenses. Mike Jacobs, though, did not part with money so easily; in fact aside from about $20,000 in token payments, he had not lived up to the agreement at all.

A few months later Gould was forced to sue Jacobs in New York Supreme Court. Braddock and Gould alleged that they were entitled to a percentage of the net profit of "ticket sales, movie, television, or radio rights for all heavyweight championship bouts" promoted by Jacobs. Jacobs came up with a clever defense. He contended that Gould had breached the agreement by "belittling publicly the skill and ability" of the recent challengers to Joe Louis's title. The publicity was not good for either side, and they quickly settled the matter – at least for the moment.

Braddock dabbled in several other business ventures. In 1940 he even promoted a few fights, featuring such stalwart sluggers as "Peanuts" Barbella and Vinnie Vines. The promotional racket did not keep his interest and after a few shows at Paterson's Hinchcliff Stadium, he moved on. In early 1941, gossip columnist Walter Winchell reported that he was a "soda water emir, making the rounds of the midtown joints and grills to peddle his product."

Braddock took a break from peddling seltzer to get in the ring one more time, fighting a five-round exhibition against Red Burman in Charlotte North Carolina. He even campaigned to be named as head of the New Jersey Boxing Commission, but he was passed over for the patronage job by the Jersey political bosses.

In October 1942 the inseparable team of Braddock and Gould made news again when both joined the military, enrolling in the Army Transportation School at Fort Slocum, New York. The evening before they reported for duty, three hundred and fifty "close friends" showed up at Toots Shor's restaurant to wish them well, demonstrating that the boxing community had not lost its appetite for rubber chicken. At the dinner, Braddock pointed out the irony of his scheduled position, telling the crowd, "I'm back on the docks again. I'm in the longshoreman's battalion of the Army Transportation Corps." Gould circulated among the captive audience, explaining the choice of service to anyone who would listen. "Braddock could have become a physical instructor, but he didn't want that," he prattled. "Jim wanted action – and I guess I do too. So we figured that the transportation corps in this world-wide war would assure us of plenty of action and at the same time make us more valuable to our country than any other department or service."

A month later both graduated officer's school with the rank of First Lieutenant. Braddock, by then promoted to Captain, would spend the war assisting in moving material through the Port of New York. Captain Braddock often found himself supervising the work at Pier Six on Brooklyn's waterfront. *New York Times* boxing writer James Dawson delighted in pointing out that "It wuz a regular pier six brawl" was the "ultimate in fight phraseology." Braddock also helped raise money for the military. His command staged a charitable boxing event in Brooklyn, Braddock and Sgt. Joe Louis refereed the bouts and Braddock sold over $1 million in war bonds.

The Army assigned Gould to an office post with the New York's Port of Embarkation, also in Brooklyn, where he passed his enlistment reviewing supply contracts for such items as rubber rafts and life preservers. In September 1944, the boxing community was shocked to learn that Gould had been arrested by Army officials and charged in connection with a conspiracy to influence the award of contracts for the sale of over $1 million equipment to the military.

Gould's court martial was convened and prosecuted in a few swift days that November. The most extravagant of the charges rapidly crumbled during the presentation of the prosecution's own case. Braddock testified on Gould's behalf, but his testimony was limited, as he knew none of the facts and was not involved in the transaction. Gould was convicted, sentenced to three years' hard labor and fined $12,000.

On appeal, the Army reduced his sentence to one year's incarceration. Joe Gould then entered the Green Haven disciplinary barracks to serve out his term. Just thirty-eight days later, he was released and dismissed from the Army, an action considered equivalent to a dishonorable discharge.

Uncle Mike Jacobs was one of the few who sought to leverage

Gould's conviction against him. After the war, and after years of sporadic payments by Jacobs, Gould once more sought an accounting as to the monies paid under the agreement relating to the Louis fight. In response, Jacobs sought to claim that because of the notoriety sure to be heaped upon Gould as a result of his conviction, Jacobs ought to be allowed to sever his association with Gould. The lawyers for Jacobs reasoned, rather elliptically, that Jacobs and his business would likely suffer if his relationship with Gould were to continue.

Gould hired former prosecutor Burton Turkus, who made his name taking down the notorious New York killing squad called "Murder Inc.," to be his counsel. Turkus had a fondness for boxers because his first famous case was a divorce involving then-middleweight champion Mickey Walker. He succeeded in having Mike Jacobs's proposed defense rejected by the New York Supreme Court.

Gould remained uncharacteristically silent throughout the entire episode. Not a single newspaper was able to quote the normally garrulous manager on the record. The word was that Gould's silence protected other important but more culpable members of the service. Nat Fleischer summed up the prevailing view of the boxing community: "He never should have done it in time of war."

On August 14, 1946, the Bayside Golf Links were a beehive of activity as amateur golfers from across Long Island and New York tried their best in the World-Telegram's thirteenth annual hole-in-one competition. One small wiry man sent the gallery into a frenzy as his drive landed on the green and made its drive for the cup. When the ball stopped just two feet from the pin, Joe Gould had the best drive of the day.

Gould's wife Lucille was with him in their apartment at 25 Central Park West when he died there, in April 1950. Ill for nearly three years, Gould had only recently been released from Mt. Sinai hospital, and still looked years younger than his age of fifty-three. On a rainy Sunday, New York's fight gang crowded the Riverside Memorial Chapel for Gould's funeral. After the services, somebody translated for Gould's friend, sports columnist Frank Graham, part of what Rabbi Morris Goldberg had intoned in Hebrew: "The Lord is my shepherd: I shall not want. He maketh me lie down in green pastures ..." The cars then left to carry Gould to Mount Neboh Cemetery in Brooklyn for burial.

Braddock and his story slowly faded from the public consciousness. By the mid-1960s, *Los Angeles Times* columnist Jim Murray could write without irony that "James J. Braddock is gray and sad and sings Irish ballads in an old man's quavering voice at fight parties."

Only occasionally would Braddock's activities appear in the news. He was named executive director of the Hebrew Boys Home in New York City. The National Sportsmen for Kennedy Committee listed him among the athletes supporting Kennedy for the presidency; old friend Joe DiMaggio also made the committee. A small group formed the New Jersey Boxing Hall of Fame and named him as one of the first inductees, along with his former trainer Joe Jeanette, who was inducted posthumously.

In the mid-1950s it was reported that Braddock and several associates were operating a ship supply and diesel parts firm. In the same article, Braddock spoke proudly about his children. "The kids were smarter than the old man. Neither of the boys went in for boxing, they picked basketball and football. Jay is twenty-five and works on plan protection for Ford Motor Company. Howard is twenty-four and has his own trucking business. Rose Marie, who is going to be twenty-three, is a secretary for the Niagara Mohawk Power Company."

By then, Braddock had gone beyond the end of the path he had so clearly foreseen as a young man: "When you go to Madison Square Garden and see it jammed to the roof, you think to yourself that the fighters in the main event are pretty lucky stiffs. The next time that thought hits you, just remember that a fighter doesn't break into the Garden overnight. He has traveled a long hard, unattractive path. The fan only sees the end of that path, but they are too far away to see the hills that we had to climb on our way to a main bout in a big club."

As the years passed, so did many of the men who had touched Braddock's life. Charlie Harvey dropped dead on his way to see a fight at the Garden; he had never managed again after Steve Hamas's loss in Germany. Uncle Mike Jacobs spent years in semi-retirement after a stroke robbed him of his ability to conduct business. Jimmy Johnston managed several fighters through the 1940s, the best of whom served as fodder for Joe Louis. Curmudgeonly press agent Francis Albertanti died in his sobbing wife's arms after a decade of illness. Max Baer, fat and wealthy, died in a Phoenix hotel room, clowning until the very end. Bill Duffy died on Long Island, where he had been providing "entertainment" in the form of illegal gambling for several years.

In 1963, at age fifty-eight, Braddock took a job manning a crane for the U.S. Steel Company, which was constructing the Verrazano-Narrows Bridge, which connected Staten Island and Brooklyn, and united all five boroughs of New York City. Writer Gay Talese told of Braddock's $150 a week salary, but warned "the Braddock story is not another maudlin epic about a broken prizefighter."

"What the hell, I'm a working man," Braddock told Talese. "I worked as a longshoreman before I was a fighter, and now I need the money so I'm working again. I always liked hard work; there's nothing wrong with it."

As Braddock toiled on the bridge, the world continued to change around him. He watched grandchildren arrive and grow, and saw a brash young fighter from Kentucky named Cassius Clay beat Sonny Liston for the heavyweight title in 1964. A decade later, Clay, now Muhammad Ali, would perform a feat nearly as unlikely as Braddock's win over Baer: he beat George Foreman in Zaire. On the evening that Ali and Foreman contested the "Rumble in the Jungle," Braddock watched the closed-circuit broadcast of the fight at Madison Square Garden. He dined first with Jack Dempsey and Gene Tunney. Columnist Red Smith overheard a man say, "There are three guys at that table who could whip Ali on the best night he ever had."

On the bookshelves at that time was what would be Braddock's valedictory interview, conducted by Peter Heller, an ambitious young ABC news writer. Heller set out with a tape recorder to track down as many former champions as he could find alive, and preserved their words in his book *In This Corner...!* He spoke with gray-haired old Cinderella Man at his North Bergen home, and listened as the stories rolled again. Braddock was typically matter-of-fact about his career. He thought Max Baer was a harder hitter than Joe Louis, and claimed he'd had an injection in his left side on the morning of the Louis fight to combat the effects of arthritis. But he had no complaints. "I come out after thirteen years, I was all right, so I figured get out of it while it's good. You got to like it to be in there. That's one business you got to like if you're going to be in it."

On November 29, 1974, Jim Braddock died in his sleep at home in North Bergen, New Jersey – the house he and Mae had lived in since Jim was champion in 1937. He was sixty-nine years old

On the day that he was buried, a boxing match at Madison Square Garden was preceded by a ceremonial ten-count on the ring bell. As the timekeeper solemnly struck each beat, most of the crowd chatted amiably with each other in Spanish. Several Latino boxers were fighting, most from impoverished backgrounds, all hoping to better themselves, to turn the power and precision of their fists into gold. Perhaps one of them would turn out to be a champion.

# Epilogue

When Parisian lawyer and author Charles Perrault wrote his version of *Cinderella* in 1691, he ended it with a moral:

> Without doubt it is a great advantage to have intelligence, courage, good breeding, and common sense. These, and similar talents come only from heaven, and it is good to have them. However, even these may fail to bring you success, without the blessing of a godfather or a godmother.

Gould would have discounted the need for such mystical intervention. "Some of you boys have been calling him the Cinderella Man," he told reporters prior to the Louis fight. "In case you've forgotten your fairy stories, Cinderella was a little housemaid who became a princess overnight. Well, as far as I'm concerned, James J. Braddock is no Cinderella Man. She had a fairy godmother, who waved a magic wand and bingo! the job was done. Jimmy didn't have a fairy godmother. All he had was a brave heart, a couple of hands and a pretty wise head. All that he is he made himself."

But Braddock knew better than to take all of the credit. "To begin with, let me bar all of that Cinderella Man talk gush that appeared in newspapers and magazines after I had turned in the biggest surprise in the history of the heavyweight championship. Sure I needed the fight, and I needed the championship. Boxing had not made me rich. [But] I did get rich.... And Joe Gould did it."

# Acknowledgements

First and foremost I would like to thank Ron Howard and the rest of his crew at Imagine Entertainment for giving me a reason to start this project. Howard's quest to get to the heart of the Braddock story for the *Cinderella Man* movie was the catalyst for me to dig deeply into the historical record. I began my research into Braddock's life believing I already knew virtually everything I needed to know about him. But as I read the books, magazines, and newspapers of the era, I began to realize that Braddock's story was not just a rehash of *Rocky*.

During my search for the truth about Jim Braddock, many historians unstintingly gave of their time and knowledge. Hank Kaplan spent several hours with me as we sifted through his massive boxing archive. Boxing researchers know that Hank is the first stop on any journey. My partner in the Cyber Boxing Zone website, Steve Gordon, always provides perceptive insights into boxing and boxers. My long time friend and mentor, Bert Sugar, could always be counted on for the most elusive pieces of information. Who else would know the name of Max Baer's dog?

I owe a huge debt to David Margolick, who shared the research he had done on the Louis-Braddock fight for his upcoming book, *Beyond Glory*. Sal Rappa graciously shared rare films of Braddock, Baer, Lasky, Loughran, and many other fighters from his immense collection. Mike Welch provided copies of many of the radio broadcasts quoted in this book. Clay Moyle reviewed his vast boxing library for obscure sources, photocopying mountains of important material for me. Kevin Smith, foremost historian of black fighters, was always ready to answer my questions, even though our conversations usually digressed from the Braddock topic. "Ric Marshall" helped track down information pertaining to Braddock's Pacific Coast trip after he won the title. Jack Kincaid had documented the dates and locations of many obscure fights; he also shared his collection of Jimmy Cannon's columns. J.J. Johnston (no relation to the Boy Bandit) provided reams of information on Charlie Harvey and Jimmy Johnston. Steve Klompton, Harry Greb's biographer, set aside his own research to track down reports of Braddock's fights in Saint Louis. Tom Carr provided several useful articles about Jimmy Slattery, who was managed by his father. *Enrique Encinosa tambien me ayudo mucho. Gracias, hermano!*

I also thank the members of the International Boxing Research Organization, led by Dan Cuoco. Through IBRO I was able to access information that otherwise would have taken several lifetimes.

Peter Walsh, of Milo Books, nurtured this project from the beginning. His patient cajoling and advice provided invaluable motivation.

Finally, a short story. When I was a boy, my father would let me play in the municipal playground directly across Metropolitan Avenue in front of his Williamsburg luncheonette. Except for the occasional double-parked sanitation truck that blocked his view, he could watch me play while feeding the denizens of Brooklyn. One day, for some forgotten reason, my personal "Elmer Furlong" shoved me, then punched me in the nose. "A lack of harmony ensued." Finally, one of the older boys broke up the fight, brought me back to my father's luncheonette, and sat me on the counter.

"Here's your boy, Mike. He was fighting in the park."

"Yeah? How'd he do?"

"He did okay but he could jab a little more."

A customer engrossed in coffee and a cruller asked: "Did he

move his head?" For the next fifteen minutes, while I sat on the counter sulking with rage, my father and half a dozen customers at Doc's Sugar Bowl carefully dissected my style and technique.

I was five years old.

This one's for you, Dad.

# Appendix

## Ring Record of James J. Braddock

BORN: James Walter Braddock, Jun 7, 1905; New York City, NY
DIED: Nov 29 1974; North Bergen, New Jersey
HEIGHT : 6' 2½"
WEIGHT : 162-199½ lbs
REACH : 78 inches
TRAINER : Doc Robb
MANAGER : Alfred M. Barnett; Joe Gould

*Career Statistics:*
86 Fights
45 W (won, 27 by knockout)
23 L (loss)
11 ND (No decision)
5 D (draws)
2 NC (No Contest)

## Professional Record

### 1926

| | | | |
|---|---|---|---|
| Apr 13 | Al Settle | Union City, NJ | ND 4 |
| Apr 22 | George Deschner | Ridgefield Park, NJ | KO 2 |
| Apr 29 | Joe Jeanette | Union City, NJ | Exh |
| Jun 18 | Leo Dobson | Jersey City, NJ | KO 1 |
| Jun 28 | Jim Pearson | Jersey City, NJ | KO 2 |
| Jul 9 | Walter Westman | Jersey City, NJ | TK 3 |

| | | | |
|---|---|---|---|
| —— | Phil Weisberger | Jersey City, NJ | KO 1 |
| —— | Jack O'Day | Jersey City, NJ | KO 1 |
| —— | Willie Daily | Jersey City, NJ | KO 1 |
| Sep 7 | Gene Travers | Jersey City, NJ | KO 1 |
| Sep 13 | Mike Rock | Jersey City, NJ | KO 1 |
| Sep 16 | Ray Kennedy | West New York, NJ | KO 1 |
| Sep 30 | Carmine Caggiano | West New York, NJ | KO 1 |
| Nov 12 | Lou Barba | New York, NY | W 6 |
| Dec 4 | Al Settle | New York, NY | W 6 |
| Dec 8 | Joe Hudson | New York, NY | W 6 |
| Dec 20 | Doc Conrad | Jersey City, NJ | ND 4 |

**1927**

| | | | |
|---|---|---|---|
| Jan 28 | George LaRocco | New York, NY | KO 1 |
| Feb 1 | Johnny Alberts | Wilkes-Barre, PA | KO 4 |
| Feb 15 | Jack Nelson | Wilkes-Barre, PA | W 6 |
| Mar 3 | Lou Barba | New York, NY | W 4 |
| Mar 8 | Nick Fadil | New York, NY | W 6 |
| Mar 15 | Tom McKiernan | Wilkes-Barre, PA | KO 2 |
| Apr 19 | Frankie Lennon | Wilkes-Barre, PA | KO 3 |
| May 2 | Stanley Simmons | Jersey City, NJ | TKO 1 |
| May 11 | Jack Stone | West New York, NJ | ND 10 |
| May 20 | George LaRocco | Bronx, NY | D 6 |
| May 27 | Paul Cavalier | Rochelle Park, NJ | ND 10 |
| Jun 8 | Jimmy Francis | West New York, NJ | ND 10 |
| Jul 13 | Jimmy Francis | Union City, NJ | ND 10 |
| Jul 21 | George LaRocco | Bronx, NY | W 6 |
| Aug 10 | Vic McLaughlin | West New York, NJ | ND 10 |
| Sep 21 | Herman Heller | West New York, NJ | ND 10 |
| Oct 7 | Joe Monte | New York, NY | D 10 |

**1928**

| | | | |
|---|---|---|---|
| Jan 6 | Paul Swiderski | New York, NY | W 8 |
| May 7 | Jack Darnell | Jersey City, NJ | KO 4 |

| May 16 | Jimmy Francis | West New York, NJ | ND 10 |
|--------|---------------|-------------------|-------|
| Jun 7 | Joe Monte | New York, NY | L 10 |
| Jun 27 | Billy Vidabeck | West New York, NJ | D 10 |
| Jul 25 | Nando Tassi | Brooklyn, NY | D 10 |
| Aug 8 | Joe Sekyra | Brooklyn, NY | L 10 |
| Oct 17 | Pete Latzo | Newark, NJ | W 10 |
| Nov 30 | "Tuffy" Griffith | New York, NY | KO 2 |

**1929**

| Jan 18 | Leo Lomski | New York, NY | L 10 |
|--------|------------|--------------|------|
| Feb 4 | George Gemas | Newark, NJ | KO 1 |
| Mar 11 | Jimmy Slattery | New York, NY | TK 9 |
| Apr 22 | Eddie Benson | Buffalo, NY | KO 1 |
| Jul 18 | Tommy Loughran | Bronx, NY | L 15 |
| | (For World Light Heavyweight Title) | | |
| Aug 27 | Yale Okun | Los Angeles, CA | L 10 |
| Nov 15 | Maxie Rosenbloom | New York, NY | L 10 |
| Dec 7 | "Jake" Warren | Brooklyn, NY | KO 2 |

**1930**

| Jan 17 | Leo Lomski | Chicago, Il | L 10 |
|--------|------------|-------------|------|
| Apr 7 | Billy Jones | Philadelphia, PA | L 10 |
| Jun 5 | Harold Mays | West New York, NJ | ND 10 |
| Jul 2 | Joe Monte | Boston, MA | W 10 |
| Aug 11 | Alvin "Babe" Hunt | Boston, MA | L 10 |
| Sep 19 | Phil Mercurio | Boston, MA | KO 2 |

**1931**

| Jan 23 | Ernie Schaaf | New York, NY | L 10 |
|--------|--------------|--------------|------|
| Mar 5 | Jack Roper | Miami, FL | KO 1 |
| Mar 30 | Jack Kelly | New Haven, CT | W 10 |
| Sep 3 | Andy Mitchell | Detroit, MI | D 10 |
| Oct 9 | Joe Sekyra | New York, NY | L 10 |
| Nov 10 | Maxie Rosenbloom | Minneapolis, MN | NC 2 |
| Dec 4 | Al Gainer | New Haven, CT | L 10 |

**1932**

| Mar 18 | Baxter Calmes | Chicago, IL | L 10 |
|---|---|---|---|
| May 13 | Charley Retzlaff | Boston, MA | L 10 |
| Jun 21 | Vincent Parille | Long Island City, NY | W 5 |
| Jul 25 | Tony Shucco | Long Island City, NY | L 8 |
| Sep 21 | John Henry Lewis | San Francisco, CA | L 10 |
| Sep 30 | Dynamite Jackson | San Diego, CA | W 10 |
| Oct 21 | Tom Patrick | Hollywood, CA | L 10 |
| Nov 9 | Lou Scozza | San Francisco, CA | LT 6 |

**1933**

| Jan 13 | Martin Levandowski | Chicago, IL | W 10 |
|---|---|---|---|
| Jan 20 | Hans Birkie | New York, NY | L 10 |
| Mar 1 | Al Ettore | Philadelphia, PA | LF 4 |
| Mar 21 | Al Stillman | St. Louis, MO | TK 10 |
| Apr 5 | Martin Levandowski | St. Louis, MO | L 10 |
| May 19 | Al Stillman | St. Louis, MO | L 10 |
| Jun 21 | Les Kennedy | Jersey City, NJ | W 10 |
| Jul 21 | Chester Matan | West New York, NJ | W 10 |
| Sep 25 | Abe Feldman | Mt. Vernon, NY | NC 6 |

**1934**

| Jun 14 | "Corn" Griffin | Long Island City, NY | TK 3 |
|---|---|---|---|
| Nov 16 | John Henry Lewis | New York, NY | W 10 |

**1935**

| Mar 22 | Art Lasky | New York, NY | W 15 |
|---|---|---|---|
| Jun 13 | Max Baer | Long Island City, NY | W 15 |
| | (Won World Heavyweight Title) | | |
| Aug 15 | Tom Patrick | Jersey City, NJ | Exh |
| Aug 15 | Jules Veigh | Jersey City, NJ | Exh |
| Aug 15 | George Nicholson | Jersey City, NJ | Exh |
| Aug 27 | Jack McCarthy | Houston, TX | Exh 3 |
| Nov 5 | Jack McCarthy | Seattle, WA | Exh 3 |

| Nov 6 | Jack McCarthy | Vancouver, Canada | Exh 3 |
| Nov 9 | Jack McCarthy | Eugene, OR | Exh 3 |
| Nov 12 | Jack McCarthy | Portland, OR | Exh 2 |
| Nov 13 | Jack McCarthy | Marshfield, OR | Exh 3 |
| Nov 15 | Jack McCarthy | San Francisco, CA | Exh 3 |
| Nov 20 | Jack McCarthy | Oakland, CA | Exh 3 |

**1937**

| Jun 22 | Joe Louis | Chicago, IL | LK 8 |

(Lost World Heavyweight Title)

**1938**

| Jan 21 | Tommy Farr | New York, NY | W 10 |

**1940**

| Oct 9 | Roy Nelson | Falls City, NE | Exh 4 |

**1941**

| Mar 26 | Red Burman | Charlotte, NC | Exh 5 |

**1969**

Jun 15    Inducted into New Jersey Boxing Hall of Fame

**1974**

Nov 29    Dies at his home in North Bergen, NJ

**2001**

Jun 7    Inducted into International Boxing Hall of Fame

**2005**

Jun 3    The movie *Cinderella Man* premieres, directed by Ron Howard and starring Russell Crowe. Braddock would have been celebrating his 100th birthday.

## Ring Record of Max Baer

BORN:     Max Adelbert Baer, Feb 11, 1909, Omaha, NE
DIED:      November 21, 1959, Hollywood, CA
HEIGHT:  6' 2 ½"
WEIGHT:  192-226
REACH:    81 inches
TRAINER:  Mike Cantwell
MANAGER: Ancil Hoffman

*Career Statistics:*
84 Total Fights
71 W (won, 53 by knockout)
13 L (loss)

## Professional Record

### 1929

| | | | |
|---|---|---|---|
| May 16 | Chief Caribou | Stockton, CA | KO 2 |
| Jun 6 | Sailor Leeds | Stockton, CA | KO 1 |
| Jul 4 | Tillie Taverna | Stockton, CA | KO 1 |
| Jul 18 | Al Ledford | Stockton, CA | KO 1 |
| Jul 24 | Benny Hill | Oakland, CA | W 4 |
| Jul 31 | Benny Hill | Oakland, CA | W 4 |
| Aug 28 | Al Ledford | Oakland, CA | KO 2 |
| Sep 4 | Jack McCarthy | Oakland, CA | LF 3 |
| Sep 25 | Frank Rujenski | Oakland, CA | KO 3 |
| Oct 2 | George Carroll | Oakland, CA | KO 1 |
| Oct 16 | Chief Caribou | Oakland, CA | KO 1 |
| Oct 30 | Alex Rowe | Oakland, CA | KO 1 |
| Nov 6 | Natie Brown | Oakland, CA | W 6 |
| Nov 20 | Tillie Taverna | Oakland, CA | KO 2 |
| Dec 4 | Chet Shandel | Oakland, CA | KO 2 |
| Dec 30 | Tony Fuente | Oakland, CA | KO 1 |

## 1930

| | | | |
|---|---|---|---|
| Jan 15 | Tiny Abbott | Oakland, CA | LF 3 |
| Jan 29 | Tiny Abbott | Oakland, CA | KO 6 |
| Apr 9 | Jack Stewart | Oakland, CA | KO 2 |
| Apr 22 | Ernie Owens | Los Angeles, CA | W 10 |
| May 7 | Tom Toner | Oakland, CA | KO 6 |
| May 28 | Jack Linkhorn | Oakland, CA | KO 1 |
| Jun 11 | Ora "Buck" Weaver | Oakland, CA | KO 1 |
| Jun 25 | Ernie Owens | Oakland, CA | TK 5 |
| Jul 15 | Les Kennedy | Los Angeles, CA | L 10 |
| Aug 11 | "K.O." Christner | Oakland, CA | KO 2 |
| Aug 25 | Frankie Campbell | San Francisco, CA | KO 5 |
| Dec 19 | Ernie Schaaf | New York, NY | L 10 |

## 1931

| | | | |
|---|---|---|---|
| Jan 16 | Tom Heeney | New York, NY | KO 3 |
| Feb 6 | Tommy Loughran | New York, NY | L 10 |
| Apr 7 | Ernie Owens | Portland, OR | KO 2 |
| May 5 | Johnny Risko | Cleveland, OH | L 10 |
| Jul 4 | Paolino Uzcudun | Reno, NV | L 20 |
| Sep 23 | Jack van Noy | Oakland, CA | TK 8 |
| Oct 21 | Jose Santa | Oakland, CA | KO 10 |
| Nov 9 | Johnny Risko | San Francisco, CA | W 10 |
| Nov 23 | Les Kennedy | Oakland, CA | KO 3 |
| Dec 30 | Arthur DeKuh | Oakland, CA | W 10 |

## 1932

| | | | |
|---|---|---|---|
| Jan 29 | King Levinsky | New York, NY | W 10 |
| Feb 22 | Tom Heeney | San Francisco, CA | W 10 |
| Apr 26 | Paul Swiderski | Los Angeles, CA | KO 7 |
| May 11 | Walter Cobb | Oakland, CA | TK 4 |
| Jul 4 | King Levinsky | Reno, NV | W 20 |
| Aug 31 | Ernie Schaaf | Chicago, IL | W 10 |
| Sep 26 | "Tuffy" Griffith | Chicago, IL | TK 7 |

**1933**

| | | | |
|---|---|---|---|
| May 28 | Jack Dempsey | Atlantic City, NJ | Exh 1 |
| Jun 8 | Max Schmeling | Bronx, NY | TK 10 |
| Jul 10 | Babe Hunt | Oklahoma City, OK | Exh 4 |
| Jul 14 | Jack Dempsey | Salt Lake City, UT | Exh 1 |
| Jul | Jack Dempsey | Salt Lake City, UT | Exh 1 |
| Jul 20 | Jack Dempsey | Louisville, KY | Exh 3 |

**1934**

| | | | |
|---|---|---|---|
| Jun 14 | Primo Carnera | Long Island City, NY | TK 11 |
| | (Won Heavyweight Championship of the World) | | |
| Dec 28 | King Levinsky | Chicago, IL | Exh 2 |

**1935**

| | | | |
|---|---|---|---|
| Jan 4 | Babe Hunt | Detroit, MI | Exh 4 |
| Jan 10 | Dick Madden | Boston, MA | Exh 4 |
| Feb 15 | Stanley Poreda | San Francisco, CA | Exh 4 |
| Jan 21 | Tony Cancela | Miami, FL | Exh 4 |
| Apr 23 | Eddie Simms | Cleveland, OH | Exh 4 |
| Apr 26 | Babe Hunt | St. Louis, MO | Exh 6 |
| Jun 13 | Jim Braddock | Long Island City, NY | L 15 |
| | (Lost Heavyweight Championship of the World) | | |
| Sep 24 | Joe Louis | Bronx, NY | LK 4 |

**1936**

| | | | |
|---|---|---|---|
| Jun 15 | Tony Souza | Salt Lake City, UT | W 6 |
| Jun 17 | Bob Frazier | Boise, ID | TK 2 |
| Jun 19 | Millionaire Murphy | Pocatello, ID | W 6 |
| Jun 23 | George Brown | Tyler, TX | KO 3 |
| Jun 24 | Wilson Dunn | San Antonio, TX | KO 3 |
| Jul 2 | "Butch" Rogers | Dallas, TX | KO 3 |
| Jul 13 | Jim Merriott | Oklahoma City, OK | KO 2 |
| Jul 16 | Junior Munsell | Tulsa, OK | KO 5 |
| Jul 18 | Cecil Smith | Ada, OK | W 4 |
| Jul 24 | Bob Williams | Ogden, UT | KO 1 |

| Aug 19 | James J. Walsh | Vancouver, Canada | KO 1 |
| Aug 20 | Nails Gorman | Marshfield, OR | TK 2 |
| Aug 25 | Cecil Myatt | Portland, OR | W 6 |
| Aug 29 | Al Frankco | Lewiston, ID | KO 2 |
| Aug 31 | Don Baxter | Coeur d'Alene, ID | KO 1 |
| Sep 2 | Al Gaynor | Twin Falls, ID | KO 1 |
| Sep 3 | Eddie Franks | Provo, UT | KO 3 |
| Sep 8 | Sammy Evans | Casper, WY | KO 4 |
| Sep 14 | "Bearcat" Wright | Des Moines, IA | W 6 |
| Sep 21 | Andy "Kid" Miller | Sheldon, IA | W 6 |
| Sep 25 | Cyclone Bench | Rock Springs, WY | KO |
| Sep 30 | Babe Davis | Keokuk, IA | W 6 |
| Oct 6 | Tim Charles | Evansville, IL | KO 4 |
| Oct 8 | Art Oliver | Platteville, WI | L 6 |
| Oct 19 | Dutch Weimer | Toronto, Canada | KO 2 |

**1937**

| —— | Bob Carville | Birmingham, England | Exh 3 |
| Apr 15 | Tommy Farr | London, England | L 12 |
| May 27 | Ben Foord | London, England | TK 9 |

**1938**

| Mar 11 | Tommy Farr | New York, NY | W 15 |
| Oct 27 | Hank Hankinson | Honolulu, HI | KO 1 |

**1939**

| Jun 1 | Lou Nova | New York, NY | LK 11 |
| Sep 4 | Ed Murphy | Silver Peak, NV | KO 1 |
| Sep 18 | Babe Ritchie | Lubbock, TX | KO 2 |

**1940**

| Jul 2 | Tony Galento | Jersey City, NJ | TK 8 |
| Sep 26 | Pat Comiskey | Jersey City, NJ | KO 1 |

**1941**

| Apr 4 | Lou Nova | New York, NY | LK 8 |

# Names Index